THE GREAT HEROIN COUP

THE GREAT
HEROIN COUP

DRUGS, INTELLIGENCE, &
INTERNATIONAL FASCISM

HENRIK KRÜGER
translated by Jerry Meldon
foreword by Peter Dale Scott

South End Press, Box 68 Astor Station, Boston MA 02123

Library of Congress Number: 80-52134
ISBN: 0-89608-031-5 paper
ISBN: 0-89608-032-3 cloth

cover collage by Susan Shup depicts Christian David
shortly after his arrest in Brazil. Background figures are
Howard Hunt and Richard Nixon.

edited by Jonathan Marshall
translated by Jerry Meldon

Typeset at Carrier Pigeon, Boston
Production at South End Press, Boston

Originally published in Danish as *Smukke Serge og Heroinen*
by Bogan in 1976.

 C-417

TABLE OF CONTENTS

To heroin's victims in the United States and Europe,
And to all veterans of the War in Vietnam,
Especially those who returned strung out,
And those who did not return at all...
To victims of torture and repression in Latin America
and elsewhere,
And to those who owe the monkey on their back,
And the scars on mind and body
To agents of the CIA and DEA.

FOREWORD

The story of Christian David, an international narcotics trafficker used by the intelligence services of at least three nations, is fascinating in itself. It is even more important for what it tells us of a larger, less documented history – the secret collaboration of government intelligence services and parallel police throughout the world, and their use of criminals, particularly from drug networks, for political countersubversion. Above all it is an important book for Americans to read, since the shadow of the CIA can be seen behind Christian David's political intrigues in countries like France and Uruguay. America's role in Christian David's strange career has never before, to my knowledge, been revealed in this country. And Henrik Krüger is able to expand the story into larger perspectives on the CIA, Watergate, and current U.S. counterinsurgency tactics.

The heavy censorship of David's story in the United States, or what may be called the media resistance to it, is perhaps the clearest symptom of America's involvement. For example, it was surely newsworthy that in June 1973 *Le Monde*, France's most respected newspaper, charged that the break-up of the Ricord French drug network in Latin America (which had included David's arrest and extradition to the United States), was the result of a "close Mafia-police-Narcotics Bureau collaboration" in the U.S. The result of this collaboration, according to *Le Monde*, was to shatter Corsican influence in the worldwide narcotics traffic, and create a virtual monopoly for the U.S.-Italian Mafia connection (whose key figures were Santo Trafficante in America and Luciano Liggio in Europe).[1]

1

Le Monde's charges, many details of which have since been cor-
roborated, were passed over in silence by the U.S. press. This studied
disinterest in the politics of narcotics (other than the propaganda,
including flagrant lies, from official press releases) is a recurring,
predictable phenomenon of our press; and it has visibly had a dele-
terious impact on U.S. politics. If the *Washington Post* and the *New
York Times*, then supposed exposers of Watergate, had picked up on
stories like the one in *Le Monde*, then the history of Watergate might
have been altered. For the history of Nixon's involvement in
Watergate is intertwined with that of his personal involvement in
drug enforcement. Nixon's public declaration in June 1971 of his war
on heroin promptly led to his assemblage of White House Plumbers,
Cubans, and even "hit squads" with the avowed purpose of combatting
the international narcotics traffic. (Among those with a White House
narcotics mission, or cover, were Krogh, Liddy, Hunt, Caulfield,
Sturgis, and Bernard Barker.)[2]

Many writers have since suggested that Nixon's war on heroin
was part of his "grand design" to develop a new drug superagency,
under direct White House control, into "the strong investigative arm
for domestic surveillance that President Nixon had long quested
after."[3] Yet the establishment press failed to look critically at Nixon's
war on heroin. Instead it blandly reported Nixon's decision in June
1971 to provide $100 million in aid to end opium production in Turkey,
a country which (according to CIA estimates) produced only 3 to 8
percent of the illicit opium available throughout the world.[4]

At the time perhaps 80 percent of the world's illicit opium was
grown, much of it by CIA-supported tribesmen, in the "golden
triangle" of Laos, Burma, and Thailand, while the Shah of Iran, who
became one of Nixon's closest foreign allies, had just announced
resumption of Iranian opium production of over 20,000 hectares (an
area 50 percent greater than the total cultivation in Turkey). As the
New Republic noted only one month later, Nixon's decision to shut
down the supply of Turkish opium was "likely to do no more than drive
the industry further east."[5]

Another, and even more cynical view of Nixon's action is to see it
as a direct attack on the French Corsican networks which relied
almost exclusively on Turkey as their source of supply, and which,
according to *Le Monde*, were being deliberately forced out of the
international drug trade as the result of a "close Mafia-police-
Narcotics Bureau collaboration." *Le Monde* stated explicitly that it
was the U.S.-Sicilian Mafia which closed down the sluice-gates of

Turkish opium production. Was Nixon personally playing a role, as Henrik Krüger suggests, in this seamy international drug war between rival networks? Such a possibility seems less remote when we recall the rivalry which had grown up in the 1960s between deGaulle's intelligence services and the CIA, and the respective reliance of these services upon the rival Corsican and U.S.-Italian crime syndicates.

Le Monde had no difficulty in spelling out the American side of the intelligence-Mafia connection, even though the CIA activities of Santo Trafficante, the alleged heir to the Luciano network, were not known to it at the time:

> Instructed by his own experience of collaboration with the American intelligence services, Lucky Luciano used to recommend to his honorable correspondents scattered from Beirut to Tangiers, via Ankara and Marseilles, to operate as he had done. It was in this way that drug dealers and couriers served as informants to [the British] MI5, to [the American] CIA, to [the French] SDECE, to the [West German] Gehlen organization, even to the Italian SIFFAR.[6]

On the French side, *Le Monde* was predictably more reticent; but from other sources we learn that at least two members of the competing Ricord network, Christian David and Michel Nicoli, were former members of the Gaullist Service d'Action Civique (SAC), the parallel police or *barbouzes* who had been used to assassinate members of the right wing Organisation de l'Armée Sécrète (OAS), in revolt against de Gaulle's accommodation with Algeria. Through SAC, David and Nicoli had come into contact with SDECE operations as well.[7]

One of the major theses of Henrik Krüger's fascinating book is that "the great heroin coup" – the "remarkable shift" from Marseilles (Corsican) to Southeast Asian and Mexican (Mafia) heroin in the United States, was a deliberate move to reconstruct and redirect the heroin trade, rather than to eliminate it, and that Cuban exiles, Santo Trafficante, the CIA, and the Nixon White House were all involved:

> It was, needless to say, *not* a willful conspiracy of *all* the above. But we can assert with reasonable certainty that the CIA, Trafficante and other mafiosi, certain Southeast Asians, and *some* people in the White House must have been in the know. (Krüger, p. 122)

As Krüger tells the story, the motivations for the alleged heroin coup were primarily political: to break the power of the old Gaullist SAC connection, which by 1970 was as distasteful to de Gaulle's pro-American successor Pompidou as it was to Nixon, and (on the

American side) to replace it by an alternative power base. In Krüger's analysis it was not so much a struggle between the French and American intelligence services, SDECE and CIA, as it was a struggle between old and new leaderships. The coming to power of Pompidou in France, and of Nixon in America, had created unprecedented tensions and suspicions between these two presidents and their old-line intelligence services: hence Nixon's desire to use the war on heroin as a pretext for a new superagency under White House control. Hence also the successive agreements between Nixon, Pompidou, and their cabinet officers to crack down on the old Corsican connection.

Once again, the U.S. press resistance to the subject matter of Krüger's book suggests that there is something to his thesis. At least two books published in America, both obviously based on U.S. government sources, discussed the arrest of David at length, without mentioning either that he had worked for SAC/SDECE or that he had confessed to involvement in the 1965 assassination of the Moroccan leftist Mehdi Ben Barka – one of the major unsolved French intelligence assassination scandals of the 1960s. The first U.S. book to mention David's confession was *Newsday*'s newspaper series *The Heroin Trail;* the *Newsday* team also told how they

> received a call from the U.S. Embassy in Paris, stating that earlier promises of French and American cooperation with our investigation would only be kept if we agreed to submit our manuscript to *both* governments in advance of publication for the correction of "erroneous information." We refused.[8]

Yet even *The Heroin Trail,* which deserved its Pulitzer prize, states only that David "confessed to participating in the plot to murder Mehdi Ben Barka, a Moroccan leftist lured to France under false pretenses by SDECE."[9]

Before Krüger's book one had had to go to books published in England or France to learn that it was not de Gaulle who wanted Ben Barka killed – quite the contrary – but some other government or governments and their intelligence services, and that a leading suspect in the case was the American CIA.

As the Oxford historian Phillip M. Williams wrote in 1969,

> Here one point is absolutely clear. The Gaullist government not only had no interest in Ben Barka's death, but had every interest in his survival. Ben Barka was a left-wing, anti-American, third-world nationalist leader with a lively admiration for General de Gaulle, and

had been received at the Elysée some time before: a natural ally for Gaullist policy. Thus any official French connivance could have come only from some section of the State machine which was acting clean contrary to the wishes of the President.[10]

Williams himself then suggests two possible hypotheses which are both compatible with each other and close to Krüger's own explanation:

> One, much favoured especially among Left Gaullists, was collaboration with the CIA to eliminate the organizer of the Havana Tricontinental Congress [i.e. Ben Barka]. Another was that SDECE were obliging either Moroccan Intelligence as such, or Oufkir [the Moroccan Intelligence Chief, whom Williams describes elsewhere as "too pro-American for the Gaullists"] in a personal vendetta against Ben Barka, in return for services rendered in the past.... That there were some SDECE officers who were violently opposed to Gaullist policy towards the United States, especially in Intelligence matters, is clear from the now celebrated "revelations" of the former SDECE agent Pierre Thyraud de Vosjoli [who was ousted from SDECE because of his services for the CIA].[11]

In other words, an Oxford don a decade ago had already explored Krüger's hypothesis that disloyal elements in de Gaulle's cabinet and intelligence service, acting at the behest of the CIA, had Ben Barka killed. Yet Krüger's book goes much further and is, to my knowledge, the first serious study of the Ben Barka mystery to be published in this country. This alone would make it an important challenge to the current stereotype of the CIA as a bunch of exotic assassination bumblers, given to armchair fantasies about thallium foot powders, exploding conch shells, or contaminated cigars.

Krüger's book is also the first in America, to my knowledge, to explore further what *Newsday* called "reports" that David, "an adventurer recruited into the French secret service for terrorist activities... assassinated a number of African officials, and, in Latin America, infiltrated Uruguay's Tupamaro guerrillas and identified several for the police."[12] Once again, a well-documented French study, *Dossier D comme Drogue,* has confirmed David's work for the French and Uruguayan secret service in penetrating and turning over the Tupamaros, for which he was equipped with a diplomatic passport.[13] But it is Krüger who supplies the details of the arms transactions by which David was able to penetrate to the very heart of the Tupamaro organization. And, once again, it is Krüger who points out that David's services against the Tupamaros were part of an effort coordinated by the notorious U.S. CIA police "advisor," Dan Mitrione – the same Mitrione who according to *New York Times* reporter A.J. Langguth arranged for the Uruguayan police to obtain superior electric torture needles through the U.S. diplomatic pouch.[14]

David's successful penetration of the Tupamaros – and, before that, of the Argentine FAL (Fuerzas Argentinas de Liberacion) – helps explain why so many U.S. and French intelligence agents have been helped, by official provision of an invaluable diplomatic passport, to become important in the lucrative international arms and drug traffic. (The two traffics are frequently interrelated, as *Le Monde* pointed out, and can help pay for each other).[15] It was as a well-connected criminal smuggler that David was able to persuade the FAL and Tupamaro leadership that he could procure arms for them; and it was after providing small arms to the Tupamaros that David became their trainer and adviser in weapons matters and turned them in. As we shall see, this *modus operandi* will be encountered frequently in Krüger's book.

When one considers that the bulk of the world's small arms traffic is dominated by the world intelligence milieu, and that the largest single wholesaler is, or was until recently, the CIA-linked multinational Interarmco (founded by former CIA agent Samuel Cummings),[16] one can see that it is difficult to rely on weapons as a major revolutionary asset without becoming dependent, at one's peril, upon one or another of the existing world powers.

Meanwhile, on the side of the police repressive apparatus, it is difficult to remain in sustained contact with the enormously lucrative narcotics traffic (particularly in countries where bribery is an accepted part of the political culture) without becoming partly or wholly corrupted by it. Thus the *New York Times* has reported how in 1974 one major narcotics trafficker obtained a diplomatic passport from the secretary to the Bolivian president for a simple cocaine shipment; while charges against another in Ecuador were dismissed at the order of Ecuador's minister of the interior.[17] As we shall see, this latter phenomenon of an "intelligence immunity" has become a recurring feature of justice inside the United States, even in major cases ranging from narcotics to political murder.

Again, it is part of Krüger's thesis that the CIA, even after it had decided to eliminate the Ricord network of which David formed part, was unwilling to destroy the international drug connection which allowed its agents to gather intelligence about insurrectionary movements through the tactic of selling arms to them; and which at the same time financed the organization of counter-revolutionary death squads and "parallel police" such as the Argentine AAA (Alianza Anticomunista Argentina). Undoubtedly, in Latin America, the stories of drugs and of death squads, such as that which arranged for the assassination of Orlando Letelier in Washington, have been closely interwoven.

As support for his argument that the traffic once dominated by Ricord was simply redirected to Cuban exiles in touch with the CIA and with Santo Trafficante, Krüger points to the extraordinary story of Alberto Sicilia Falcon. Somehow Sicilia, a twenty-nine-year-old Cuban exile from Miami, was able to emerge as the ringleader of the so-called "Mexican connection" which promptly filled the vacuum created by the destruction of the Ricord network in 1972. Lucien Sarti, a top Ricord lieutenant, was shot and killed by authorities in Mexico on 27 April 1972, after being located there by U.S. agents.[18] The new Sicilia network, according to DEA Chief Peter Bensinger, was operating by May 1972, and had "revenues reliably established in the hundreds of millions of dollars" by the time of Sicilia's own arrest in July 1975.[19]

Once again, it is virtually impossible to find any extensive treatment in the U.S. press of the mysterious Alberto Sicilia Falcon, even though his arrest led to no less than 104 indictments, 73 of them in the United States.[20] From the noted German magazine *Der Spiegel,* however, one learns that Sicilia told the Mexican authorities who arrested him that he was a CIA agent, and had been trained at Fort Jackson (as had at least one of Nixon's Watergate Cubans) for possible guerilla activity against Cuba. Allegedly he had also worked in Chile against the socialist government of Salvador Allende until he returned to the U.S. in early 1973. He also, according to Mexican police, spoke of a special deal with the CIA; the U.S. government had turned a blind eye to his heroin shipments, while his organization supplied CIA weapons to terrorist groups in Central America, thereby forcing the host governments to accept U.S. conditions for security assistance.[21]

DEA Chief Bensinger was quite circumspect in his testimony about Alberto Sicilia Falcon, merely calling him "a Cuban national" and alluding to his possible "revolutionary activity in Central and South America." From this it was easier to deduce that Sicilia was a Castro agent than the reverse.[22] In fact, Sicilia was a Cuban exile who had come to Mexico from Miami, where he had links to the Cuban exile community, and had personally negotiated for manufacturing rights to the celebrated 9mm Parabellum machine pistol, better known as the Ingram M-10.[23]

Parabellum was a Miami-based arms sales firm set up by soldier-of-fortune Gerry Patrick Hemming, and headed by Cuban exile Anselmo Alliegro IV, whose father had been close to Batista.[24] Parabellum in turn was sales representative for Hemming's friend Mitch WerBell III, a mysterious White Russian, OSS-China veteran, small arms manufacturer, and occasional U.S. intelligence operative, with unexplained relations to the CIA, DEA, and the major drugs-for-arms deal for which he was indicted but acquitted.[25] (The government's case failed after the chief government witness, arms and dope smuggler Kenneth Burnstine, was killed in the crash of his private plane.)[26] As we shall see, another client interested in producing the Ingram M-10 machine pistol in Latin America, under license from WerBell, was the international fugitive and Nixon campaign contributor, Robert Vesco.

Like other European journalists, Krüger notes that the same 9mm automatic pistol, better known (after its inventor) as the Ingram M-10, was found in February 1977 among the effects of the Italian neo-Fascist, Luigi Concutelli, of Ordine Nuovo, who had used it in the July 1976 political murder of the Italian centrist judge Vittoria Occorso.[27] Its presence among Concutelli's effects was considered especially significant because the M-10, manufactured by WerBell's former firm the Military Armaments Corporation, was supposed to be delivered only to intelligence services (such as Spain's D.G.S.), and every sale of the M-10 required a special permit from the Munitions Control Branch of the U.S. State Department.

According to the Spanish Minister of the Interior, Concutelli's Ingram M-10 had been modified in a clandestine arms factory in Madrid, discovered in a raid by Madrid police on 22 February 1977.[28] Arrested in connection with that raid were six Italian leaders of Ordine Nuovo and Mario Sanchez Covisa, the leader of a Spanish terrorist group (the Guerrillas of Christ the King, or GCR) which had just assassinated a number of left wing Spanish activists on the eve of Spain's first general election after the death of Franco. According to a detailed study by the French journalist Frédéric Laurent, the two chief advisers to Sanchez Covisa, the Italian Stefano Delle Chiaie and the Frenchman Yves Guérin-Sérac, escaped arrest with the others. In turn, all but one of the rest were released three months later. The reason for this leniency, according to Laurent, was that the GCR had served as a parallel police for the Spanish intelligence service (DGS) in its murderous repression of the Basque (ETA) separatist terrorist network.[29]

Clearly the Sanchez Covisa episode had international overtones, and a number of newspapers, even including the *New York Times,* mentioned speculations that the GCR might be functioning in coordination with a newly created "Fascist International." Such notions gained credence when Spanish police discovered among the GCR's assets three gold ingots which had been stolen the preceding summer by a group of French rightists and OAS veterans in a spectacular $10 million robbery of the Société Générale de Nice.[30] The leader of this well-organized group was Albert Spaggiari, veteran of an OAS assassination attempt against de Gaulle. When Spaggiari was captured by the French police in October 1976, the British press service Reuter noted reports from police sources that Spaggiari "had links with an international organization with members in right-wing circles in Italy, Lebanon, Britain and elsewhere."[31]

Spaggiari's international milieu acquired an even more intriguing dimension when it was revealed that in September 1976, after the robbery, Spaggiari had flown to Miami and offered his services as a mercenary to the CIA, citing his role in the Nice robbery as among his qualifications. Contrary to what he had expected, the CIA chose to transmit this information to the FBI, who in turn notified the French police through Interpol. It was this contact with the CIA which thus led to Spaggiari's arrest one month later.

After thirty-seven hours of noncooperation, Spaggiari suddenly admitted his role in the Nice robbery. According to *Le Monde,* this was part of a negotiated deal with the French police: Spaggiari would plead guilty to the $10 million dollar robbery, and thereby escape indictment on a still more serious charge of international arms trafficking. Spaggiari gained acceptance of this proposal after citing "the name of an important personage in the Ministry of the Interior, sometime participant in the cabinet of [French Interior Minister] Michel Poniatowski, who, for various reasons, was aware of the traffics in which he [i.e. Spaggiari] was involved."[32]

Five months later, in March 1977, Spaggiari escaped by jumping through the second-story window of the Nice Palais de Justice, landing on the roof of a waiting truck. Meanwhile the French weekly, *L'Express,* revealed that Spaggiari had been in contact in 1976 with a gang in Rome, "the Marseilles clan," who in turn had been close to Concutelli, and had been indicted by the latter's victim, Judge Occorsio.[33]

As Henrik Krüger points out, CIA-trained Cubans and their new patrons from the intelligence service and parallel police of the military police-states of Chile and Argentina, were also directly in touch with the so-called "Fascist International" milieu of Concutelli's Ordine Nuovo, Sanchez Covisa's GCR and Spaggiari's connection. As he points out (Krüger p. 204), an Argentine, Jorge Cesarsky, and a Cuban, Carlos Perez, were arrested in January 1977, in connection with one of the murders organized by Sanchez Covisa's GCR.[34] Carlos Perez is of particular interest to U.S. readers, because he was the Madrid representative of the Movimiento Nacionalista Cubana (MNC), an ideologically Fascist Cuban exile group, two of whose leaders (Ignacio and Guillermo Novo Sampol) have recently been convicted in connection with the assassination in Washington, in September 1976, of former Chilean foreign minister Orlando Letelier and Ronni Moffitt.

As has now been confirmed in part by a U.S. court, the assassination of Letelier by MNC members and Chilean intelligence agent Michael Townley was one of a series of "crimes in which Cuban exile terrorists and Chilean officials have collaborated since 1973."[35] Senior members of the Chilean junta intelligence service (DINA) initiated the Letelier murder, while junta leader Augusto Pinochet himself, according to a U.S. government official, was personally responsible.[36] One of these shootings, that of former Chilean Christian Democratic leader Bernardo Leighton and his wife (who was left paralyzed for life) took place in Rome in October 1975. Zero, a Cuban exile terrorist group allied to the MNC, took credit for the shooting in a well-informed communique. American sources have claimed that the attack was arranged through either Michael Townley or his wife Mariana Callejas, working for two Chileans who had collaborated earlier on the murder of Chilean General Rene Schneider.[37] European journalists have added that the terrorists in Rome were connected to a former mercenary group, once based in Lisbon, known by its cover name of Aginter-Press, and more particularly to Aginter's Italian "correspondent" Stefano Delle Chiaie.[38] Both Aginter-Press and the Townleys had collaborated in the 1973 Chilean coup group Patria y Libertad (a group indirectly subsidized by the CIA), while Delle Chiaie and his friend, the Italian Fascist Prince Valerio Borghese, had visited the Chilean junta in 1974.[39]

Delle Chiaie has already come to our attention as the Italian attached as senior adviser to the GCR in Spain, along with Yves

Guérin-Sérac, the former leader of Aginter-Press and, like most Aginter members, a veteran of the OAS. We should like to recall that Delle Chiaie and Guérin-Sérac escaped because of their relationship to the Spanish DGS arrest for the same murder in Madrid which led to the temporary arrest of Cuban MNC representative Carlos Perez. In other words the Letelier killing, horrible in itself, was only one incident in a larger web of international conspiracy.

The Latin American aspect of this larger story has already been told in the United States: the creation of an international Cuban exile terrorist network at the service of dictatorships such as Cuba, Brazil, and Nicaragua (under the Somozas), in exchange for payments in arms and future support in actions against Fidel Castro. Thus the Letelier killing has been traced back to the creation of a Cuban exile umbrella organization, CORU (Coordinacion de Organisaciones Revolucionarias Unidas), in the Bonao mountains of the Dominican Republic, in June 1976, under the leadership of Cuban exile terrorist Orlando Bosch, who had visited Chile in December 1974 with Guillermo Novo, and had spent a year there at junta expense.[40]

Bosch himself spoke to *New Times* reporter Blake Fleetwood about these activities. While declining to talk about the Letelier killing which was then under investigation, he cheerfully admitted setting up the murder of two Cuban diplomats in Argentina, in conjunction with the Argentine right wing terrorist AAA (to which Jorge Cesarsky, arrested in Spain, belonged).[41] Government sources told Saul Landau of the Transnational Institute in Washington that the Bonao meeting, attended by a U.S. Government informant, broke down into workshops for the planning of specific crimes, including the murder of Letelier and the October 1976 bombing of a Cuban airliner, in which seventy-three people were killed.[42] Bosch returned from the Bonao meeting to Venezuela, at the invitation, he maintains, of the Venezuelan intelligence service DISIP, who gave him a DISIP identification card.[43]

Given the nature, and the scope, of this network of government-assisted terror, of which the U.S. government was well-informed, it is interesting to recall the initial charade which the U.S. intelligence agencies put on for the benefit of the U.S. press:

> On October 11, 1976, *Newsweek* magazine reported that "the CIA has concluded that the Chilean secret police were not involved in the death of Orlando Letelier." The CIA also reassured the U.S. Department of Justice of this "fact." A Washington *Star* reporter (8 October 1976) was told by FBI sources that "Letelier might just as

well have been killed by leftist extremists to create a martyr." David
Binder of the *New York Times* reported (12 October 1976) that
"intelligence officials" were "pursuing the possibility that Mr.
Letelier had been assassinated by Chilean left wing extremists as a
means of disrupting U.S. relations with the military junta"[44] .... But
the biggest flood of distortion and rumors came from former and
retired FBI and CIA officials.... Members of such groups as the
Association of Former Intelligence Officers headed at that time by
David Phillips (Phillips, incidentally, headed the CIA's Latin
American covert action department at the time of the Sept. 11, 1973
coup in Chile) delivered documents from Letelier's briefcase [to
suggest, falsely] that Letelier was... not only a Cuban agent, but...
a Soviet agent as well.[45]

After persistent pressure from Letelier's U.S. associates and
friendly journalists, Letelier's principal assassin (Michael Townley)
has received a 10 year sentence (he will be eligible for parole in 1981).
For some reason the CIA was withholding relevant information from
the Justice Department at the same time it publicly advocated its
theory of DINA's innocence. Those who ordered Townley's crime
have not even been indicted. On the contrary, a related case against
another Cuban exile for receiving heavy-caliber arms, reportedly in
"part payment for the Letelier-Moffitt murders," was unsuccessful;
largely, it has been charged, because the CIA helped throw the case.[46]

As I write these words, a Congressional Committee has just
released a bill which responds in part to mounting pressures to
"unleash" the CIA. Thus Krüger's book is urgent and timely: it lifts the
veil on the global networks of these parafascist terrorists who can so
frequently plot and murder with impunity, thanks to their relationships and services to the intelligence agencies of the so-called "free
world." In short, it tells a story which our own media have
systematically failed to tell.

I cannot promise that his account is flawless. He writes about
intrigues where disinformation is rife and the truth about an event is
frequently misunderstood even by its participants. But he has
brought together a prodigious amount of information, supported by
shrewd analysis, particularly with respect to the European scene
which he knows best. As for the American scene, it may be difficult on
first reading to accept his hypothesis of a huge "Miami conspiracy",
now "reaching out with a vengeance to Latin America" (Krüger p.
204). Other observers of the so-called "Fascist international"
phenomenon (to use the term first given respectability by *Le Monde*),

have seen it as more polycentric, continuously divided by sectarianism, paranoia, and the ultimate inadequacy of national socialism as an international ideology.[47] But, even if nationalist ideologues continue to clash, there is unquestionably increasing international unity among the professional terrorists. I prefer to call the latter *parafascists* rather than Fascists because their primary concern is neither ideology nor a mass movement, but rather to function covertly in the service of, or parallel to, intelligence bureaucracies. Among parafascists there is a tendency toward international cohesion, even if this is fluid, and requires no one single capital or base. Where Krüger focuses on Miami, others have focused on Madrid, Costa Rica or Washington.

Krüger's invaluable contribution is to have spelled out the pervasive role of narcotics in supplying finances, organization, and sanctions to this parafascist network, from the Argentine AAA to the World Anti-Communist League (WACL) founded by KMT intelligence personnel on Taiwan. Before World War II the KMT regime in China was perhaps the best example of political manipulation of the narcotics traffic, under the guise of an "opium suppression campaign," to finance both a political and an intelligence apparatus (under General Tai Li).[48] This practice spread after World War II to a number of other WACL member countries and groups. Today there is cause to fear that Nixon's superagency, the Drug Enforcement Administration, has, like other narcotics enforcement agencies before it, come to use corrupt personnel who are actually part of the traffic, as part of a covert war against revolution.

This is easiest to argue in the case of corrupt police forces overseas, such as the DEA-supported Thai Border Patrol police who, by a massacre of unarmed Thai students, contributed to the overthrow of Thai democracy in October 1976.[49] But, in addition, *Harper's* Washington editor Jim Hougan has raised the possibility that a supersecret *internal* DEA intelligence group called "Deacon 1," consisting of thirty former CIA officers, all of them Cuban exiles, was "taken over by Cuban exile extremists" who "may have felt a greater loyalty to the politics of Orlando Bosch than to the goals of the DEA."[50] Hougan and Krüger cite the example of Deacon 1 operative Carlos Hernandez Rumbaut, a convicted narcotics trafficker who became second-in-command of the Costa Rican Narcotics Division and allegedly also joined a local death squad. Hougan asks whether the plans for Bosch's CORU and the DEA Deacon 1 operation in Costa Rica may not together explain the convergence in Costa Rica in

1974-76 of Robert Vesco, Mitch WerBell, Santo Trafficante and Orlando Bosch – all of whose activities "impinge on the same areas... exile politics, smuggling, and the CIA."[51] In support of this disturbing question, one can note that Bosch was given no less than three passports by Costa Rica in August 1976, right after the Bonao CORU meeting; and also that ten months later Bosch's daughter and son-in-law were both arrested on charges of smuggling cocaine.[52]

The U.S. government's narcotics Mafia connection goes back, as is well known, to World War II. Two controversial joint operations between OSS (Office of Strategic Services) and ONI (U.S. naval intelligence) established contacts (via Lucky Luciano) with the Sicilian Mafia;[53] and (via Tai Li) with the dope-dealing Green Gang of Tu Yueh-Sheng in Shanghai.[54] Both connections were extended into the post-war period as the Luciano and KMT networks slowly resumed their pre-war contacts. In Washington, in 1947, State Department official Walter Dowling noted with concern the efforts of an ex-OSS officer to reactivate the wartime OSS-mafia connection. Future CIA officer James Angleton (then in an interim agency, SSU) appears to have shared Dowling's repugnance; but one of the principal ex-OSS agents concerned, Max Corvo, now enjoyed influential private backing as a consultant to Italian-American industries in Sicily.[55]

The deportation of Lucky Luciano to Sicily in 1946 was followed by that of more than sixty other American *mafiosi*, some of whom, like Frank Coppola, became not only key figures in the postwar Luciano-Trafficante narcotics connection, but also political bosses whose Mafia muscle ensured the election of Christian Democrat M.P.s.[56] Coppola's name has been linked, together with that of Interior Minister Mario Scelba, to a May Day 1947 massacre at Portella delle Ginestre, in which eight people were killed by machine-gun fire, and thirty-three were wounded. In all 498 Sicilians, mostly left wingers, were murdered in 1948 alone, a revealing footnote to former CIA operative Miles Copeland's benign assurance that "had it not been for the Mafia the Communists would by now be in control of Italy."[57]

Meanwhile, in the United States, KMT agents helped establish a powerful China Lobby, and collaborated with friends in U.S. agencies to target, and in some cases drive from government, old foes of the former U.S.-KMT-Tai Li alliance including those inside the OSS. A scholarly book in 1960 noted that "the narcotics business has been a factor in some activities and permutations of the China Lobby," thus challenging the official Narcotics Bureau myth that KMT dope in this country was "Communist Chinese".[58]

The Luciano and KMT networks had been in contact for U.S. dope distribution in the 1930s. Although there is no evidence of substantial collaboration between them in the 1950s, there are symptoms of increasing convergence, partly through agents who dealt with both. There is the example of George White, an FBN official and former OSS agent who testified to the Kefauver Committee that he had been approached on behalf of Luciano in 1943 by an old China trafficker, August del Grazio.[59] White worked closely with the CIA in the post-war years and (under FBN cover) ran one of their LSD experiments in Project MK/ULTRA.[60] In 1948 White was back in Europe, intending to check up personally on Luciano and his narcotics associate Nick Gentile, another former U.S. gangster who (like Vito Genovese) had worked for the Allied Military Government in Sicily.[61] Soon afterwards Mafia traffickers in the United States began to be arrested, but not men like Luciano, Gentile, or Coppola.

By the time of White's visit to Marseilles, the CIA and AFL organizer Irving Brown were already subsidizing the use of Corsican and Italian gangsters to oust Communist unions from the Marseilles port. Brown's CIA case officer, Paul Sakwa, has confirmed that by the time CIA subsidies were terminated in 1953, Brown's chief contact with the Marseilles underworld, Pierre Ferri-Pisani, no longer needed U.S. support, because of the profits his newly-gained control of the port supplied from the heroin traffic.[62] Under the oversight of Ferri-Pisani and the Guerini gang, Corsican traffickers worked with the Luciano network and in the 1950s were its chief source of refined heroin. This alone might help explain the apparent immunity of Luciano's network, to which *Le Monde* alluded, along with that of its Corsican suppliers, about which *Le Monde* was silent.

Although White worked on the Luciano and Corsican cases, his FBN reputation had been made in 1937 by smashing a major distribution network headed by the pro-KMT Chinese tong (gang) in San Francisco, the Hip Sings.[63] But by 1951 the CIA was closely allied with KMT drug operations in Burma and Yunnan, through a Miami-based proprietary, Sea Supply, Inc., organized by OSS veteran Paul Helliwell.[64] In 1959 the FBN and White again arrested a new generation of Hip Sing officials, but only after the ringleader (Chung Wing Fong, a former Hip Sing president and official of the San Francisco Chinese Anti-Communist League, a KMT front) had yielded his passport to the U.S. consul in Hong Kong and then travelled as ordered to Taiwan.[65] In this way Fong became no more than an unindicted conspirator and the KMT disappeared from view; White, meanwhile, turned around and told the U.S. press the heroin came from *Communist* China ("most of it from a vast poppy field near Chungking").[66] In China, if not in Italy, White's concern about dope seems to have centered on networks within U.S. borders, not on the international suppliers.

In 1953-54 the CIA drew on old China hands with exposure to KMT traffic (Chennault, Willauer, William Pawley, Howard Hunt) to set up the overthrow of the Arbenz government in Guatemala, an operation which at least contemplated the use of "Puerto Rican and Cuban gangsters."[67] As part of this operation, we see CIA officer Howard Hunt, a veteran with his friend Lucien Conein and Conein's friend WerBell of OSS operations in China under Helliwell, helping in 1954 to set up what would eventually become the Latin American branch of the KMT-backed World Anti-Communist League. (Four years later the chairman of this group was the Guatemalan attorney of New Orleans Mafia leader Carlos Marcello.[68]) Nevertheless, in the late 1950s it seemed unlikely that the heroin connection, outside of countries directly involved, like Laos, would either have a major impact on U.S. policy or become a significant alternative to it. With the decline of cold war paranoia, events seemed to be moving towards normalization.

All this changed with the 1960s, when the CIA reassembled for the Bay of Pigs the old Guatemala team (including Hunt, Willauer, and Pawley, who oversaw Cuban recruitment). With the failure of the Bay of Pigs Cuba became to America what Algeria had been to France. The explosive political controversy meant that thousands of Cuban exiles, many of them with backgrounds in the Havana milieu, were trained by the U.S. as guerrillas and/or terrorists, then left in political limbo. Many of them soon turned to smuggling to augment their finances, and in some cases supplant their original political objectives. At least one CIA project growing out of Operation 40 (the control element in the Bay of Pigs invasion force), had to be terminated, when the drug activities of its members became too embarrassing.[69] In 1973 *Newsday* reported that "at least eight percent of the 1500-man [Bay of Pigs] invasion force has subsequently been investigated or arrested for drug-dealing."[70]

By this time many Bay of Pigs veterans were working for either Vesco or Trafficante.[71] Both the lucrative drug traffic and its anti-Communist politics began increasingly to get out of U.S. control. This was particularly true when, after the death of President Kennedy, the

U.S. lent a hand to military coups in Brazil, the Dominican Republic, and Greece, nations which in turn became bases for further right wing activities in other countries. America's lack of enthusiasm for the Fascist clients it had helped to procreate, only had the effect of encouraging them to plot more energetically with each other, and to lobby lavishly for more right wing policies in Washington. It was in this period that mercenary terrorism, illicit arms traffic, and drug traffic, consolidated into one increasingly global milieu. The long-delayed founding of the World Anti-Communist League in Taiwan in 1967 may be a less significant symptom of this trend than the Greek coup of the same year, after which the KYP (the Greek CIA) became an active fomenter of parafascist terror tactics in the rest of Europe.[72]

The official termination of the CIA MONGOOSE project against Cuba in the same year left a colossal disposal problem: what to do with the estimated 7000 trained Cubans? Here America seems to have followed the example set by de Gaulle. Some of these Cuban exiles were absorbed into other CIA and Pentagon operations, some went to work as did David for intelligence services in Latin America, some were retained by the CIA to report on their former colleagues and even to eliminate the more troublesome of them. But each of these solutions ran the risk of giving more power to the very elements whom the CIA wished to disperse. This was the situation faced by Richard Nixon on his election.

Several studies of Richard Nixon have focused on his contacts since 1946 with elements from organized crime, mostly through his early political adviser Murray Chotiner, and his close friend and business associate Bebe Rebozo. Kirkpatrick Sale has suggested that "It is possible that Richard Nixon was one more of the large number of politicians in this country who have been bought or cajoled into the service of the ends of organized crime."[73]

Yet this dark hypothesis is, I think, as oversimplified as its opposite. Like every one of his predecessors since at least World War II, Nixon, to become elected, had made accommodations to all of the prominent political forces in the coalition he represented, including the inevitable connection to organized crime. It may well be that in his early career these connections were more prominent than in the case of Lyndon Johnson, who started as FDR's protegé, or John F. Kennedy, who was born wealthy (and could leave dirty business connections to his father). But it was also apparent, even before he was elected in 1968, that Nixon sought to pursue a foreign policy that would be independent of the early KMT, and other money which had first helped him to become a national political figure.

Faced with the growing and closely related problems of right wing terrorism and of the international narcotics traffic, Nixon's approach seems to have been that of a self-perceived political realist: to gain control of, redirect, and manipulate the problem forces, rather than to somehow make them magically disappear. It is unlikely that these objectives were unrelated to his foreign policy efforts to establish links to mainland China, for this policy challenged the powerful China lobby which had supported him in the past. It may be no coincidence that the proclamation of the war on drugs, Kissinger's secret trip to Peking, and the establishment in the White House of what the president called "a non-legal team" (the Plumbers), including Hunt and Conein, all took place within a month of each other in mid-1971.

Thus in Miami Nixon appointed an energetic U.S. attorney, Robert Rust, who in June 1970 rounded up ex-CIA Cubans like Juan Restoy in Operation Eagle: this unusual zeal, according to Hank Messick, made Rust an exception to the South Florida "don't-rock-the-boat" tradition.[74] But Nixon's appointments to the Federal Court in the Miami area (one of whom was close to Paul Helliwell and had served as director of a bank accused of laundering money for Meyer Lansky) were not so gung-ho; and eventually most of Rust's indictments in Operation Eagle were overturned in court. Meanwhile the "non-legal team" at the White House, thanks to Howard Hunt, began to recruit men like Frank Sturgis, whose FBI file linked him to possible "organized crime activities," and Felipe de Diego, a colleague of Restoy in the CIA's Operation 40 project which had to be closed down because of its narcotics involvement.

Nixon, following de Gaulle's example, seems to have taken steps to restore control by the White House over a milieu which the U.S. government itself had helped to create. Like the French, he seems to have turned to elements of the milieu to work against it; but he seems to have had worse luck in those whom he picked. In his memoirs Nixon tells how, less than two weeks after the Watergate break-in

> Haldeman said that the whole thing was so ludicrous that Dean had not discounted the possibility that we were dealing with a double agent who purposely blew the operation. Otherwise it was just too hard to figure out.[75]

Eight years of journalistic books on Watergate, most of which barely mention the narcotics responsibilities of the so-called Plumbers, have not come up with any better explanation.

Edward J. Epstein's book on Nixon's drug policies, which *ipso facto* is a book about Watergate, analyzes this shortcoming of the journalists:

> The White House timetable for consolidating its power over the investigative agencies of the government was rudely interrupted on June 17, 1972, when Washington, D.C., police arrested five men in the national headquarters of the Democratic Party in the Watergate apartment and office complex.... With Nixon's impending reelection threatening the very independence of the power base of the investigative agencies, there were strong forces within the executive branch of the government which would not only refuse to help cover up the embarrassing connection but would actively work to disclose it.... Richard Helms... had been told that Nixon planned to replace him immediately after the election, and he feared, as he told me subsequently, that Nixon also planned "to destroy [his] agency.".... The "battle of the leaks," as Colson called it... began to sink the Nixon Administration....
>
> Consider, for example, the problem of Woodward and Bernstein, of the Washington *Post*. Woodward was receiving information from Robert Foster Bennett, of Robert R. Mullen and Company, that focused the blame for Watergate on Charles Colson. If he had assumed that Bennett was providing him with this information for anything more than a disinterested purpose, he would have had to ask whom Bennett worked for, what the true business of Mullen and Company was, and why Bennett wanted him to steer his investigation away from the CIA and toward Charles Colson. He then would have found that Mullen and Company was a CIA front organization and was aware that Bennett was giving information to Woodward; and that the CIA was trying to divert attention from itself (and succeeding, in the Washington *Post*) because a number of the conspirators involved in the Watergate burglary had also been involved in operations that the CIA had directly supported, such as the Plumbers. Moreover, the very fact that a CIA front group was providing information that was undermining the Nixon administration pointed to a conflict between Nixon and the CIA. Woodward and Bernstein, however, could not have reported these implications and thus could not have depicted the power struggle between the president and the CIA without revealing one of their prime sources. For the same reason, the reporters who received Nixon's tax returns from officials of the Internal Revenue Service could not have revealed this as evidence of a struggle between disgruntled members of the Treasury Department and the president without also revealing that they were no more than messengers for insurgents struggling against the president. By not revealing their sources, they received the Pulitzer Prize...[76]

Epstein views Watergate as optimistically as Edmund Burke saw the Whig Revolution of 1688 – as a restoration of decorum after tyrannous encroachment, a revolution not so much made as prevented: "The revolt of the bureaucrats thus succeeded in blocking Nixon's plan to gain control over the investigative agencies of the government in his second term."[77] This optimism assumes that Nixon himself was the problem, not the monster DEA agency which outlasted him or the CIA Cubans it recruited. It is true that the Watergate exposures put an end to Hunt's little known "recruitment of a secret army of Cuban exiles [no fewer than 120, according to CBS], answerable only to the White House, and equipped to assassinate foreign leaders."[78]

But some of the old China hands with network connections began moving to the new DEA. As we have seen, Hunt secured a post for his old OSS-Kunming friend Lucien Conein in what eventually became DEA, and Conein in turn recruited his own band of CIA Cubans in Deacon I, at least one of whom, according to CIA reports, has already taken part in a death squad operation.[79]

Nor did Watergate have a good effect on narcotics enforcement. On the contrary, the Watergate disclosures were followed by a marked drop-off in high-level drug conspiracy arrests. Senate investigator Philip R. Manuel reported in 1975 that "from 1917 through early 1973 Federal narcotics enforcement had its period of greatest success," but failed to hold its gains thereafter.[80] The new DEA soon came under both Senate and Justice Department scrutiny for a series of irregularities, including what one Senate staff report called "unprofessional conduct" in failing to pursue a Vesco narcotics lead.[81]

The terrorism connection which would survive Nixon's departure from office was not confined to Conein's Cuban squad in DEA. In 1975, when one Aginter-Press operative was overseeing the attempted murder of Bernardo and Anna Leighton in Rome, another was consulting in Washington with right wing Senator Strom Thurmond and with an official of President Ford's National Security Council. The second Aginter operative was former OAS member Jean-Denis Raingeard, and he sought (but failed to obtain) U.S. support for a plan by which the Azores would secede from Portugal; Aginter's Plan Usine for the secession involved a deal whereby a U.S. firm, with links to a New York Mafia family, would obtain rights for a casino, a bank, and (as one might have predicted) two diplomatic passports.[82] Although the Ford Administration did not ultimately buy the illegal proposal (they were more worried by the Portuguese reaction) neither did they discourage Raingeard's lobbying efforts among the Republican right wing. The next year U.S. agencies helped cover up the murder of Letelier by Aginter's Cuban allies in CORU, in a plot of which they may have had foreknowledge.

Whatever one may think of the Carter administration, it does not seem to have been as protective of Aginter, CORU, or their connections in the international arms and drug traffic. There are, however, two separate reasons why Henrik Krüger's exposé of the international parafascist connection is a timely one, and particularly important to U.S. readers. The first reason is that a number of recent revelations, which I have explored elsewhere, link those in the Aginter-CORU connection to the assassination of President John F. Kennedy. At least three Cubans prominent in the Letelier case have also been revealed, by the recent publications of the House Select Committee on Assassinations, to have been allied in a 1963 Cuban exile junta which, the Committee reported, warranted a "thorough investigation" in the Kennedy assassination case. Lee Harvey Oswald's activities in New Orleans brought him into contact with an anti-Castro group financially backed by this junta, and to Americans with links to the future Aginter community and possibly the OAS. And on 23 November 1963, Jean René Souetre, an OAS terrorist and future Aginter operative, was, according to recently declassified CIA reports, allegedly "expelled from the United States at Fort Worth or Dallas 18 hours after the assassination."[83]

More currently, there are press reports that Ronald Reagan, if elected president of the United States, would appoint Richard V. Allen to succeed Kissinger and Brzezinski as his special assistant for national security affairs. Richard Allen (who had been Nixon's first choice for the Plumbers' unit) is known to have represented Robert Vesco in Washington back in 1972, the year in which Vesco flew from a meeting with Lansky's representative Dino Cellini to Costa Rica, and initiated the contacts which later led to the proposed deal to manufacture Ingram M-10s in Costa Rica, between Vesco and Parabellum, Alliegro, and WerBell. Allen is also said to have been one of the U.S. contacts of the Aginter Plan Usine lobbyists who were proposing an economic free zone for the Azores (and the U.S. Mafia) much like that which Vesco, at Allen's suggestion, was proposing for Costa Rica.[84]

Richard Allen, to be sure, is no Vesco or Raingeard, but a professional cold warrior who in 1975 helped organize the Committee on the

Present Danger – a coalition against detente, uniting such veterans of the CIA-military-financial establishment as Paul Nitze, Gordon Gray, Gen. Maxwell D. Taylor, Arthur H. Dean, and Vesco's attorney Edward Bennett Williams. Nevertheless, unlike any previous national security adviser, but very much like some of the younger intellectual members of CPD, Allen comes out of the circle of ideological right wing think tanks which have advocated rollback rather than containment, which have collaborated with the Chilean junta, and which have been in touch with their European opposite numbers who in turn have had contact with Aginter and/or the OAS.

Whether or not he has a future in the White House, Allen's past involvement with both the Vesco milieu and the Wall Street establishment should remind U.S. readers that there is much more to the former than Caribbean exoticism, and much more to the latter than Council on Foreign Relations meetings and the sedate journalism of the *New York Times*. As long as the CORU planners of Letelier's assassination remain protected and unindicted, we must accept that terrorism in this country still enjoys the intelligence immunity which it did in the 1960s in Italy and France. With the advantage of his European experience, Henrik Krüger has seen the full scope of this international parafascism, more clearly than any U.S. journalist I know of. If we in this country wish to do something about the problem he describes, we will do well to begin by studying this book.

Peter Dale Scott
Berkeley, June 1980

NOTES

1. *Le Monde,* 17-18 June, 1973, pp. 11-12.
2. Edward J. Epstein, *Agency of Fear: Opiates and Political Power in America* (New York: G.P. Putnam's Sons, 1977), p. 299.
3. Epstein, p. 252.
4. Epstein, p. 86.
5. Epstein, p. 86; Eliot Marshall, "Heroin: the Source of Supply," *New Republic,* 24-31 July, 1971, p. 24; cf. Peter Dale Scott, *The War Conspiracy* (New York: Bobbs Merrill, 1972), p. 212.
6. *Le Monde,* 17-18 June, 1973, p. 11.
7. Newsday, *The Heroin Trail* (New York: New American Library, 1974), p. 124.
8. *Heroin Trail,* p. 108.
9. *Heroin Trail,* p. 110.
10. Phillip M. Williams, *Wars, Plots and Scandals in Post-War France* (Cambridge: Cambridge University Press, 1970), p. 115.

11. Williams, pp. 118-19.

12. *Heroin Trail*, p. 155.

13. Alain Jaubert, *Dossier D... Comme Drogue* (Paris: Alain Moreau, 1973), pp. 302-03, 352.

14. A.J. Langguth, *Hidden Terrors* (New York: Pantheon, 1978), p. 251.

15. Of the U.S. Treasure Department's list of 710 key illicit arms dealers, in 1977, 108 were drug smugglers, 24 percent of them Class I (U.S. Congress, Senate, Committee on Government Operations, *Illicit Traffic in Weapons and Drugs Across the United States-Mexican Border, Hearing*, 95th Congress, 1st Session, 12 January 1977, p. 31; cited hereafter as Bensinger Hearing).

16. George Thayer, *The War Business* (New York: Simon and Schuster, 1969), p. 43.

17. *New York Times*, 21 April 1975, pp. 1, 26.

18. Evert Clark and Nicholas Horrock, *Contrabandista* (New York: Praeger, 1973), p. 215.

19. Bensinger Hearing, pp. 9, 11.

20. Bensinger Hearing, p. 16.

21. *Spiegel*, 9 May, 1977, pp. 136-137, 148.

22. Bensinger Hearing, pp. 10, 14. Indeed, the *Los Angeles Times*, expanding on Bensinger's description of Sicilia as a "Cuban national," noted "reports that the subcommittee is trying to determine whether Cuba and the Soviet Union are involved in smuggling firearms into Mexico and narcotics into the United States" (13 January, 1977, II, 6).

23. Bensinger Hearing, pp. 42-44.

24. Interview of Gerry Patrick Hemming, *Argosy* (April 1976), p. 52; Jim Hougan, *Spooks: The Haunting of America – The Private Use of Secret Agents* (New York: William Morrow, 1978), p. 46. Anselmo Alliegro Senior was also a member of the shadowy Ansan investment group in Miami, suspected by a 1948 IRS report of being a front for Luciano funds (Steve Weissman ed., *Big Brother and the Holding Company*, Palo Alto, Ramparts Press, 1974, pp. 124, 259-60).

25. Hougan, pp. 46, 15ss.; Hank Messick, *Of Grass and Snow: The Secret Criminal Elite* (Englewood Cliffs, N.J.: Prentice-Hall, 1979), pp. 81-83.

26. Messick, p. 83.

27. Frédéric Laurent, *L'Orchestre Noir* (Paris: Stock, 1978), p. 366.

28. Laurent, pp. 362-63.

29. Laurent, pp. 311, 363.

30. Laurent, p. 401; Wilfred Burchett and Derek Roebuck, *The Whores of War: Mercenaries Today* (Harmondsworth, Middlesex and New York: Penguin, 1977), p. 155.

31. Reuter, 31 October 1976, quoted in Burchett, p. 156.

32. *Le Monde*, 18 May 1977, quoted in Laurent, pp. 398-99.

33. *L'Express*, 21 February 1977; cf. Laurent, pp. 365-66, 400.

34. *New York Times*, 1 February 1977, p. 8.

35. Saul Landau, *They Educated the Crows: An Institute Report on the Letelier-Moffitt Murders* (Washington: Transnational Institute, 1978), pp. 28-29.

36. Landau, pp. 4-13.

37. Donald Freed, with Dr. Fred Simon Landis, *Death in Washington: the Murder of Orlando Letelier* (Westport: Lawrence Hill and Associates, 1980)

38. Laurent, pp. 137, 312. Since the writing of this preface, a new book has identified Delle Chiaie as a key figure in the Leighton shootings; and adds that his group had informal ties to Italy's intelligence apparatus: John Dinges and Saul Landau, *Assassination on Embassy Row* (New York: Pantheon, 1980), pp. 117n, 196.

39. U.S. Congress, Senate, Select Committee to Study Government Operations with Respect to Intelligence Activities, *Intelligence Activities: Senate Resolution 21*, Hearings, 94th Congress, 1st Session, Volume 7, p. 171; Laurent, p. 312.

40. *New Times*, 13 May, 1977, p. 48; Landau, p. 27.

41. *New Times*, p. 48.

42. Landau, p. 27.

43. *New Times*, p. 51.

44. Ironically, Ignacio Novo's conviction for perjury derived from having suggested the same flagrant falsehood ("Maybe the communists did it to create problems") to the Washington Grand Jury.

45. Landau, p. 33

46. Dinges and Landau, pp. 242, 379; William Schapp, "Throwing a Case: The Trial of Armando Lopez Estrada," *Covert Action Information Bulletin*, (July 1978), pp. 8-14.

47. *Le Monde*, 1 April, 1975; Laurent, pp. 291, 307.

48. Alfred McCoy, *The Politics of Heroin in Southeast Asia* (New York: Harper and Row, 1972), pp. 380-83; Jonathan Marshall, "Opium and the Politics of Gangsterism in Nationalist China, 1927-1945," *Bulletin of Concerned Asian Scholars* (July-September 1976), pp. 19-48.

49. Noam Chomsky and Edward S. Herman, *The Washington Connection* (Boston: South End Press, 1979), p. 227. The Thai Border Police were supported in the 1950s by a Miami-based CIA proprietary, Sea Supply Inc., headed by Paul Helliwell (cf. footnote 64 below.)

50. Hougan, pp. 198-99.

51. Hougan, p. 197.

52. *New Times*, p. 51; *Miami News*, 27 July 1977. "Pinochet [chief of the Chilean junta] turned over to the United States drug enforcement administration a planeload of cocaine dealers rounded up after the coup. Their drug dealing could be blamed on Allende's ousted government. Then Pinochet's right-hand man, Contreras, could set up his own men with DINA protection in the same cocaine factories and shipping points. The anti-Castro Cubans had a piece of the action. The enormous profits went to supplement DINA's clandestine budget. The Cubans' share went into individual pockets and to the anti-Castro cause." (Dinges and Landau, p. 264n.).

53. Rodney Campbell, *The Luciano Project: The Secret Wartime Collaboration of the Mafia and the U.S. Navy* (New York: McGraw Hill, 1977), p. 176.

54. Marshall, p. 42; Richard Harris Smith, *OSS: The Secret History of America's First Central Intelligency Agency* (Berkeley: University of

California Press), p. 245; Milton Miles, *A Different Kind of War* (New York: Doubleday, 1967), p. 508.

55. Roberto Faenza and Marco Fini, *Gli Americani in Italia* (Milan: Feltrinelli, 1976), pp. 13, 138; David C. Martin, *Wilderness of Mirrors* (New York: Harper and Row, 1980), p. 18.

56. Gaia Servadio, *Mafioso: A History of the Mafia from Its Origins to the Present Day* (New York: Dell, 1976), pp. 72, 108; *Le Monde,* 17-18 June 1973, p. 11.

57. Servadio, pp. 125-28; Miles Copeland, *Beyond Cloak and Dagger: Inside the CIA* (New York: Pinnacle Books, 1975), p. 240. The bandit Giuliano who was responsible for the 1947 May Day massacre is said to have received "aid and support from former OSS members (who in the past had furnished him with the arms of the division of [Polish General] Anders), and, it appears. of OSS Chief William Donovan personally" (Faenza, p. 138, citing a conversation with OSS veteran Earl Brennan).

58. Ross Y. Koen, *The China Lobby in American Politics* (New York; Macmillan, 1960), p. ix; cf. Scott, *War Conspiracy,* pp. 203-04.

59. The effect of White's testimony was to suggest that OSS had rejected the proposal, or, as Smith (a CIA veteran) put it (p. 86), "OSS remained aloof, partly at the insistence of Major George White." But the lawyers implicated by White denied his charges altogether. "Three years afterward, when [New York State Commissioner of Investigation] Herlands questioned White under oath about this charge, White did not produce any kind of corroboration" (Campbell, p. 278).

60. John Marks, *The Search for the Manchurian Candidate: The CIA and Mind Control* (New York: Times Books, 1979), p. 89.

61. George White letter to Harry Anslinger, 10 June 1948, George White papers, Foothill College, Los Altos, Cal.; Servadio, p. 102. The AMGOT recruiter of Vito Genovese and other mafia figures was Charles Poletti, described by Lucky Luciano as "one of our good friends" (Servadio, p. 88). Poletti, a Democratic politician under Roosevelt and law partner of his son, went on to be an overseer of Harvard University."

62. Allan Francovich and Howard Dratch, "On Company Business" (Filmed for television) KQED, 16 May 1980. Sakwa's statement lends credibility to a French report that in 1952 Brown attended a Bordeaux meeting with Antoine Guérini (the chief Corsican mafia contact of Ferri-Pisani), and Jo Césari (the Marseilles chemist supplying Luciano with heroin), before Brown moved on to contact mafia personnel in Italy (Jaubert, p. 46n).

63. Will Oursler and L.D. Smith, *Narcotics: America's Peril* (Garden City, N.Y.: Doubleday, 1952), p. 87.

64. Scott, p. 211; McCoy, p. 130; As head of OSS S1 Branch in Kunming, China, Helliwell used to pay for intelligence with opium (*Wall Street Journal,* 18 April 1980). cf. footnote 49.

65. *San Francisco Chronicle,* 15 January 1959, pp. 1, 4.

66. *New York Times,* 15 January 1959, p. 4.

67. Susanne Jonas and David Tobis (eds.) *Guatemala* (Berkeley: NACLA, 1974), pp. 63, 67, 71.

68. Peter Dale Scott, *Crime and Cover-Up: The CIA, the Mafia, and the Dallas-Watergate Connection* (Berkeley: Westworks, 1977), p. 16.

69. *New York Times,* 4 January 1975, p. 9.

70. *Heroin Trail,* p. 169.

71. Hougan, pp. 195-196.

72. London *Observer,* 7 December 1969; Laurent, pp. 11, 217-43.

73. Kirkpatrick Sale, *Power Shift* (New York: Random House, 1975), p. 205.

74. Messick, p. 179.

75. Richard Nixon, *Memoirs* (New York: Grosset and Dunlap, 1978), pp. 643-44.

76. Epstein, pp. 235-38, 309-10.

77. Epstein, p. 241.

78. Jonathan Marshall, "The White House Death Squad," *Inquiry,* 5 March, 1979, p. 15.

79. Hougan, p. 199; *Washington Post,* 13 June 1976, C5. Nixon's own ambassador to Costa Rica, Viron Vaky, was aware of Carlos Hernandez Rumbaut's activities and in 1973 ordered DEA to have no more to do with him. But DEA disregarded Vaky's order.

80. U.S.-Congress, Senate, Committee on Government Operations, *Federal Drug Enforcement, Hearings,* 94th Cong., 1st Session, pp. 10-11, cf. pp. 26, 70, 251.

81. U.S. Congress, Senate, Committee on Government Operations, *Staff Study of the Frank Peroff Case,* 94th Congress, 1st Session, p. 198.

82. Fred Strasser and Brian McTigue, "The Fall River Conspiracy," *Boston* (November 1978), pp. 124, 180, 182.

83. Peter Dale Scott, Paul L. Hoch, Russell Statler, and Josiah Thompson, *Beyond Conspiracy: The Hidden Dimensions of the John F. Kennedy Assassination* (Berkeley: Westworks, 1980), cc. 12-14.

84. Hougan, pp. 205-06; U.S. Congress House Committee on Judiciary, Impeachment Hearings, Statement of Information, (Washington: G.P.O., 1974), Book VII, p. 602. Michael Oliver, the American adventurer behind the New Hebrides "free zone" secession movement of June 1980, had collaborated in an earlier WerBell project for an independent Abaco in the Bahamas, and is said to have inspired, with Allen, Vesco's Costa Rica project. (Hougan, *Spooks,* pp. 96-98, 206-07). According to the *Wall Street Journal* (14 July 1980), Vesco himself had been interested in the Azores in 1972-3 and, through his attorney, Howard Cerny, hired Allen to explore the financial prospects there. In the same period, Allen was a paid consultant to both the Vesco organization and the Nixon White House. Moreover, while still Nixon's deputy assistant for international economic affairs, Allen flew across the Atlantic with Vesco in Vesco's private plane.

PART I
BEAU SERGE

ONE
THE PRISONER

It must have been prisoner 77,343's worst dream come true when, on 1 October 1979, he was transferred to Hell's waiting room, the federal penitentiary in Atlanta.

In Atlanta's nightmare of a maximum security prison, Dominique Orsini, prisoner 77,343's friend and partner in the branch of the French Mafia known as Grupo Francés, had been murdered in an isolation cell on 12 April 1978. In the same prison six months earlier their heroin customer, Vincent Papa, had been eliminated by contract killing.[1] And before that, Orsini's lawyer, Gino Gallina, had been shot down in New York.[2]

Of nine murders committed within Atlanta's walls over a seventeen-month period in 1977-78, at least four were contracts on Mafia connected narcotics dealers, of whom Orsini and Papa were among the elite.[3] Since then the killings have continued, despite federal investigation of the obsolete seventy-eight year old prison.[4]

To the "honorable men" who drive up in black cars and flash their CIA, FBI, and DEA IDs, prisoner 77,343 remains the subject of intense interrogation, and that is another reason for his constant fear all these years. He knows prison walls won't stop his enemies or, for that matter, his friends – in his business there's little difference. Thus each time a guard sends in food he sniffs it, pokes at it, tastes it cautiously. That is how it's been for seven years. Only now, in Atlanta, the odds are worse than ever.

The prisoner who knows too much is Christian David, age fifty, French, known among friends as "le Beau Serge," and by more recent acquaintances in Latin America and the U.S. as "Eduardo" and "Jean-Pierre." Among French Connection notables he's a legend, a man whose mystique grows with each new tale of his exploits.[5]

He's been a pimp, robber, hired assassin for French intelligence, hatchet man in Algiers torture chambers, arms trader, spy, narcotics trafficker and, true to form, lover of beautiful women. He's one of the few alive who knows the truth about the Ben Barka affair that shook France in 1965;[6] he knows details of the brutal power struggle within French intelligence agency SDECE; of SDECE collaboration with the Corsican Mafia; and of secret CIA operations in Latin America. Ample grounds for anyone's paranoia. But David is cunning and tough, and that is why he's still alive.

He arrived in the U.S. on 17 November 1972 from Brazil, where he'd been arrested as the head of the huge narcotics smuggling ring, the Brazilian Connection. International law actually gave extradition priority to France, where he'd been sentenced to death *in abstentia* for murdering a police officer. But the Americans were not about to let the drug kingpin slip through their fingers.

When fetched from his cell in Brazil, David was desperate. Unsure of his destination, fearing it was France and a guillotine, he smashed a light bulb and swallowed the fragments. Even so, as he later claimed, "the Americans . . . filled me with drugs and carried me off to a military plane which flew me to the USA."[7]

Following a short hospital stay, he was hauled to a Brooklyn courthouse where the judge set bail at $2.5 million. Fearing the amount was not beyond the means of David's connections, authorities rammed his case through the labyrinth of justice. Within two weeks of his arrival, federal judge Jacob Mishler sentenced Beau Serge to twenty years in prison for smuggling half a ton of heroin into the United States.

During his trial, proof was obtained of David's activities on behalf of a very special branch of French intelligence known as Service d'Action Civique (SAC). His tri-colored SAC ID placed on display, David explained: "I was taken from prison in 1961 to work for an organization called SAC. It was arranged by someone with connections in the highest political circles."[8]

Of his confinement in Brazil, he had this to add: "I was tortured by the Brazilians for thirty days and fed nothing for twenty-six days. They stole all my money. Today I can't afford a lawyer, I haven't a cent."[9] According to Armand, his compatriot and prison mate for the trial, "When I saw David in the West Street jail, I could hardly recognize him, so terribly had the Brazilians mauled him."[10]

This doesn't quite jibe with David's later writing a Parisian friend of his desire to be transferred back to Brazil. But the ways of Christian David are often inexplicable. And for some the thought of torture is more bearable than that of death.

After his arrival in the U.S., David's attitude often shifted, depending on where he saw the greatest dangers. After his sentence was pronounced, he told FBI detectives: "If I had been extradited to France instead of abducted from Brazil, I would only have gotten three years. They would have forgotten about Galibert" (the police lieutenant he'd murdered in Paris). But he later wrote the writer Daniel Guerin: "If you get me a guarantee I won't be extradited to France, I'll tell you the truth about the Ben Barka affair."

The French government's two official attempts to have David extradited failed. And the French press has been surprisingly indifferent. One year after David was jailed in the U.S. (at first in the Marion, Illinois pen), *France Soir* reported he had shaved his beard, lost weight, complained of heart trouble, and sought admission to Springfield military hospital. On examination, however, the prison doctor found him in excellent health.

Another year passed and the following item appeared: "David acts deranged...darts about his cell, knocks his head against the wall, gesticulates weirdly, tears at his hair and screams he's being devoured by rats..."[11]

Then, in the summer of 1975, the beautiful Simone Delamare, his mistress in Brazil, came to Paris to plead David's cause with the press. In a letter to her dated 29 January 1975, he had written: "I'm doing all I can to avoid extradition to France. All I ask is to be treated like any other inmate. I'm locked in a windowless 2x2 meter cell, never see a ray of sunshine, have no idea of day or night. I hardly sleep anymore because of the evil atmosphere around me. I'm afraid they'll poison my food... The doctor examines me in two minutes. I speak no English and he knows no French. So he can't understand I have heart pains."[12]

After a long silence it was finally reported that on 6 December 1979 Ms. Delamare had visited Beau Serge in Atlanta. In a photo she had taken of their reunion, he no longer seemed particularly handsome. The loss of nearly all his hair had been compensated by a full beard. He reportedly wore strong glasses and was in bad health. A cancer specialist was said to visit him regularly.[13]

Despite appearances, few believe that David is truly incapacitated. He will stop at nothing, the authorities suspect. After all, he escaped from prison earlier in his career by playing mad. But would it really be so strange if he were disturbed? Few can take the constant fear of a sudden death, fed by memories of a life such as his.

Christian David fears both his friends from the Mafia and SAC and his enemies from the SDECE and CIA. But some of them are equally afraid of him. Why? This book does not provide the ultimate answer, but it will lift a corner or two of the veil placed over his record.

Notes

1. *New York Times*, 6 May 1979.

2. *France Soir*, 13 April 1978.

3. *Boston Globe*, 10 August 1978; *New York Times, op. cit.*

4. In a report issued 12 January 1980 the Senate Governmental Affairs subcommittee concluded that the Atlanta prison "serves to stimulate criminal activity rather than diminish it" and should be closed down no later than 1984. The Marion, Illinois pen, to which David was first sent, is regarded as the U.S.'s toughest prison and known among inmates as "the end of the line." The successor to Alcatraz, it was built to confine the most hardened and escape-minded prisoners, 100 of whom are housed in an ultrasecurity unit within the maximum security prison. After the bloody February 1980 riot in a New Mexico state prison, 21 inmates there were transferred to Marion, where they joined 400 other convicts in a three-week strike, beginning on St. Patrick's Day 1980, mostly to protest living conditions.

5. There was even a persistent rumor in 1979 that David had been smuggled back to France as an undercover agent for the DEA, and had opened up a restaurant in Marseilles.

6. The "Ben Barka affair" refers to the mysterious October 1965 kidnaping of the exiled Moroccan political leader Mehdi Ben Barka in Paris. Ben Barka had led the preparations for the Third World's first Tricontinental Congress in Cuba, which took place in early 1966. His disappearance, which involved more than one Western intelligence agency, is one of the great scandals of the century; see chapter six.

7. *France Soir*, 9 July 1975.

8. The Newsday Staff: *The Heroin Trail* (Souvenir Press, 1974).

9. *L'Aurore*, 20 November 1972.

10. R. Berdin: *Code Name Richard* (Dutton, 1974).

11. *France Soir*, 7 February 1974.

12. *France Soir*, 9 July 1975.

13. *VSD* (Vendredi-Samedi-Dimanche), 28 December 1979.

TWO
THE DUBIOUS ALLIANCE

The love affair of French intelligence and the underworld, the catalyst for Christian David's ascent in gangland, was a product of Franco-American ingenuity. In 1942 Thomas Dewey was the governor of New York. In an earlier role as district attorney he'd won fame battling organized crime. He'd put his most infamous victim, top mafioso Lucky Luciano, away in 1936 for "white slavery." However, Syndicate superstrategist Meyer Lansky had vowed to get his partner out of jail; and Dewey did an about-face when he found himself dependent on the Mob as election time approached.

Naval intelligence badly needed the assistance of Luciano, who held sway over New York's longshoremen. One word from the capo and they would rid the harbor of Axis powers' agents and saboteurs who threatened the war effort. The navy approached Dewey, who in turn arranged a meeting with Lansky and Moses Polakoff, Luciano's lawyer. They agreed that since only Lansky could prevail upon Luciano, he would visit his boss in prison. When Lansky proposed a deal guaranteeing him his freedom at war's end, Luciano agreed to cooperate.[1]

Thus began Operation Underworld. Luciano ordered his men to obey Lansky, who became the liaison with naval intelligence. Moreover, Luciano's contacts ensured the Allies a soft landing for their invasion of Sicily.

In early 1946 Luciano saw his reward. Dewey pardoned and deported him along with some of his lieutenants, but not before he met with agents of the CIA's forerunner, the Office of Strategic Services (OSS). When Luciano's ship embarked for Italy, the U.S. appeared to be taking leave of an honored guest. Besides Lansky, Frank Costello, and other Mafia dons, a host of politicians bade him farewell, as longshoremen kept reporters at bay.

Social unrest was then sweeping Europe, particularly France and Italy, where Communists, respected for their anti-Fascist resistance during the war, were fast gaining ground. The renowned Wild Bill Donovan, wartime head of the OSS, conceived the idea of using the Mob to battle the "Reds." Though enormously successful, the strategy also resulted, albeit inadvertently, in Mafia inroads in intelligence and politics, both in Europe and the United States.

In 1947 the Central Intelligence Agency (CIA) was established, just at the peak of France's political crisis. The center of unrest was Marseilles, where U.S. intelligence agents were already on the job. Jay Lovestone and Irving Brown, under cover of the International Ladies Garment Workers Union (ILGWU), had infiltrated French trade unions and were handing out money left and right.[2] In November 1947, the CIA's first director, Admiral Hillenkoetter, sent a team of experienced anti-Communist agents to Paris and Marseilles. It consisted of three OSS veterans and three "representatives" of the American Federation of Labor (AFL). They were told to "do something, anything."[3]

Pitched battles disrupted Paris the day the team arrived. The Communists had called for a struggle against the "parti Americain" and the Ramadier government had been toppled. When the agents hit Marseilles, the red flag waved over the Palace of Justice, and the leftists appeared in control of the city. The six agents wired home that the situation was desperate and that drastic measures were needed.

Those measures required gangsters from the Italian and Corsican underworld, hordes of whom were sent into battle. Their methods were brutal, the fight short but bloody. Within weeks the hoods had the situation under control. The CIA had been able to mobilize them so rapidly thanks to an important local ally. In early 1947 General de Gaulle had formed a right wing anti-Communist front, the Rassemblement du Peuple Francais (RPF), forerunner of the present-day Gaullist party (UDR). It soon established a security corps known as the Service d'Ordre du RPF (SO du RPF).

The corps made extensive use of Corsican gangsters against its political enemies. Dominique Ponchardier, its commander, later glorified the escapades of his Gorilles in a series of novels; other ringleaders included Roger Frey, Roger Barberot, Alexandre Sanguinetti, Paul Comiti and Jacques Foccart.[4] The Socialist party also plunged in headlong against the Communists, and worked especially closely with the CIA. Its security corps, the SO de la SFIO, also numbered Corsican hoods in its ranks.

Among the criminals recruited in 1947 by the CIA and SO du RPF were the Guerini brothers, the Francisci clan, Jo Renucci and Jo Attia, pillars of the underworld about whom we'll say more in the chapters that follow.

Unfortunately for the six-man CIA team, word of their underworld partnership arrived before them in Washington, where they were fired on the spot.[5] But that did not stop the CIA from maintaining contact with gangsters at home and abroad. On the contrary, the partnership expanded with time.

Notes

1. H. Messick: *Lansky* (Berkeley, 1971).
2. A. Jaubert: *Dossier D...comme Drogue* (Alain Moreau, 1974).
3. M. Copeland: *Beyond Cloak and Dagger* (Pinnacle Books, 1975).
4. P. Chairoff: *Dossier B...comme Barbouzes* (Alain Moreau, 1975).
5. Copeland, *op. cit.*

THREE
THE FRENCH UNDERWORLD

The French underworld is divided into two main groups: the Corsican Mafia and the independent, non-Corsican gangs. The latter are undisciplined and lack political influence. The Corsican Mafia, on the other hand, is as well-organized as the Sicilian and probably wields even greater political clout.

The story of the Corsican Mafia recalls that of the Sicilian. It was started by immigrants who left an island of hunger, underdevelopment, and desperation. At the turn of the century the Corsicans poured into France, particularly Marseilles. At first it was everyone for themselves. Then blood-bound clans emerged to control prostitution and the smuggling of alcohol and cigarettes. The take was initially divided equitably, but dissension soon broke out and the years since have been marked by a succession of bloody interfamily feuds.

Narcotics, heroin above all, brought the Corsicans their wealth and power. Marseilles became the heroin stronghold, as local underworld chemists learned to turn out the drug with pure, chalk-white quality. Most of it was sold on the U.S. market, where Italian and Cuban wholesalers entered the scene. In 1971 the Corsican Mafia delivered 80 percent of the heroin on the U.S. market. They deposited their millions in Bahamian, Swiss, and Lebanese banks, reinvesting some of it later in legal enterprise.[1]

Drug trader Richard Berdin, a non-Corsican gangster, described his Corsican colleagues as follows: "Most of them began as or still were pimps...they generally regarded anyone who did not have a Marseilles accent, didn't drink pastis or swoon over bouillabaisse, as suspect... We in Paris, especially we young hoods who came of age in the sixties, in our own way felt just as superior; we dressed mod, they dressed hood; we spoke decent French, they spoke broken Midi; we knew how to order good food and wine, they reeked of garlic and pastis; we knew how to escort and talk to women, they considered them all as hookers... Our 'profession' often brought us into contact... But it was a shaky marriage at best..."[2]

Not all Corsicans fit Berdin's description. Corsican capos live lives of fabulous luxury, with vast palaces outside Marseilles, and similar abodes in Paris and Corsica. They throw lavish parties teeming with politicians, or invite them for cruises aboard their yachts.

The Guerini clan was the first to truly dominate the Corsican Mafia. It centered around the brothers Antoine, Barthélémy ("Mémé"), Lucien, Francois, Pascal, and Pierre Guerini, who had been shepherd boys on Corsica before coming to Marseilles in 1912. By the close of the twenties, after prolonged and bloody vendettas, the Guerinis and their allies had risen to the top. There they remained for over thirty years. Throughout their reign Antoine, the oldest, headed the clan, and the Corsican Mafia as a whole.

The Guerinis were among the first to systematically organize the smuggling of opium and morphine base from Turkey and other Middle Eastern countries. They also started the production and marketing of heroin. Heroin laboratories sprouted all over Marseilles, where there was ample room for other gangs to operate either independently or in collaboration with the Guerinis.

The legendary Jo Cesari ensured the famous and coveted quality of Marseilles heroin. A self-taught chemist, he was a true master in the lab. No one in the world could teach him about the art of making heroin. He built and ran the great majority of Marseilles heroin labs until 1972.

Wisely, the Guerini brothers cultivated allies among politicians. Because of Marseilles' traditional socialist allegiance, they supported Gaston Deferre, mayor of Marseilles since 1953 and, in 1969, the Socialist party's presidential candidate. Beyond France's borders the Guerinis were in contact with the CIA, with whom they battled Communists in 1947. Even master heroin chemist Cesari allegedly had CIA connections.[3]

World War II brought a number of changes in the Marseilles underworld. The Carbone-Spirito gang, number two in the hierarchy, was decimated during the postwar purge for its collaboration with the Gestapo.[4] Joe Orsini and Auguste Ricord, two of its lieutenants, fled respectively to Canada and South America, there to become important international narcotics figures. This allowed Jo Renucci's gang to assume the no. 2 spot. Renucci, Lucky Luciano's French contact, was politically active for the right wing SO du RPF.[5] His lieutenants included Marcel Francisci and the brothers Dominique and Jean Venturi.

Francisci was born in Corsica in 1919 and demonstrated great organizational talent from an early age. He spun a web of connections on his native island. He fought with the Free French forces in Italy during the war and won medals for valor. After the armistice he joined Renucci's Marseilles gang and began smuggling cigarettes and silk stockings. He also made good narcotics contacts in the Arab lands.[6]

Starting in 1947 Renucci lent Francisci and other underlings to the SO du RPF as campaign guards and anti-Communist strongmen. Seizing the opportunity, Francisci befriended members of the coterie surrounding Charles de Gaulle – future secretary general Sanguinetti, future interior minister Frey, future police chief Jean Bozzi, future Parliament chairman Achilles Peretti, future minister for African Affairs and intelligence chief Jacques Foccart, and future chief bodyguard for de Gaulle, Paul Comiti, to name a few.[7] Francisci himself was to become a leader of the Gaullist party on Corsica and sit prominently on the island's administration, his residency in Paris notwithstanding.

Renucci's death in November 1958 spawned the Francisci-Venturi clan. The nation-hopping Joe Orsini returned to join the organization in 1964, while Jean Venturi left for Canada to assume control of the U.S.-bound narcotics traffic. Though Francisci was in charge, he returned to Paris and left the dirty work in Marseilles to the others. That work consisted almost exclusively of the production and smuggling of heroin. In Paris, Francisci spent much of his time playing politics and investing his wealth in restaurants, casinos, and real estate. His influence in the Gaullist party grew with his bank account.

To play it safe the Francisci-Venturi clan took out two political insurance policies. Dominique Venturi stuck with Marseilles' Socialist mayor Deferre, as had the Guerinis before him.[8] Though his men served in the Socialist security force, Venturi himself worked for the Gaullist SAC.

At some point in the mid-sixties the Francisci-Venturi clan decided to push the Guerini brothers out of the picture. Two masked motorcyclists shot down Antoine Guerini on 23 June 1967. Weeks later Marcel Francisci was shot at during a political meeting in

Ajaccio, Corsica, but managed to reach cover. Four Guerini lieutenants were killed in the next three months.

On 14 December 1967 two men were blown to bits planting a bomb
in Francisci's home near Paris. No one else was hurt. Francisci's com-
ment: "I forgive them."

On 21 June 1968 Francisci again escaped with his life, this time
from a restaurant in Corsica as five men sprayed machine gun bullets
in his wake. Passersby weren't as fortunate. One was killed, five
others were wounded. The machine gunners were taken care of four
months later in a Montmartre bar, by police-clad gangsters.

Mémé Guerini's efforts to avenge his brother's death ended with
his twenty-year murder sentence on 16 January 1970. With brother
Francois' death in prison one year earlier, the Guerinis no longer
stood in the way of the Francisci-Venturi mob.

U.S. narcotics police have long eyed Marcel Francisci, the man
they refer to as "Mr. Heroin." Whenever they try nailing him, however, they run into a roadblock. According to Francisci's supporters in
French politics, he's a respected businessman, not a gangster.[9] At
Fouquet, the flagship of his restaurant chain on Paris' Champs
Elysées, politicians and businessmen make important deals over
dinner.

Francisci's direct underworld contacts are people he can trust
completely: his brothers Jean, Francois, and Roland, with whom he
meets almost daily. Under President Valery Giscard d'Estaing (who is
not a Gaullist), Francisci has become even more careful. Furthermore, since 1972 the police have closed down many of his heroin
operations. But Francisci has the wherewithall to survive hard
times.[10]

Of the non-Corsican gangsters, the greatest was Jo Attia,
France's most colorful criminal until his death in 1972. Though mentioned primarily because he was responsible for Christian David's recruitment as a barbouze (specialist in undercover political violence,
spook), he was also the first gangster to become an international
espionage agent.

He was born on 10 June 1918. His mother was a worker in Rennes,
his father a Tunisian passing through. He was raised in a convent until
age twelve, when he was sent to earn his keep on a farm. Out of the
hard grind came the magnificent physique that would become his
underworld trademark. But by age sixteen he'd had it with farm life.
He headed to Marseilles and joined a gang of youths. Within a year
police caught him red-handed in a break-in. He was sent to North

Africa with a penal batallion. There he learned to box and to kill, and became a close friend of Marseilles gangster Pierre Loutrel. Upon their release, Attia plunged back into the Marseilles underworld and Loutrel headed to Paris.

During the war Attia worked with the French resistance force, the Maquis. His main contribution was to confine his thievery to Germans and their French collaborators. But he allegedly also helped hundreds of Jews to cross the border to Spain.

In July 1942 the Gestapo arrested him and sentenced him, first to death, later to the concentration camp at Mathausen. Within days of his arrival there, Attia glanced through his barracks window to discover an SS agent beating a defenseless prisoner. Infuriated, he sprang through the door and knocked the SS man down with a booming right. Had it not been for high-ranking German officers impressed with his valor, Attia would have been executed on the spot.

Fear did not stop Jo Attia. From the German supply depot he stole food for fellow inmates and medicine for the ill among them. Indebted to Attia for their survival of Mathausen were future justice minister Edmond Michelet and Mirage jet manufacturer Marcel Dassault. The Hero of Mathausen, Attia became the prisoners' spokesman.

Following the war Charles de Gaulle himself appointed Jo Attia to the Legion of Honor. Still, a hero's glory buys no bread. Jo thought of entering the boxing ring, but the first manager he approached broke up at the sight of Attia's tattoed body. "We're looking for a boxer," he said, "not a roadmap."

By chance Jo ran into his old friend from the penal batallion, Pierre Loutrel. In the meantime Loutrel had become one of Paris's leading crooks, "Pierrot le Fou" (the crazy). During the war Loutrel and his right-hand man Georges Boucheseiche had collaborated with the Gestapo. But Jo let bygones be bygones and joined the Auto Gang which was then laying France to waste with a string of murders and bank robberies.

On 25 September 1946 police finally caught up with the Auto Gang in the town of Champigny, southwest of Paris. Three hundred policemen were dispatched in armored cars to the hotel where the gang was holed up. There followed an exchange of fire in the classic Chicago tradition. Other than a few underlings, the only gangsters present were Attia and Boucheseiche. Pierrot le Fou was dining at a nearby restaurant.

When the sound of gunfire reached him, Loutrel sprang into his brand new armored Delahay, not to flee, but to rescue his pals. At top speed he swung through the bullet shower at the hotel entrance and jammed on the breaks long enough for Attia to jump in. He then floored the gas pedal and disappeared. The gendarmes were left gaping. Boucheseiche, by hiding in a water barrel and breathing through a hose, also managed to escape. When the police left the scene, he emerged.

Their luck ran out a few months later. They assaulted and shot a jeweler. Carrying the take to the car, Pierrot le Fou stuffed his pistol under his belt. It fired, stopping him in his tracks. His partners buried him on an island in the Seine.[11] Attia took over, but some of the wildness had left him. He opened a chain of bordellos and nightclubs. He also began to push drugs, while maintaining relations with the Corsican Mafia, especially the Guerinis.

In 1949 Attia was sent to prison for four years for concealing a body (that of Pierrot le Fou) and illegal possession of weapons. The prosecutor, charging Attia with murder, had asked for a life sentence. But Attia got off lightly thanks to the intervention of one Colonel Beaumont, alias Bertrand, of the SDECE, whose life Attia had saved during the war. Behind bars in Fresnes in 1952, Jo married the mother of his daughter, Nicole.[12]

When released, Attia was tracked down by his friend Beaumont, who had become the head of an SDECE division. The colonel offered Jo a large fee to locate a Moroccan terrorist hideout in French North Africa. Attia agreed. He took a whirlwind course in secret agentry, and left that year on several missions, mostly in Africa. Sometimes he parachuted, other times he came by land. At times he worked for Beaumont, at others he was in the employ of Colonel Fourcaud, another top man in the SDECE. Always, however, the mobster roamed free under the wings of the intelligence establishment.

In 1956 Attia was sent to Morocco to kill the Moroccan rebel leader Alal el-Fassai.[13] But he was arrested by Spanish authorities for blowing up the hotel in Spanish Morocco where Alal was holed up.[14] To ensure extradition to France he confessed to murdering two Frenchmen who had sold weapons to the Algerian revolutionaries of the FLN. The trial in France was a mockery of justice. Before long he was released.

In 1957, while Jo was on an SDECE mission in Tunisia, a member of Defense Minister Chaban Delmas' staff "accidentally" set eyes upon the SDECE gangster roll, and demanded to be told why Attia was working for the agency. Colonel Fourcaud defended him as a "marvelous personality, an admirable man and one of our best agents."

After 1958 Attia worked primarily for the secret intelligence network of Jacques Foccart, the Minister of African Affairs. In 1959 Jo surfaced first in Katanga, then in Abidjan, the capital of the Ivory Coast, where he purchased a nightclub, the Refuge. It became the headquarters of Foccart's African spy ring. Several attempted assassinations of black political leaders were planned in its back rooms. Attia also established an espionage center in his Gavroche restaurant in Paris's Montmartre quarter. It became the haunt of gangsters and agents, and those who were both.[15]

There are those who believe Attia also worked for the CIA in the same period. The Church committee report on assassinations of foreign leaders reveals the agency's recruitment of a European gangster for the murder of Patrice Lumumba of the Congo. The hit man, code named QJ/WIN, was described as a convicted criminal who could be dispatched on high-risk missions. Although Attia was probably not the killer in question, both QJ/WIN and a second potential assassin, referred to as WI/ROGUE, are likely to be found in a census of the French underworld.[16]

Around 1960 Jo Attia met Christian David, who was then just a smalltime hood. Together they worked as barbouzes in Algeria and were involved in a long series of shady intelligence capers including the infamous kidnapings of Colonel Antoine Argoud and Mehdi Ben Barka. (See chapters five and six.)

After 1962 Attia was in and out of prison, but that was probably more for his own protection than anything else. He had all the freedom necessary to carry out his intelligence missions, though eventually he was officially banned from France. He then roamed through the Congo, Morocco, and the Ivory Coast, but returned to Paris when so inclined. Police knew of his presence but did nothing.

On 22 June 1972 Jo Attia died of throat cancer. But before he did he settled a score with a rival gang led by Georges Segard and Christian Jubin. Jubin had raped Nicole, the daughter of Jo the Terrible. Segard and Jubin were handed over to the police.

Within hours of his death there were break-ins at Jo's apartment and at his restaurant, Gavroche. Someone wanted to be satisfied that no compromising material would end up in the wrong hands. Was it the SDECE?

Notes

1. Some sources estimate the amount of Marseilles heroin smuggled in 1971 at three tons, others at over six. The second figure is more likely, given the official 1972 figure of 7300 kilos; see The Newsday Staff: *The Heroin Trail* (Souvenir Press, 1974).

2. R. Berdin: *Code Named Richard* (Dutton, 1974).

3. A. Jaubert: *Dossier D...comme Drogue* (Alain Moreau, 1974).

4. The exploits of the Carbone-Spirito gang are romanticized in the film "Borsalino" with Alain Delon and Jean-Paul Belmondo.

5. Jaubert, *op. cit.*

6. The Newsday Staff, *op. cit.*

7. Jaubert, *op. cit.*; P. Chairoff: *Dossier B...comme Barbouzes* (Alain Moreau, 1975).

8. The Newsday Staff, *op. cit.*

9. Francisci has sued *Time* magazine and a number of French journalists for trying to connect him to the drug trade, but each time he has retreated in the eleventh hour.

10. According to journalist Nicholas Gage (*New York Times*, 12 January 1980), there is increasing evidence, including the uncovering of several heroin labs in Marseilles, Nice, and Milan, of a revived French Connection. Francisci himself has apparently not been active in French politics since 1974, but remains a man of considerable influence. The last heard of him was when his restaurant, Fouquet, denied access to unaccompanied women in 1979.

11. S. Vincentanne: *Ea bande a Pierrot-le-Fou* (Champ Libre, 1970).

12. N. Attia: *Jo Attia* (Gallimard, 1974).

13. P.T. de Vosjoli: *Le Comité* (Éditions de l'Homme, 1975); The Newsday Staff, *op. cit.*

14. Jaubert, *op. cit.*

15. Attia also owned the nightclub "Number Ten" in Leopoldville, which was often frequented by Lumumba.

16. *Les Complots de la CIA* (Stock, 1976); *Le Meilleur*, 10 June 1976.

FOUR
THE FRENCH INTELLIGENCE ZOO

Trying to make sense out of French intelligence activities is like trying to find one's way out of a maze knowing there's no exit. All told, there are four intelligence services, and at various times they work together, independently, and against one another in an atmosphere of scandal and intrigue. The four are: the foreign espionage agency, Service de Documentation Exterieure et de Contre Espionage (SDECE); the domestic security agency, Direction de la Surveillance du Territoire (DST); the police intelligence force, Renseignements Généraux (RG); and the Gaullists' para-police force, Service d'Action Civique (SAC).

Charles de Gaulle reigned over the Golden Age of French espionage. The president was enamored of cloaks and daggers and could not get enough security from the dangers left and right...including those responsible for his security. Though he determined overall policy, de Gaulle kept his own hands off intelligence activities, leaving the nuts and bolts to loyal followers.

The rules had been written during World War II, when de Gaulle and his followers were located in London's Free French house. De Gaulle saw a double agent in every unannounced Channel crosser and, not infrequently, had that individual executed without regard to the petty details of justice. After the war, anonymous corpses were exhumed from the cellar of the London abode.

The SDECE emerged shortly after World War II. It consisted of seven departments that handled intelligence analysis, Eastern and Western Europe, Africa, the Middle East, the Far East, and America. In addition there is a special action group within the SDECE, the Service d'Action du SDECE. It's not to be confused with SAC, though it is sometimes difficult to distinguish between their operations.

The SDECE employs some 2000 men and has a yearly budget fixed at $25 million. Another $50 million can be tapped from a secret reserve.[1] Its headquarters are next to a large bathhouse in the Paris suburb of Les Tourelles. The French call it "the swimming pool."

In its thirty years of existence the SDECE has had six chiefs. De Gaulle's first, General Grossin, lasted until 1962. General Paul Jacquier, his replacement, was dropped without so much as a handshake following the 1965 Ben Barka affair. The next chief, General Eugene Guibaud, didn't last much longer. He left in 1970 when Georges Pompidou became the president. Pompidou was convinced that SDECE figures had led a smear campaign to keep him out of Charles de Gaulle's shoes. He chose the aristocratic pro-U.S. Alexandre de Marenches to purge the intelligence agency.

A dynasty of military officers has run the various SDECE departments. The names heard most often in connection with assassination, kidnaping, and other scandals are: Colonel René Bertrand alias Beaumont, Colonel Nicolas Fourcaud, Colonel Marcel Leroy alias Leroy-Finville, Colonel Paul Ferrer alias Fournier, and Colonel Marcel Mercier, who headed the neo-Fascist Red Hand that was responsible for a string of political murders.[2]

The SDECE story is one of continuous scandal. Murder plots, kidnapings, drug deals, and extensive collaboration with the underworld have been brought to light, but are only part of the story. France has never shown the tendency toward open government that has, for example, produced public hearings in the U.S. on CIA and FBI crimes. What light has been shed in recent years is due mostly to Phillipe Thyraud de Vosjoli, a former SDECE agent in Cuba and Washington. His books, *Lamia* and *Le Comité*, raised a furor in France. It was he who tipped off the United States about the presence of Russian rocket bases in Cuba while stationed there as a French agent. He was fired in 1963.

According to de Vosjoli, under de Gaulle a murder committee existed consisting of the president's closest political allies and intelligence officers. It plotted extreme measures against nations or individuals who threatened de Gaulle or his policies. At one point, the hit list included as many as thirty names. They included Guinea's chief-of-state Sekou Touré and Tunisia's Habib Bourgiba, both of whom survived. Others did not, though their deaths have been recorded as accidents.

SDECE agents working for the committee, according to de Vosjoli, were responsible for the 1962 plane crash which took the life of

Italian oil magnate Enrico Mattei. Mattei, then Italy's strong man, was on the verge of engineering an Italian takeover of French oil interests in Algeria. A French agent code-named Laurent tinkered with Mattei's aircraft, which crashed en route from Catania to Rome. William McHale, a *Time* magazine reporter writing a series about Mattei, was among the other dead. Apparently a similar fate awaited the journalist Mauro de Mauro who, while investigating the Mattei affair in 1970, disappeared without a trace.

The committee also had tasks other than murder. When a newly designed Russian military jet broke down during a visit to France and was to be sent home over land, Marcel Leroy of the SDECE went into the moving business. He was hired to move the jet from the airport to the freight train the Soviets had rushed to Paris. As unsuspecting Russian guards sat in a car trailing the freight truck, the jet was placed in a second truck identical to the first, in which French agents scampered about with cameras. The two trucks were switched back when the Russians were delayed at an intersection.

During a 1961 conference in Cannes, an SDECE agent broke into the hotel room of U.S. Assistant Secretary of State George Ball, and photographed all his documents while Ball snored peacefully. Similarly, an agent once rummaged through the baggage of the Moroccan ambassador to France. His eyes lit up when he opened the lock of an attaché case. Inside were nothing but pornographic photos and an ivory penis together with a user guide, in a package addressed to Madame Oufkir, the wife of the notorious Moroccan security chief, Mohammed Oufkir.

In his first book, *Lamia*, de Vosjoli also claimed that the de Gaulle regime for a long time chose to ignore the presence of Soviet spies on French soil, and perhaps even fed them information. De Gaulle, with nationalistic pride over France's development of an A-bomb, ignored John F. Kennedy's warnings about the Russian agents. He was tired of listening to Washington. With France about to become a great power again, the United States became its number one rival.

De Gaulle also had ideas of his own on how to win the Third World over to France. At one time France was the greatest colonial power in Africa. However, in 1961-62 de Gaulle gave autonomy to nearly all its African possessions. His policy of creating a French "Commonwealth" was clever in principle. But the man to whom de Gaulle entrusted his Third World plans was intelligence whiz Jacques Foccart, the Gaullist Grey Eminence. The policies carried out by Foccart bore little resemblance to de Gaulle's guidelines and the newly created French Community of Nations soon fell apart at the seams.

Behind Jacques Foccart was the loyal core of his own espionage ring, and the entire SAC staff, which he'd gradually expanded into an apparatus that permeated French society and foreign locales as well.[3] SAC had appeared in 1958, the crisis year in which de Gaulle assumed power by a *coup d'etat*. The RPF became the official Gaullist party, and SAC became its security force. The men who founded SAC were for the most part those who had also dominated the SO du RPF: Foccart, Frey, Ponchardier, Sanguinetti, Bozzi, Comiti, and Charles Pasqua.[4] Comiti and Charles Lascorz were the first to direct the para-police force. However, ultimate control always remained in the hands of Foccart.

The official task of SAC was to protect Gaullist politicians in travels and at meetings. However, by the end of its first year of existence, 1958, SAC had joined the battle against the Algerian revolutionary movement, FLN, and even then it was studded with gangsters. In the final phase of the war in Algeria, SAC agents – les barbouzes – were pitted against the mutinous Secret Army Organization (OAS) whose murderous resistance was choked off with equal brutality.

When de Gaulle granted Algeria its independence in 1962, the barbouzes turned their wrath against de Gaulle's political enemies. They became the instruments for the dirtiest of Gaullist tricks. Murder, corruption, industrial espionage, election fraud – SAC agents could do it all.

Foccart assigned his best SAC men to key posts on French commissions for developing countries, and in offices charged with the allotment of public funds. He also dispatched them to infiltrate African regimes, where pro-French governments allegedly paid them enormous kickbacks in return for economic assistance from Paris.

At its peak SAC comprised a core of 120 directors in immediate contact with Foccart, plus some 20,000 associates, three-quarters of whom were estimated to have been criminals, many of them heroin smugglers.[5] (French intelligence has frequently been accused of having both organized and profited from the trafficking of heroin.) SAC was used at home to instigate and then crush left wing disturbances, such as the time a SAC agent took potshots at a peaceful demonstration in La Mure and struck down a renowned athlete, and the knifing of a left wing activist by a SAC agent in Drancy.[6] Foccart's SAC agents are especially active at election time. In Socialist and Communist-dominated areas they've often been caught stealing and burning ballots.

In 1968 SAC terrorized the student rebellion. The DST handed its SAC colleagues lists of suspected de Gaulle foes in Marseilles, Lyons, and Grenoble, as part of a SAC plan to detain political "subversives" in stadiums and camps, similar to what happened in Chile.[7]

Through the years Jacques Foccart was not only in charge of SAC, but he also had many of his top men assigned to key positions in the SDECE. While many SAC agents were also SDECE agents and *vice versa,* there were always SDECE men opposed to Foccart (as there are now), and that has long been a source of intrigue. In de Gaulle's time both SAC and the SDECE worked against the CIA, though several French agents played footsy with the Americans. The criminal elements were available to anyone for the right price.

Under Pompidou, and more so now under Giscard d'Estaing, the goal has been centralization of intelligence activities. The U.S. is no longer considered the number one enemy, and the SDECE has been ordered to cooperate with the CIA. Pompidou fired 7000 of SAC's crooks. Although Giscard d'Estaing would like to eliminate SAC altogether, he dares not legislate it out of existence.[8]

At 66 Jacques Foccart hangs on as one of France's most powerful men. After the deaths of de Gaulle and Pompidou, he had thousands of documents destroyed, documents that would have exposed the Gaullists' dirtiest tricks. But Foccart has not shred all his papers. He allegedly has a file on every French politician and officeholder since 1974, which puts him in a position to blackmail many of them.

In 1974 Giscard d'Estaing replaced Foccart, as his advisor on African affairs, with Foccart's underling, René Journiac. Foccart retired after an additional number of years in a similar position with Omar Bongo, the corrupt ruler of Gabon.

On 6 February 1980, Journiac perished in a mysterious plane crash in Northern Cameroon.[9]

Notes
1. J. Hoagland, *Politiken,* 14 June 1976.
2. P.T. de Vosjoli: *Le Comite* (Editions de l'Homme, 1975); A. Jaubert: *Dossier D...comme Drogue* (Alain Moreau, 1974); N. Fournier and E. Legrand: *Dossier E...comme Espionage* (Alain Moreau, 1977).
3. P. Chairoff: *Dossier B...comme Barbouzes* (Alain Moreau, 1975).
4. UDR member Charles Pasqua held a seat in Parliament and chaired a 1969

committee investigating France's narcotics problem. From 1952 to 1967 he held various high-ranking positions in the big wine firm, Ricard Pastis. When the known heroin trafficker Jean Venturi came to Montreal in 1962 to establish a new smuggling network, his cover was as a representative for Ricard Pastis, where his immediate superior appears to have been Pasqua – see The Newsday Staff: *The Heroin Trail* (Souvenir Books, 1974).

5. Chairoff, *op. cit.*

6. Jaubert, *op. cit.*

7. Chairoff, *op. cit.*

8. As late as the summer of 1976 Marseilles' Socialist mayor Gaston Deferre, and other left wing politicians, charged in Parliament that the Gaullists were about to rebuild SAC, and that murderers and thieves were again being recruited out of prison as in 1961. In the last few years, however, the Gaullists have lost much ground, whereas France's non-Gaullist Right, with OAS figures in the fore, has gotten a shot in the arm. Many former SAC goons are allegedly currently working for this movement.

9. E. Ramaro: "Un Petit Mort Sans Significance," *Afrique-Asie*, 3 March 1980. For a review of French dirty work in Africa pre- and post-Foccart, see K. Van Meter: "The French Role in Africa", in *Dirty Work 2, The CIA in Africa*, edited by E. Ray, W. Schaap, K. Van Meter and L. Wolf (Lyle Stuart, 1979).

FIVE
ASSASSIN IN ALGIERS

Christian David was born in 1929 in the city of Bordeaux in the south of France. Like most youths destined to underworld stardom, he was wild and incorrigible, picked up for pickpocketing on more than one occasion. His Bordeaux chums recall him as ostentatious and hot-headed. By age twenty-one he had parlayed good looks and charm into a budding career as a pimp.

Not long thereafter he purchased the Whiskey A Go-Go night-club.[1] But the proceeds from the whores and the club were not enough. Greed was another of his traits. He had tasted the life of a playboy and his need for excitement bordered on the pathological. Beau Serge began to mastermind bank heists. At age twenty-six he was arrested and sentenced to a stay at Besancon prison on a score of counts ranging from procuring to armed assault.[2] One year later he escaped and was on the loose for several months. When recaptured he was jailed on Ile de Ré outside the city of La Rochelle.[3]

He escaped once more in the fall of 1960. This time he remained longer in hiding with the help of his friends in the underworld. It was probably then that he impressed the gangster kingpin Jo Attia, who would greatly influence Beau Serge's career. In February 1961 David was again taken prisoner and returned to Ile de Ré, where he was placed under close guard. Escape number three would demand all his cunning and a dash of theatrics.

His behavior slowly altered. He uttered strange things, trembled uncontrollably, communicated with no one, and smashed his cell in fits of hysteria. The doctor became convinced of his derangement. In the summer of 1961 he was moved to the Cadillac mental hospital.

Within months a nurse became his accomplice in escape. But all was in vain. A chase through the woods and Beau Serge was soon back in his cage on Ile de Ré.

All the while, however, and unknown to him, plans for David's future were being made just outside prison walls. Serious men were gathered in a house on Ile de Ré to discuss a list of names. The house belonged to France's ambassador to the Central African Republic, Colonel Roger Barberot – a hero of World War II and Indochina, and chief of the Black Commandos in Algeria.[4] Most of the men were members of the inner circle of the ruling Gaullist party. Others were princes of the underworld. One of the latter was Jo Attia. And one of the names on the list was Christian David's.

One day in October 1961 David was taken from his cell to government offices in La Rochelle, and seated in a comfortable chair opposite a man of influence and power. The man was Pierre Lemarchand, a high-ranking Gaullist betrothed to de Gaulle's adopted daughter.[5] When presented with Lemarchand's proposal, Christian David was dumbfounded. Freedom would be his if he agreed to join a terror corps assembled to put an end to the Algerian operations of the ultranationalist, anti-de Gaulle Secret Army Organization (OAS). The corps was a division of SAC, the semiofficial security and intelligence unit of the Gaullist party.

Beau Serge joined SAC at once. Though admission normally required two sponsors, the rules were waived in times of crisis. During the May 1968 student insurrection one merely had to declare oneself anti-Communist and look like a bruiser.

In the de Gaulle era an almost religious aura surrounded SAC just as it did the towering president himself. The new recruit, David, was placed on a red carpet in the middle of a room with drawn, thick curtains. Two or three SAC leaders, facing a wall, listened to the enlistee as he swore allegiance with his hand upon a Cross of Lorraine and dagger. A leader would then declare: "You are now our follower in life and death."[6]

Christian David, and hundreds of others plucked from prison for an Algerian rendezvous, were sent to a camp in Satory. There they were run through a crash training course in weaponry, sabotage, and hand-to-hand combat. It left little doubt that their *métiers* would be murder and torture.

On December 1 the "barbouzes" landed in Algiers. Headquarters were set up in Villa A – for Andrea – at 8 Rue Fabre in the El Biar district, and Villa B on the corner of Chemin Reynaud and Rue

Faidherbe.[7] David was installed at Andrea; its real name, Dar Es Saada, means the house of bliss. The name fit. A pretty lane led to its main entrance and to a large garden stocked with orange trees. But the interior of this house of bliss would soon resound with the screams of those tortured in its cellar.

OAS terrorist activities, led by Jean-Jacques Susini and Roger Degueldre, were at their peak. Bombs hurled at Algerian restaurants, buses, and public squares killed hundreds of innocent bystanders. An explosion in Paris' Charone Metro station killed eight passengers and wounded thirty. The order to the barbouze corps was clear: the OAS had to be halted at all costs.

The ensuing struggle between the barbouzes and OAS terrorists was brutal in the extreme. Resembling more a bloody vendetta than the usual sort of war, it became a test of one's imagination for atrocity. When seven barbouze bodies were found hanging from lamp posts less their ears and noses, no one doubted a more gruesome fate awaited the OAS. On 22 December 1961 the barbouzes exploded a bomb at the Grand Rocher restaurant, a known OAS haunt, killing twelve. Eight days later a large OAS force attacked Villa B. The barbouzes were about to ring in the New Year when bazooka blasts echoed all around them. Fourteen were killed and two were wounded.

On 27 January 1962 the barbouzes captured several high-ranking OAS officers, among them Alexandre Tisslenkoff, who had directed illegal radio broadcasts. The captives were taken to the basement of Villa A and tortured. Tisslenkoff later related his days of suffering at the hands of three men: a Vietnamese, a Frenchman who ran a karate school in Paris, and a third man who swaggeringly identified himself as the "intellectual of the barbouzes." Four years later, in Paris, Tisslenkoff would recognize the last-mentioned hatchet man as Christian David.

In his book *J'Accuse Lemarchand*, which was banned and destroyed in France, Tisslenkoff described being tortured by thrashing, suffocation, and electrocution, and claimed that Pierre Lemarchand was present for part of it.[8] The latter, together with Dominique Ponchardier, headed the Mouvement Pour la Communauté, an *ad hoc* Gaullist group under whose auspices the barbouze corps was formed. SAC agents ransacked the publishing house as Tisslenkoff's book was about to go to press.

29 January 1962, like any other day at Villa Andrea, was filled with cries of pain, profanity, and black humor. David and Lemarchand were away. Inside were a total of twenty-nine barbouzes

and prisoners. At 5:00 PM there was a violent explosion. The villa rose like a rocket as men and concrete were hurled dozens of yards through the air. The OAS had decimated Villa Andrea with 150 kilos of explosives. Miraculously, ten men survived. Seven were barbouzes, among them Dominique Venturi, who later became one of France's leading drug merchants; three were prisoners, among them Tisslenkoff. All had been in the garden at the time.

In reacting to such violence, Christian David showed no restraint. The death of a friend could drive him berserk. Former SAC agent Patrice Chairoff, alias Dominique Calzi, claims that David was responsible for the murder of fifty-four people in his seven to eight months in Algeria. "He was a born killer," says Chairoff.[9]

When Beau Serge returned shortly after the explosion, he saw red at the sight of the prisoners who had escaped the fate of his nineteen comrades, whose remains were splattered everywhere. Demanding summary execution of the prisoners, he lunged at Tisslenkoff. Had it not been for officers who intervened, wrote Tisslenkoff, David would have killed him with his bare hands.

The OAS success was short-lived. The barbouzes, until then regarded in France as a shady outfit, were buried as heroes. Their leaders cried for revenge. But the barbouzes needed no prodding. They gained more than their revenge. When the smoke cleared five months later on 3 July 1962, Algeria was independent, and the vendetta had claimed the lives of 110 barbouzes, over 400 OAS terrorists, and a far greater number of bystanders. Six years later a pile of bodies was found buried in the garden surrounding Villa Andrea's remains. Many had skulls riddled with high-caliber bullet holes.

A new world had opened up to Christian David in Algeria. He established many contacts crucial to his later career. Among his fighting buddies had been: Michel Nicoli, Ange Simonpieri, André Labay, Michel Victor Mertz, Roger Delouette, Jo Attia, Jean Palisse, Georges Boucheseiche, Francois Marcantoni, Dominique Venturi, Jean Auge, Roger Dadoun, Louis Nesmoz, Didier Barone, Paul Mondolini, and Marcel Francisci. All eventually rose to the top of the French underworld. All trafficked in narcotics, and nearly all remained in touch with French intelligence.

Beau Serge had quickly ascended to the ranks of the barbouze elite. He had become the friend of such notables as Lemarchand, Ponchardier, and Barberot. Overnight he was transformed from a *voyou* (punk) into a man to be respected.

In the months following his return from Algiers, David lay low to avoid a vindictive OAS. He lodged incognito in Marseilles' Saint Victor quarter, and soon had two prostitutes working for him.[10] However, David had performed so impressively in Algeria that he was urged to become a full-time agent of the SDECE.[11] He jumped at the chance and was given the complete training course at the Saint-Cyr-au-Mont d'Or police academy.[12]

Upon graduation David went on a long series of missions in Africa, particularly in Morocco. It's also believed he was sent to Latin America twice between 1962 and 1965. He specialized in weapons deals and the elimination of independent dealers who encroached on SDECE territory. Mostly he took on missions for Jacques Foccart's special forces; he also temporarily slid back over to SAC. In France he helped the Gaullists fix elections. Under questioning in the U.S. in 1972 he admitted often stealing opposition ballots.[13]

Between intelligence assignments David minded not only his own affairs, but also those of Jo Attia, who was officially in prison and, for a period, in exile in Africa. David ran two of Attia's houses of ill-repute. In the evenings he could often be seen at Attia's Gavroche bar in the company of gangsters Georges Figon, Georges Boucheseiche, and Julien le Ny.[14]

In those years Beau Serge played strange games in the underworld, gaining a footing in the Guerini clan, and eventually becoming boss Mémé Guerini's confidante.[15] A Corsican gangster later told police of a curious summit on 14 January 1965 in Antoine Guerini's house in the La Galenzana district of Marseilles. Corsican leaders were contemplating the liquidation of former police superintendent Robert Blémant, who had carved his own successful niche in the underworld.

"All the criminal bosses of France were there, and some from Germany and France as well. Everyone awaited the arrival of the Guerini brothers. Suddenly the door opened and in walked a man with an 11.43 caliber in one hand. It was Beau Serge. He ordered all of us to reach for the sky while he frisked us. When he was through Antoine and Mémé Guerini came in.[16]

At the meeting David allegedly angered the Guerinis by voting against Blémant's elimination.[17] Nonetheless three hit men shot Blémant down shortly afterward. One of the murderers, Pierre Colombani, was tortured and slain in Ajaccio, Corsica a few months later. Several Guerini clan members suspected that David had done him in.[18]

From 1962 to 1966 David could be found everywhere. Jo Attia's band of thugs was then known primarily for their political dirty work. While Jo the Terrible was in protective confinement or exile, Boucheseiche was in charge. But the latter was usually in Morocco tending his chain of brothels, and David often worked instead for the young Lyons-based Lesca gang, centered around Felix Lesca, Didier Barone and Louis Nesmoz.[19] Together they pulled off one of the period's most audacious, well-executed heists, the 1964 armed robbery of the Colombo jewelers in Milan, which netted them between $2 and $2.5 million.

During a badly needed vacation in Biarritz on the Atlantic, David took time off to relieve an armored car from the Brequet factory of $50,000.[20] Shortly thereafter Beau Serge was a frequent guest at Leon le Juif in Paris.[21] He also met with SAC leader Charley Lascorz. If the police had wanted to arrest him, they could have.

It is also likely that Christian David was with Attia's gang when they abducted OAS colonel Antoine Argoud from West Germany to France on orders from Jacques Foccart. Defeat in Algiers had not spelled the end of the OAS, which continued sporadic terrorist actions while in exile. Its members bombed restaurants and movie theaters in France, and made numerous daring attempts on the life of President de Gaulle. Colonel Argoud, a highly intelligent and intriguing figure, headed the organization in exile. He was the brains behind its terrorist activities and assassination attempts.

On 14 February 1963 de Gaulle's security forces uncovered a new conspiracy to murder the president. A sharpshooter was to fell the president from behind as he delivered a speech at a military academy. Infuriated, de Gaulle summoned the man responsible for security, Interior Minister Frey. The French president had had his fill of assassination attempts. Frey went to Foccart, who put his intelligence agents to work. On February 22 one of Foccart's men in Rome reported that Argoud was en route to Munich, where he would stay for the carnival.

Foccart contacted the West German intelligence czar Reinhard Gehlen, a former general under Hitler, and requested his help in bringing Argoud to France. But Gehlen would have nothing to do with the plan, making its execution all the more difficult now that German intelligence was tipped off. Foccart still had his barbouze army to turn to, and chose Jo Attia's mob for the job. Jo the Terrible, then in exile in Africa, got the green light to return.

On February 25 Argoud arrived in Munich from a Rome huddle with OAS leaders. Driving from the train station to the Eden-Wolff hotel, he could not have known that half-a-dozen disguised barbouzes awaited him. Handed the key to room 434, Argoud was about to enter the elevator when he was accosted by two men in leather pants and Tyrolian hats. The receptionist later recalled assuming the men were friends of the Colonel's and off to have some fun; after all, it was carnival time and the beer was flowing.

Argoud himself suddenly felt as if both his arms were in a vise. Leaving the hotel one of the men pressed a finger against the pressure point under his ear, causing Argoud to faint. The barbouzes placed their arms around his shoulders, walked over to a Renault Frigate, and drove off. The car headed out of Munich towards the Europa Bridge between Kehl and Strassbourg, France, racing down the "third lane" reserved for allied forces in Germany. Its license plate revealed its attachment to the French army.

The next day Parisian police received a strange phone message about a blue truck parked at the entrance to Notre Dame cathedral. Inside was a package the police were sure to find interesting. The man on duty was inclined to disregard the call, but sent two patrolmen to inspect the truck. It was parked as described. When the policemen broke open the door they found a man lying bound and gagged, his face crimson from a bloody nose.

"Mon dieu!" cried one of the officers, "It's Colonel Argoud!"

The abduction became an international scandal. Diplomatic wheels rolled. The Bonn regime, supported by the United States, addressed a sharply worded note to the French demanding Argoud's return to Munich. Cynics who believed the CIA had taken part in attempts on de Gaulle's life, charged that the Americans had been in touch with Argoud.

But the Paris regime refused to release the OAS colonel. He was imprisoned, but pardoned in 1968 after de Gaulle issued a general amnesty for former OAS members – when forced to do so by French officers who had made it a condition for their support during the 1968 student-led strike. After his release, Argoud announced he had recognized Jo Attia as one of his kidnappers. It wasn't the first time Jacques Foccart had treaded on the feet of foreign governments and intelligence services, and it wasn't the last time gangsters would be his tools.

NOTES

1. A. Jaubert: *Dossier D . . . Comme Drogue* (Alain Moreau, 1974).

2. *L'Aurore*, 16 June 1975.

3. According to French journalist Jean Montaldo, David was also jailed temporarily in Poissy Penitentiary outside Paris. His cellmates there were the gangsters Goerges Figon, who was later murdered, probably by Beau Serge, and Francois Marcantoni, a key figure in the strange case of the murder of Stefan Markovic, the bodyguard of the Actor Alain Delon.

4. R. Barberot: *A Bras le Coeur* (Robert Laffont, 1972). The Black Commandos, the intelligence agency SDECE's special infiltration units in Algiers, were attached to the 11th Parachute Shock Brigade.

5. *Newsday*, 14 February 1973.

6. The Newsweek Staff: *The Heroin Trail* (Souvenir Press, 1974).

7. L. Bitterlin: *Histoire des Barbouzes* (Éditions du Palais Royal, 1972).

8. A. Tisslenkoff: *J'Accuse Lemarchand* (Éditions Saint-Just, 1966).

9. From the author's interview with Chairoff.

10. L. Durand: *Le Caid* (Denoel, 1976).

11. Others also took notice of the barbouze elite, whose terror pacification tactics were innovative: "Ed Lansdale, Desmond Fitzgerald, Colby and others took it over as part of their own method of operation. Pacification in this special sense became part of the U.S. Army Special Forces training doctrine. The Phoenix Project was the assassination (to use Lyndon Johnson's terms, 'The Murder Inc.') part of pacification." (L.F. Prouty, *Ramparts*, October 1973).

12. Jaubert, *op. cit.*

13. The Newsday Staff, *op. cit.*

14. Jaubert, *op. cit.*

15. Sarazin, *op. cit.*

16. M. Accosta: "Smukke Serge," *Kriminal Journalen*, March 1978.

17. *Ibid.*

18. David might well have been doubling as an informer. Recall that through his intelligence work and guerilla activities for SAC, David was working for the Gaullist inner circle. The latter group supported the Francisci clan in its power struggle against the Guerinis, who backed the Socialists. David often frequented the Leon le Juif bar in Paris' Seventeenth District, the known rendezvous of the assistant chief of police intelligence, Jean Caille, Pierre Lemarchand, and their underworld connections. Sarazin, *op. cit.*

19. The Lesca gang, also known as the "Bricole" gang, was also connected to Lemarchand and Foccart's intelligence network (D. Guerin: *Les Assassins de Ben Barka*, Guy Authier, 1975) and worked especially closely with the Lyons SAC chief, Jean Auge (Sarazin, *op. cit.*).

20. Jaubert, *op. cit.*

21. Sarazin, *op. cit.*

SIX
NIGHTMARE OF THE AGENTS:
THE BEN BARKA AFFAIR

The October 1965 kidnaping of the Moroccan exile leader Mehdi Ben Barka was the most controversial and daring affair involving Christian David. Of the twentieth century's most consequential political melodramas, the Ben Barka case ranks with the murder of John F. Kennedy. It remains an unsolved puzzle, with unexploded fireworks that still haunt spooks on both sides of the Atlantic.

There is a semiofficial scenario, but it is full of holes. To make the story hold water many of the involved have been killed, threatened, or ruined. In 1980, fifteen years after Ben Barka's disappearance, that story remains as dubious and full of holes as ever.

The current version goes something like this:

The Moroccan King Hassan II, Interior Minister General Mohammed Oufkir, and his security chief, Colonel Ahmed Dlimi, conspired with members of the French government and its intelligence arm, the SDECE, to lure Ben Barka to Paris, where he would be turned over to Moroccan espionage agents.

The abduction was executed as planned on October 29. Ben Barka was taken to a house in the Paris suburb, Fontenay-le-Vicomte. The following evening General Oufkir, Colonel Dlimi, and Moroccan intelligence agents arrived. Soon thereafter Ben Barka was tortured and killed by Oufkir himself, and buried by hired crooks.

Implicated were the Moroccan government, certain leading French politicians, the French intelligence agency SDECE, and gangsters connected to it; no one else, according to the official version, was involved.

De Gaulle believed, with good reason, that he had been hood-winked by some of his own men who had been in cahoots with the CIA, which he blamed for the entire affair. Amazingly, though, the CIA came out smelling like a rose. The only ones to be disgraced in the en-suing trial were the Moroccans and French intelligence, their under-world allies having long since been compromised. Not coincidentally, the trial was punctuated by interruptions, postponements, the liqui-dation of two star witnesses, the disappearance of a number of the implicated, and the deaths of three French attorneys for the Ben Barka family.

Oufkir and members of his security staff were sentenced *in ab-sentia* to life in prison. Several Frenchmen, among them police and in-telligence agents, received up to eight years. SDECE chief Paul Jacquier was sacked. Prime Minister Georges Pompidou, Interior Minister Roger Frey, and de Gaulle's son-in-law, member of Parlia-ment Pierre Lemarchand, were all blasted by de Gaulle.

To the stunned populace that was as far as the scandal went, and it was far enough. But what really happened? Why did so many strug-gle so desperately to keep the lid on? So far the succession of theories and rumors have all lacked credibility. However, in recent years addi-tional aspects of the Ben Barka affair have come to light through scat-tered details in many books and articles. Alone, these facts seem in-significant. Together they form a lead that can be followed.

I emphasize strongly that the following scenario is *my own*. My linking of the many facts is *hypothetical*. The following, therefore, is not necessarily "the truth about the Ben Barka affair" nor an exhaus-tive account of what occurred, because this is not a book about the Ben Barka affair. Rather, I try to show that *we still haven't been told the truth*, that the CIA was involved, and that the Ben Barka affair has to this day left some unfinished business in the netherworld of spooks. Furthermore, this will clarify one reason for Christian David's anxie-ties in jail.

Mehdi Ben Barka was forty-four years old when he disappeared. From an early age he had been a zealous champion of Moroccan inde-pendence and of a Socialist future for his country. For a period in the late forties he was the mathematics instructor of Hassan, son of Mohammed V, who became the present King Hassan II. In 1952, with Morocco still under French rule, Ben Barka was banished to the desert, and there he devoted much of his time to study.

In 1956 Morocco gained its independence. Three years later Ben Barka founded the Union Nationale des Forces Populaire (UNFP). In

1961 Hassan was crowned and appointed himself the prime minister.

In the 1963 National Assembly election Ben Barka's party, the UNFP, won twenty-eight seats, while another reformist party, Istiqlal, gained forty-one. The two were expected to form a coalition, which was a threat to the king's ruling party, FDIC, which itself claimed sixty-nine seats.

In July 1963, two months after the election, security chief Oufkir disclosed a "plot" against the king. A sworn devotee of feudal rule and a flaming anti-Communist, Oufkir cracked down hard against the "conspirators." In March 1964 the court of Rabat sentenced seventy-seven opposition politicians. Eleven were condemned to death, though eight had already fled. Among those sentenced to death *in absentia* was Ben Barka. According to a report of the International Commission of Jurists, which followed the trial, evidence for the plot was scanty at best.

Whether or not the plot was Oufkir's fabrication, its uncovering was a boon to his career. From 1964 on he was Morocco's interior minister and strong man, the man the CIA supported and worked with in Morocco. At the time Ethiopia and Morocco were America's two most important African allies. They received the lion's share of U.S. economic and military aid, and Morocco's Kenitra air base was a focal point of CIA activity in Africa and the Middle East.

The U.S. ambassador to Morocco in 1965, Henry J. Tasca, later became known for his service in Greece, where he supported the colonels' junta. The CIA station chief, Robert Wells, coordinated CIA assistance to the Moroccan security police in eradicating political opponents of the regime.

The Americans took a keen interest in Ben Barka in 1965 when he set up a Geneva base for his Third World travels. Ben Barka had been elected chairman of the steering committee for the first Tricontinental Congress, to be held 3-10 January 1966 in Havana, Cuba. The conference was slated to be a Third World milestone, demonstrating solidarity and brotherhood in the battle against imperialism. It was a thorn in the side of the U.S. in more ways than one. The Americans hadn't given up hope of "liberating" Cuba. Moreover, Washington had good reason to fear that the budding Third World solidarity would lead to a strong, united front against the U.S. and American business interests abroad.

In 1965 King Hassan began airing the possibility of pardoning Ben Barka and allowing him to return to participate in politics, under the king's conditions. Hassan went so far as to send an emissary to

Geneva to negotiate with Ben Barka. It's impossible to know whether the king's gesture was sincere. Hassan might have been part of the plot from the very beginning. More likely, though, the king was hoping to entice Ben Barka back to Morocco of his own free will, but needed the help of the French.

The hoodwinking grew out of discussions between Oufkir and the CIA. Ambassador Tasca inquired at CIA Paris headquarters about the possibility of helping return Ben Barka to Morocco.[1] The CIA was primarily interested in preventing Ben Barka's attendance at the Tricontinental Congress, and in learning of preparations already under way. Moreover, the CIA wanted to keep Ben Barka out of Moroccan politics. All three goals could only be realised by liquidating him or taking him to Morocco and putting him under permanent house arrest.

Oufkir was most concerned with ensuring Ben Barka's permanent absence from Moroccan politics. His second priority was serving the CIA. The possibility cannot be overlooked that the CIA and Oufkir had already made plans for Morocco's future . ∴ plans that led to Oufkir's catastrophic coup attempt seven years later.

And what of the affair's scapegoats? How did France feel about Ben Barka's return to Morocco and his trip to the Tricontinental Congress? In my opinion France was led by the nose by its own intelligence agents who were actually cooperating with the CIA. After all, the Ben Barka affair took place at the nadir of Franco-American relations. De Gaulle, intent on strengthening France's Third World relations to the detriment of the USA's, had just returned from Latin America, where he had expressed whole-hearted support for Third World nationalism.

De Gaulle was very much interested in the Tricontinental Congress, and even more so in Ben Barka's reconciliation with King Hassan and subsequent return to Moroccan politics. That would undermine the U.S. position in North Africa and weaken Oufkir, whom de Gaulle despised for aiding OAS figures following the war in Algeria. It was not in France's official interest to have Ben Barka killed. But within de Gaulle's own party hierarchy were people who went their own way, at times working with the CIA.

As usual, one can't help suspecting de Gaulle's grey eminence, Jacques Foccart, who was going his own way, at the time, in Latin America. However, Foccart had just seen his African policies backfire, and would likely hesitate before risking another major blunder. Moreover, until then Foccart had been secretly supplying Ben Barka with money and arms.[2]

It must have been either King Hassan or his trusted Colonel Dlimi who, in search of French assistance, presented a plan for collaboration to the likes of Interior Minister Roger Frey, Jacques Foccart, and Pierre Lemarchand. The plan, however, was hardly as elaborate as the one hatched by Oufkir and the CIA, with or without King Hassan's consent. The plan shown to de Gaulle's people probably was limited to bringing Ben Barka to Paris and holding him there on suspicion of narcotics smuggling, until he and the Moroccans had reached an agreement on Hassan's offer.[3] What's most important is that the plan involved the French and the Moroccans only. Judging from appearances, Hassan even asked Lemarchand at the start to negotiate with Ben Barka. Papers later found on a murdered key witness indicate that Lemarchand had jotted down the king's conditions for presentation to Ben Barka.

The French agreed to lure Ben Barka to Paris, in the belief it would help both the king and the exiled leader. Foccart and Lemarchand also anticipated viewing plans for the Tricontinental Congress so that they could suitably adjust French policy.

According to plan, both Moroccan and French espionage agents shadowed Ben Barka in Geneva. But Oufkir sought independent intelligence – intended neither for Hassan nor for the French. Had he assigned the job to the CIA, it would have been too risky, since it would quickly have aroused French suspicions. He requested instead the aid of the Israeli intelligence agency, Mossad.[4] Though it might sound strange today, Israel and Morocco were on excellent terms in the sixties – so excellent that Moroccan espionage agents were trained in Israel.

Oufkir, claiming his own men were not up to the assignment, requested the loan of Israeli agents from Mossad chief Meir Amit. Amit agreed and sent a team of agents to shadow Ben Barka in Geneva. A few days later they phoned in a report that French and Moroccan agents were stumbling over one another's feet. The Mossad chief called off his men and told Oufkir he didn't need three sets of agents to spy on one man.

Oufkir entrusted his business in France to his agent Mohammed Miloued, code named "Chtouki". The two spun a web of conspiracy involving exclusively Frenchmen who either were deceived by or were working with the CIA. Getting Ben Barka to Paris would be taken care of by de Gaulle's unsuspecting staff. For the practical details the French hired the gangster Georges Figon, an acquaintance of Lemarchand's who moved in many different circles.

Quite casually they located the film director Georges Franju, who was then planning an antiimperialist film and fancied having Ben Barka in a starring role. It was excellent bait, for if Ben Barka agreed to come to Paris to discuss the film, he would bring his file on the approaching Tricontinental conference. The go-between was reportedly Phillipe Bernier, a friend of Figon's who knew Ben Barka personally.

Ben Barka took the bait. Enthusiastic about the movie, he agreed to meet in Paris with Franju, Bernier, and Figon on 29 October 1965 at the "Drugstore" restaurant on Boulevard Saint-Germain-des-Prés.

Prior to Ben Barka's arrival, however, Georges Figon caused trouble. Nervous, he asked to be remunerated for services rendered. In Jo Attia's bar, Le Gavroche, he confided to acquaintances that he'd soon be paid a small fortune. Among those acquaintances was Christian David. Oufkir decided he'd had it with Figon, who he most likely knew was working for Lemarchand.[5] Oufkir offered him a lucrative job in Morocco, but Figon declined, having been ordered to hang on.

Around noon on October 29, Ben Barka was walking through Paris with his friend Azemouri, a Moroccan student. The two were on their way to meet with the filmmakers. A patrol car pulled up in front of the Brasserie Lipp restaurant on Boulevard Saint-Germain-des-Prés. Two men hopped out, flashed police badges, and asked Ben Barka to join them.

There were already three men in the car: Orly airport chief Antoine Lopez, French narcotics lieutenant Louis Souchon, and the latter's assistant, Roger Voitot. An agent for the SDECE, Lopez was close to Oufkir, who had promised him the directorship of Royal Air Maroc if anything went wrong. Georges Pompidou had Lopez working closely as a special agent with America's Paris narcotics office, a beehive of CIA activity.[6] Souchon and Voitot were similarly collaborating with U.S. narks. Lopez, however, had apparently convinced them the action was sanctioned by Jacques Foccart.

The abduction was initially camouflaged as a drug raid. Had anything misfired at the start, they could always have claimed, truthfully enough, that Ben Barka was a suspected trafficker.

The car with Ben Barka and the three cops headed out of Paris, followed closely by another containing Georges Boucheseiche, Julien le Ny, Pierre Dubail, and Jean Palisse – all from Jo Attia's gang. Like Attia, Boucheseiche had worked for the SDECE. However, his true loyalty was to General Oufkir, under whose wing he ran nightclubs and brothels in Morocco.

The two cars drove twenty kilometers out of Paris to Fontenay-le-Vicomte, where Ben Barka was led into a house owned by Boucheseiche. Lopez, Souchon, and Voitot drove away immediately, leaving behind the four gangsters and two Moroccan agents. Shortly thereafter Lopez phoned Commandant Finville of the SDECE, alias Marcel Leroy, and delivered the message: "Pedro to Thomas – the package has been delivered."

At the time, Marcel Leroy, who was later fired and imprisoned for his complicity in the Ben Barka affair, was highly valued by the Americans. The CIA got him out of jail by blackmailing the SDECE and French politicos through Phillipe Thyraud de Vosjoli, the French spy who became friendly with the CIA after uncovering the Soviet rocket bases on Cuba. De Vosjoli's *Le Comité*, which the French press speculated was ghostwritten by Leroy,[7] discloses the previously mentioned French murder committee whose job under de Gaulle was to cut down the president's enemies.[8] In the book de Vosjoli insists that Colonel Marcel Mercier, not Leroy, was the "evil SDECE man" in the Ben Barka affair.

In a curious chapter apparently added to *Le Comité* at the eleventh hour, Leroy describes being summoned, shortly before the Ben Barka incident, to the Matignon building where Pompidou had his offices. There, to his surprise, he was ordered by a certain Monsieur Legros to collaborate with Antoine Lopez on a drug control measure, Ben Barka's abduction. Leroy claims to have refused unless the order came directly from his immediate supervisor, which it later did.

The Legros whom Marcel Leroy met in the Matignon office may well have been Fernand Legros, the playboy, millionaire, art dealer, CIA agent, and member of Pompidou's entourage who later crossed paths with Christian David under unusual circumstances. Legros was a double agent. Appearing to work for both the SDECE and CIA, his loyalty rested with the Americans. A personal friend of Henry Kissinger's, Legros was the man the CIA assigned to snoop on UN secretary general Dag Hammarskjöld. Legros helped the CIA kidnap the African leader Moise Tshombé. And in 1965 Legros was in personal contact with Ben Barka in Geneva, where Legros maintained a residence and a large art gallery.[9]

When Leroy receives the "Pedro to Thomas" message, a big question mark arises. Was the "package" delivered to the appropriate place? Should Ben Barka have been taken to an altogether different location by agreement with the French? And did Lopez really tell

Lemarchand that Ben Barka had been "freed" by passengers (Boucheseiche's mugs) in another car and hidden from the police?

Everything suggests something happened which the police could do nothing about. Telephone wires began humming and the Moroccans dashed into Paris, perhaps to appear as much overcome by panic and dismay as were the French. First came Chtouki, then, hours later, security chief Dlimi. Finally, a day after the kidnaping, General Oufkir himself arrived.

From here on no one seems to agree on anything. There's absolutely no proof for the official version that put Oufkir in Fontenay-le-Vicomte to murder Ben Barka that same evening. The only basis for that theory is a 10 January 1966 *L'Express* article in which Figon recounts seeing Oufkir torture and murder Ben Barka in the Paris suburb on the evening of October 30. However, the article's origin is a mystery. A copy of Figon's account was delivered to the editors of *L'Express* by gangster Joseph Zurita of the Felix Lesca mob, whose members had strong ties to Pierre Lemarchand.[10] Figon's eyewitness account of Oufkir murdering Ben Barka was later disavowed by the magazine, but not before it gained acceptance. Moreover, there was no official disavowal by the French government.

One thing is certain. Oufkir would not have murdered Ben Barka before the eyes of someone like Figon – whom he mistrusted and had tried to eliminate, whom he knew would run to Lemarchand. Had the unthinkable in fact occurred, had Figon accidentally seen Oufkir murder Ben Barka, then Figon would not have lived to tell about it.

One more thing about Figon's article sounds implausible. It says he took a taxi to Boucheseiche's house. In such a delicate matter, that would have sufficed to seal not only Figon's fate but the taxi driver's as well. I believe the article can be discounted.

Alternatively, Chtouki, Dlimi, and Oufkir might well have come to France to ensure Ben Barka's transfer to Morocco. Either Dlimi or Oufkir were to have held the French in check as Ben Barka was taken away, and it would have to have been Dlimi, since he was the one who later avoided prosecution.

The French might have become suspicious, with Figon panicking and running to Lemarchand. The Lesca gang, with Christian David, could then have entered the plot at this early stage. Lemarchand might have tried to prevent the abduction to Morocco by sending his Lesca gang barbouzes to Fontenay-le-Vicomte. That could easily have led to conflict. Ben Barka could have been killed during the struggle, or someone could have murdered him and made it appear an accident.

Ben Barka could have been killed by Oufkir, a Moroccon security agent, the CIA, one of Boucheseiche's hoods, or one of Lemarchand's barbouzes. All were candidates, but the French, naturally, were most suspicious of Oufkir.

Moreover, none of the following, publicly aired hypotheses can be totally disregarded: that the French murdered him because he possessed information embarrassing to high-ranking individuals – perhaps regarding international narcotics trafficking; that Ben Barka committed suicide upon realizing he was bound for Morocco; or that he was murdered not in France, but in Morocco. Each contains a grain of plausibility.

In an interview published on 19 October 1966 in the Lebanese daily *El Hayat*, Colonel Dlimi maintained that Ben Barka was still alive when he and Oufkir left France, and was to have been flown to Morocco on the evening of 3 November 1965. He allegedly waited in vain that entire night at a tiny airport in the town of Msili.

Eleven days passed before rumors of Ben Barka's disappearance began to leak out. He could have been kidnaped or murdered any time within those eleven days, and by any of the parties involved. Among them, however, Oufkir and the CIA had by far the strongest motives.

It's my firm belief that the CIA was behind the whole affair, that Oufkir and possibly some of his men were CIA tools, and that the French, with stunning naiveté, allowed themselves to be duped into the CIA's ingenious scheme. . . all of which, of course, could only happen because a number of French agents were working with the CIA. Whether Oufkir, a gangster, or a CIA agent killed Ben Barka is secondary. What's important is that the agency was behind it.

In order to back up this claim it's essential to focus on the period immediately following the murder. All the participants were busy covering their tracks. Only the CIA succeeded, because the agency had made exclusive use of Moroccans and Frenchmen. The French, on the other hand, appear to have been caught with their pants down.

De Gaulle was fuming. "Somebody's taken me for a complete idiot," he raged, vowing to get to the bottom of the affair. He was convinced the CIA was involved, but could not touch them. All he could do was crack down on Frenchmen he suspected were CIA lackeys. Collaboration with the CIA went beyond certain French intelligence units to the highest government circles – the men closest to de Gaulle. That is precisely what the president suspected, and why he felt so powerless.

If one believes Leroy when he says his orders to cooperate with

Antoine Lopez on the Ben Barka affair came directly from "a certain Monsieur Legros" in a Matignon office, then one can't help but trace CIA tracks directly to Prime Minister Pompidou. The connection becomes crystal clear in light of the clash between de Gaulle and Pompidou that grew to implacable hate in de Gaulle's last years – and in light of Pompidou's later cooperation with the Americans – especially in the area of narcotics.

Why, then, didn't Lemarchand step forward to tell his story and pull the French out of the fire? In the first place, until the affair leaked out he was busy camouflaging his own role and trying to determine what really happened to Ben Barka. He knew very well that the French had been woven into the web, and probably feared it was worse than it seemed.

Furthermore, Lemarchand's CIA counterparts had better cards to play. They knew all about Lemarchand's hiring Georges Figon to entice Ben Barka to Paris, since the Moroccans had talked Lemarchand into doing so. If that information slipped out, Lemarchand, Foccart, and de Gaulle would all be up the creek without a paddle. There would be no way for them to retaliate. And that wasn't the only trump in the hand of the Americans. They could finger Lopez, Souchon, and Voitot – all French cops – as Ben Barka's kidnappers. But the ace up the CIA's sleeve was the uncertainty of de Gaulle's people about what really happened to Ben Barka. All the French could do was clam up and try to cut their losses.

Gangster Figon, a key to the mystery surrounding the actual Ben Barka kidnaping, remained a question mark in the ensuing drama. Though the Moroccans had promised him a fortune, Figon never saw a cent. While fellow thugs Boucheseiche, le Ny, Dubail, and Palisse had their pockets full and enjoyed asylum in Morocco, Oufkir refused to pay Figon. This again underscores that either Figon had given Oufkir reason for suspicion, or that Oufkir simply didn't bother paying a Lemarchand man who was not a sworn conspirator.

Money had been Figon's only motive. As to Lemarchand, he now had to think twice before passing out traceable funds. Figon became increasingly embittered and finally decided to make the best of the situation.

I suspect Figon committed two major blunders. His first was to speak to reporters, not seriously, but enough to cause some confusion. The second was to put the squeeze on Lemarchand for money. Judging from appearances, Lemarchand responded by having his Lesca gang barbouzes soften up Figon, who then decided it was time to become scarce. Though Figon had given several acquaintances the impression he feared the Lesca gang, he went into hiding with Joseph Zurita and Louis Nesmoz, two thugs who claimed they'd broken with Lesca in anger.[11] That was mistake number three, because Zurita and Nesmoz never did lose touch with the mob and Lemarchand.

Meanwhile de Gaulle's crowd concluded, perhaps after gaining wind of certain "rumors," that Ben Barka had been knocked off by Oufkir. That suited them just fine. Moreover, someone, it seems, persuaded Figon to dictate his account into a tape later transcribed for an article. The article might also have been edited prior to delivery, since it was submitted by gangster Zurita and not Figon himself. On 10 January 1966 *L'Express* published the celebrated story which blamed Oufkir for killing Ben Barka in front of Figon.

Though the thought of Figon witnessing the murder was hard to swallow, the CIA could not rebuff him just then without coming out in the open. And Oufkir's own denial landed on deaf ears.

In a letter produced at a later trial, *Newsweek*'s Paris correspondent, Edward Behr, claiming to have heard the Figon tape, said there was no mention on it of the latter's witnessing Oufkir murder Ben Barka. The tape itself proved useless, as something was later recorded over the conversation with Figon. Behr was transferred to *Newsweek*'s Hong Kong bureau shortly after the Ben Barka incident.[12]

As to Figon, he seems to have gone along with the article's fabrication. Immediately following its publication his finances took a sharp turn for the better. He sported a new false passport and told friends he'd either travel abroad or move to a luxurious apartment. He was called in for interrogation but never got a chance to explain the article to the police. On 17 January 1966 he was found in his 14 Rue des Renaudes apartment with a bullet in his head.

Rue des Renaudes had been swarming with police supposedly there to protect Figon, and no one else was seen entering his apartment. The police listed his death as a suicide and swept the loose ends under the rug. In Figon's suitcase they found King Hassan's conditions for the return of Ben Barka to Moroccan politics. They were on documents drawn up by Lemarchand.[13]

During the trial of the Ben Barka case, orders were issued for the arrest of General Oufkir and Colonel Dlimi, both of whom were safely in Morocco. Nonetheless, on 18 October 1966 Dlimi came secretly to Paris and registered in a hotel, the Peter the First of Serbia. This hotel was distinguished as the haunt of spooks, and the home of a mercenary recruiting office for Moise Tshombé's Congolese army. The office's directors, André Labay, Thierry de Bonnay, Michel Leroy, and Lucien Swarm, were all close friends of CIA agent Fernand Legros.[14] The next day, October 19, Dlimi reported to French police for interrogation.

In October 1972, following six uneventful years, a bomb exploded in far away Brazil. Mobster/spook Christian David, one of Lemarchand's and Foccart's most trusted agents, confessed, allegedly under torture: "I saw to it Ben Barka's body disappeared. General Oufkir paid me 15 million old francs for the job...and I, together with a certain Monsieur X, broke into the apartment on Rue des Renaudes minutes before Figon 'committed suicide.' The police didn't notice us because we went through building no. 11 on the parallel Rue Theodule-Ribot."[15]

The confession of Beau Serge is nothing short of fantastic. It reveals how intelligence agents operate, especially under duress. Those few lines contain a gross lie, an important message, and a warning. And I would even insist that the confession was composed in detail by the CIA. It's puzzling how the French and American press could have swallowed it whole.

First there's the torture business. Newspapers on both sides of the Atlantic dwelt on David's mauled appearance upon arrival in the U.S., and on the agonies inflicted upon him in the torture chamber. I've learned enough about Brazilian torturers and police to know that these experts don't leave marks, and under no circumstances would they molest a prisoner bound for extradition to either France or the United States.[16]

Another intriguing fact about David has never been mentioned. A few months after his extradition to the U.S., it was disclosed that the chief whipping-boy for the Brazilian security force in Sao Paulo, Sergio Fleury, along with several of his men and their colleagues in the narcotics squad, had accepted bribes to protect David's drug ring.[17] Moreover, three of David's SAC brethren were closely connected to Fleury. They served as advisors to, and more than once personally assisted the chief hatchet man in the torture of prisoners.[18]

No, Christian David was not tortured in Brazil. His horrible appearance upon arrival in the U.S. stemmed, instead, from a desperate attempt – that included slashing his wrist and swallowing glass – at hospitalization and access to escape.[19] Something else, then, was in the air. Why would the Brazilians force a confession on a matter, like the Ben Barka affair, in which they had no interest? And why was the prisoner's statement immediately publicized when it had nothing to do with the charges levelled against him?

The revelation that David was tortured certainly did not come from the Brazilians, who to this day deny that such things happen. It could only have come from one source, the CIA. That is the only way to explain reports of a hardened criminal and experienced spook opening up on an ever-explosive subject. Let us not forget that, in 1972, CIA agents were still sent out by the dozens to be interrogators and advisors in Brazilian police headquarters.[20] According to *Le Monde* reporter, James Sarazin, CIA agents were in fact present at the interrogation of Christian David.[21] No such important information could have unintentionally slipped through their fingers into print.

There remains another, even more important aspect that seems to have totally escaped notice: a very special agent of the CIA was then spending much of his time in Brazil. That agent was Fernand Legros, perhaps the same Legros whom Marcel Leroy eventually fingered as the man who gave the orders for the Ben Barka kidnaping.

Although Christian David's "confession" was probably composed meticulously to suit the aims of the CIA, that does not mean it contains no truth. That would not have been very smart. One thing, however, was astounding: Oufkir took the ultimate blame. That had happened often enough in the past – but never at the hands of his old bedfellows and protectors in the agency. Why?

For that there's a simple explanation: Oufkir's death two months earlier, on 16 August 1972, in the wake of an unsuccessful coup d'état against King Hassan.[22] The CIA, which had engineered the attempt, had nothing more to lose in Morocco. It was now in the agency's interest to bury the Ben Barka affair with Oufkir.

Furthermore, French President Pompidou had just cleaned house at the intelligence agency SDECE, which was now coming to terms with the CIA. Having David implicate Oufkir was the CIA's way of extending its hand to the French. Beau Serge, moreover, had been working not for Oufkir, but for Lemarchand.

All too little attention has been focussed on the latter underworld connection. The gangsters who it can be proven were bought and paid for by Oufkir – and therefore perhaps by the CIA – all fled to Morocco. On the other hand, Lesca gang thugs, closely associated with Lemarchand, wound up in Latin America, where they regrouped around David and continued to work for SAC and the SDECE.

Oufkir's fate was shared by gangsters Boucheseiche, le Ny,

Dubail, and possibly Palisse as well. All were executed in a Moroccan prison, on orders from Dlimi, for complicity in the Oufkir/CIA coup attempt. The witnesses closest to Oufkir in the Ben Barka affair, and protected by him afterward, were thus put out of the picture.[23]

International spook Luis Gonzalez-Mata, a close friend of General Oufkir's, claims the latter told him the CIA had planned to murder Ben Barka and had constantly plotted behind his (Oufkir's) back: "Ben Barka was alive when I left him in Paris," insisted Oufkir.[24]

Another striking aspect of David's "confession" is its undisguised warning to Monsieur X. If X doesn't play ball, he'll be exposed; and Monxieur X certainly knows that the CIA is aware of his identity. If he believes the business about the torture, he's also aware that torturers don't deal in unknowns like X and Y. If he doesn't believe it, then he must know that the CIA made a deal with Christian David for information – a deal that saved David from extradition to France and a possible date with the guillotine. The fact that Monsieur X is mentioned at all can only mean he played an important role in the affair and perhaps in French politics as well. The CIA, furthermore, followed up the warning with reports that Figon's pistol was found in the possession of Christian David.[25]

I won't hazard a guess as to Monsieur X's identity, only that he might well belong to the older wing of the Gaullist party that can't come to terms with rapprochement with the Americans. That is why he's told to watch his step.

In the interim there has been a notable shift in CIA posture on the Ben Barka affair. In 1975 Daniel Guerin published *Les Assassins de Ben Barka*, also alleging CIA involvement. *Time* magazine promptly published a curious article purporting to prove that Ben Barka had been murdered by either Oufkir or Dlimi. In fact, the article contained no new facts. What was new, though, was that the Americans were pointing the finger at Dlimi, without justification – perhaps as a warning.

This caused matters to take a grotesque twist. As Guerin later informed me, both Antoine Lopez and the widow of Boucheseiche told him they would be willing to testify that Ben Barka had been kidnaped from Boucheseiche's house by other gangsters, and that Oufkir and Dlimi had never seen Ben Barka in Paris. Here we observe Dlimi hard at work defending himself against U.S. allegations. Having become good friends with the CIA, the French were suddenly out of the picture. Now the CIA's formerly good friends and presently not-such-good friends in Morocco had their turn to be run through the treadmill. Back to square one: the Moroccans and the CIA.

I believe Figon was murdered because nobody could count on his silence, under interrogation, about the fabrication of the story against Oufkir. Too much was at stake. If it leaked out that the pro-de Gaulle faction had fabricated the story, it would have been hard to convince people of the same faction's innocence in the Ben Barka assassination.

And I believe Christian David helped knock off Georges Figon. Otherwise the CIA's warning to Monsieur X would be meaningless. And otherwise David would not have acted the way he did on 2 February 1966 – fourteen days after Figon's "suicide." On that day, the head of the police department's antigangster squad, Lieutenant Maurice Galibert, received a tip that a man implicated in the Ben Barka case could be found at the Saint Clair restaurant.

Galibert dashed off with officers Gouzier and Gibeaux. Upon arrival at the Saint Clair, they spotted Christian David playing cards with Belkacem Mechere, the deputy prefect of the interior ministry police.[26] When Galibert asked David to come downtown, Mechere protested. David flashed his SAC ID, but Galibert stood his ground. David shrugged his shoulders and fetched his coat from the checkroom.

Suddenly he stuck his hand in his coat pocket, drew a pistol and shot all three policemen. Galibert died on the spot. The other two were badly wounded.

And Beau Serge got away.

Notes

1. *Time*, 29 December 1975.

2. *Ibid.*

3. Some of the funds for Ben Barka's revolutionary activities allegedly came from the smuggling of morphine base.

4. *Time, op. cit.*

5. C. Clement: *Oufkir* (Éditions Jean Dullis, 1974).

6. See chapter fourteen.

7. The book *Le Comité* is dedicated to the family of Marcel Leroy.

8. *Le Comité* hit the market just as the U.S. was deep into its investigation of the CIA. The strategy behind that was simple: it's easier to defend oneself from attack when one can claim the others are doing the same. The CIA, most likely, was also behind de Vosjoli's first book, *Lamia*, which inspired Leon Uris's *Topaz*.

9. In an interview especially for this book, Legros confirmed that the Geneva

gallery was a base for his espionage activities on behalf of the CIA; see also R. Peyrefitte: *La Vie Extraordinaire de Fernand Legros* (Albin Michel, 1976).

10. D. Guerin: *Les Assassins de Ben Barka* (Guy Authier, 1975).

11. A. Jaubert: *Dossier D . . . comme Drogue* (Alain Moreau, 1974).

12. Guerin, *op. cit.*

13. *Ibid.*

14. Peyrefitte, *op. cit.*

15. Writer/philosopher Daniel Guerin, who has dedicated his life to unraveling the Ben Barka affair, and is gathering material for a reopening of the case on behalf of Ben Barka's son Bachir, told me he had tested out the claim in David's confession. He had confirmed that it's possible for an adroit man to go through the backyard of 11 Rue Theodule-Ribot and then climb up cornices to Figon's apartment.

16. H. Krüger: *Doktoren* (Bogan, 1975) and *Likvider Boilesen* (Breien, 1978).

17. A. Lopez: *L'Escadron de la Mort* (Casterman, 1973). According to the 23 May 1973 *Nouvel Observateur*, Sergio Fleury led the group which did in the David gang in Brazil. It was also Fleury and his men who questioned David.

18. P. Chairoff: *Dossier B . . . comme Barbouzes* (Alain Moreau, 1975).

19. *L'Aurore*, 20 November 1972.

20. CIA agents were not only advisors and interrogators in the traditional sense. In Latin America they were both instructors in and practitioners of torture – see A.J. Langguth, *New York Times*, 11 June 1979. Furthermore, those who have difficulties comprehending anti-U.S. feelings in Iran will be interested to know that a senior CIA official instructed agents of SAVAK, the Iranian secret police created by the Shah in the late fifties with assistance from the CIA, on techniques for torture. According to Jesse J. Leaf, for five years the chief CIA analyst on Iran before his 1973 resignation, the CIA's methods "were based on German torture techniques from World War II" – see S.M. Hersh, *New York Times*, 7 January 1979.

21. J. Sarazin: *Dossier M . . . comme Milieu* (Alain Moreau, 1977).

22. Oufkir ordered jet fighters into the air to shoot down the king's plane. According to French general Claude Clement (Clement, *op. cit.*), when that failed, Oufkir was executed by King Hassan himself. Colonel Dlimi first shot Oufkir in the back and shoulder, dropping him flat on his stomach. The king then took Dlimi's pistol and fired at Oufkir's neck. The bullet exitted through the general's left eye, shattering the sunglasses that had been his trademark.

23. *L'Aurore*, 24 August 1972.

24. L. Gonzalez-Mata: *Cygne* (Grasset, 1976).

25. Chairoff, *op. cit.*

26. The Newsday Staff: *The Heroin Trail* (Souvenir Press, 1974).

SEVEN
BEAU SERGE,
SCOURGE OF THE PARTISANS

The murder of police lieutenant Galibert caused a major sensation in France. Despite what seemed to be an all-out manhunt, the wily Christian David, aided by friends, eluded Galibert's colleagues in the antigangster squad. In the Fetich Club of Neuville-Sur-Ain, outside Lyons, Beau Serge bided his time. A big-time bordello and haunt of the Guerini clan, the Club was a frequent rendezvous of David's friends in SAC.

Reportedly, Mémé Guerini at first favored delivering his body to the police. But powerful forces must have intervened, as Mafia bosses were persuaded to help Beau Serge flee from France.[1] One day in March 1966 a car picked him up at the Fetich Club and drove him to a Guerini post on the outskirts of Marseilles.

In early May David sent word to Simone Mauduit, one of his Parisian mistresses, asking her to fly down to Marseilles with a bundle of money.[2] From Marseilles David's friend Francois Orsoni drove her to a restaurant on the road from Cannes to Nice. There she handed Beau Serge the cash and bade him a fond farewell.[3]

Later that month David was driven to Genoa, Italy, where he boarded a ship bound for Latin America. A new career in the shadows awaited him. Beau Serge had with him from Marseilles a letter of introduction to the former French mafioso and Gestapo collaborator Auguste Ricord. The mobster was then organizing a major narcotics network that would smuggle heroin from Marseilles to the U.S.A. via Argentina and Paraguay.

His reputation having preceded him in Latin America, David was welcomed into the Ricord organization with open arms and soon moved into its highest ranks. Also part of Beau Serge's reception committee were agents of the SDECE and SAC. His arrival coincided with a powerful French diplomatic offensive in Latin America. With the U.S. wading into a quagmire in Indochina and otherwise preoccupied with the Soviet Union, de Gaulle, and more so Jacques Foccart, sought to entrench themselves as deeply in Latin America as they had in Africa.

De Gaulle planned to come on like the Great White Father, the Third World's only friend, but Foccart felt that wouldn't suffice. He moved several of his most trusted men from Africa to Latin America. Between 1965 and 1968, for example, we find the notorious Colonel Roger Barberot as France's ambassador to Uruguay, and Dominique Ponchardier its man in Bolivia.[4] If anyone stands for cloaks and daggers it's these two, whose names turn up in a string of France's most sensitive espionage scandals.

Foccart's men moved where they saw the greatest openings: supporting right wing forces in a region already in the grip of military dictatorship. Barberot and Ponchardier offered to help these regimes break the back of left wing insurgency. For that they needed men without scruples, men like Christian David.

On arrival in Argentina, David met Francois Chiappe, wanted in France for a pair of murders. Chiappe, also known as "Big Lips," had worked for the Guerini mob and was on excellent terms with politicians and right wing militants in Argentina.[5] He was also a top member of the Ricord organization.

The Ricord network was divided into four teams that operated independently out of separate headquarters. Ricord himself ran the main team from Asunción, Paraguay, and oversaw the entire operation. Chiappe and Michel Nicoli led another team, Dominique Orsini and Louis Bonsignour a third, and André Condemine and Lucien Sarti a fourth.[6] Other important names in the organization were Claude-André Pastou, Didier Barone and Michel "Bouboule" Sans. It was Murder Incorporated in French. Nearly all had been sentenced to death in France.

Barone, besides belonging to the Felix Lesca gang, had teamed up on art swindles with the aforementioned CIA agent Fernand Legros and with Legros' forger, Elmyr de Hory.[7] Pastou is similarly interesting. In December 1968 Enrico Passigli, a weapons-smuggling friend of Christian David's, was murdered in Rome.[8] Almost simultaneously, Thierry de Bonnay, another close associate of Legros',[9] died in a mysterious auto accident. Italian police suspected Pastou in both killings, which were committed while he was on a trip back to Europe.

The Ricord network operated freely south of the border because its members helped repressive regimes fight the left and smuggle arms, sometimes combining the two profitably. While he was helping intelligence groups infiltrate guerilla movements, Christian David found new customers for his weapons. The major arms deals, though, were with militant fascist groups in Argentina and Chile.

Through connections, Chiappe secured David an Argentine passport in the name of Carlos Eduardo Devreux-Bergeret. Beau Serge then went on secret missions for French intelligence. His first assignment, to infiltrate Douglas Bravo's Venezuelan urban revolutionaries, led nowhere. In early 1967 Bravo was expelled from the Venezuelan Communist party and police smashed his organization. Once relocated in the hills, Bravo was wary of spies.

Following the false start in Venezuela, Beau Serge flew to Mexico and met with two African agents. They handed him a contract to eliminate African politicians. It's not clear whom he was to murder and whether or not he succeeded, but he was in Africa several months, and murder was a task he rarely muddled.[10] Upon returning to Latin America he joined Ricord in Ascunción before planting himself in Argentina.

In late 1967 David – alias Eduardo Devreux-Bergeret – managed to infiltrate the Forcas Argentines de Liberacion (FAL), one of the most active guerilla groups in stormy Argentina from 1967 to 1971. Among other actions, it kidnapped Auguste Ricord's close friend and Paraguay's consul in Argentina, Waldemar Sanchez.

Relying on his experience with the instruments of death, David soon became the FAL's arms instructor and ingratiated himself with its members. In the end he made off with its files and a cashbox containing $250,000.[11] While fleeing he allegedly slew an FAL leader and a lookout.[12] He headed with his prize to Central America. Eventually the SDECE made a deal for the papers with the Argentine government, which led to the arrest of several guerillas and the death by torture of one.[13]

Soon thereafter David went to Uruguay, where the French ambassador was Roger Barberot – the same Barberot who four years later would be associated with the French Connection heroin affair that also involved Beau Serge.[14] In May 1968 Barberot and Dominique Ponchardier were unexpectedly rushed home to Paris to help quell French student unrest, forcing Foccart to put his plans for Latin

America on hold.[15]

After 1968 Beau Serge was more or less a free-lance agent. While remaining in close touch with the Foccart network, he also took on assignments for security police and political death squads in Argentina, Uruguay and Brazil, and thereby, inevitably, for the CIA. In Montevideo he reconnected with his mistress Theresa, who just happened to be a member of the Tupamaros. Through her Beau Serge infiltrated Latin America's best-organized band of guerillas.

Uruguay's President Pacheco Areco had already begun a determined struggle against the revolutionaries. Assisting his police and armed forces was a squad of CIA agents expert at torture and anti-guerilla warfare. Two of those agents, Dan A. Mitrione and Claude L. Fry, were captured by the revolutionaries. Mitrione was given the death penalty by a people's court, while Fry suffered a heart attack and was released.[16]

Beau Serge appears at first glance to have done more for President Areco than the entire conventional CIA team. But on this job he probably collaborated with U.S. intelligence. Also assisting him was Jacques Foccart's full-time man in Uruguay in Roger Barberot's absence, Jean-Baptiste Listroni, who became David's go-between with the Uruguayan government.[17]

David must have been quite an actor, since he even fooled the legendary Tupamaros leader Raul Sendic. After robbing a bank, the guerillas handed Beau Serge $400,000 for the purchase of weapons. He then flew off, as if to complete the deal, to Foccart's personal fiefdom and beehive of the weapons trade, the African nation of Gabon.[18]

While he was away, however, the guerillas somehow learned, not of his escapades in Argentina, but of his role in the Ben Barka affair. They decided to set a trap for him. But once back in Uruguay, Beau Serge smelled trouble and rushed to the security police, who soon arrested 150 guerillas in the strongest blow they'd dealt the revolutionaries. It was a handsome feather in the cap of President Pacheco Areco.

For his troubles David was reportedly given $200,000 in addition to the $400,000 of which he had relieved the partisans, plus a Uruguayan diplomatic passport in the name of Edouard Davrieux.[19] The passport made David the heir-apparent of Auguste Ricord. With it he travelled freely to the U.S. and Europe, controlling and expanding the international narcotics network.

There's also a somewhat unbelievable story about David's departure from Uruguay. In the transit hall of Montevideo airport, a stewardess reportedly brought him a package. Suspecting a bomb, Beau Serge had the stewardess open it herself. She screamed when she did. Inside was the head of Theresa, a goodbye gift from the Tupamaros.[20]

President Pacheco Areco's glee was short-lived. Within two years nearly all the guerilla's David had sent to prison would escape. In March 1971, thirty-eight Tupamaros women fled through a tunnel from a Montevideo jail. The president fumed. As to the police, they were sure the men locked up in Punta Carretas had similar plans. Within weeks they felt vindicated. At a river sewage outlet they discovered a package containing frogmen gear and a plan of the Montevideo sewer system. An escape by the Tupamaros had apparently been foiled. Jokingly, the warden told the press that the Tupamaros' map of the sewers was superior to the city's. Using it, the police had discovered electric drills and other tools meant for the escape.

The authorities took no chances. They reinforced surveillance of Punta Carretas with tanks and police dogs, as President Areco looked towards the approaching October election. If Sendic and his guerillas slipped away, he'd be finished.

At 4:10 AM on 6 September 1971, Billy Rial, a prison neighbor, phoned the prison to announce that a group of inmates had just run through his house.

"Yeah, tell us another one," was the answer. "Nobody runs off from our prison."

But Rial insisted and the watchman decided to check out the guard room.

"Everything quiet," was the response.[21]

The watchman told Rial off for trying to make fools of the authorities. One hour later, though, his tune changed. An entire prison wing had been emptied of inmates, Raul Sendic included.[22] The police dashed off to Rial's house. There they found 106 prison uniforms in a 6x3 feet heap. A 2-foot wide, 100-yard long tunnel ran from the basement of Rial's home, below the garden, the street, the prison walls and yard, to the building which had housed the fugitives. Their escape had taken nine hours.

According to Rial, his house had been overrun by partisans who held his family hostage. Equipped with walkie-talkies, they were in radio contact with those still within prison walls.[23]

"They treated us well," said Rial, "but wouldn't even have a cup of coffee."

As the prisoners gradually appeared, they had exchanged their uniforms for civvies. When all were present, they embarked peacefully in stolen busses.

The authorities were helpless laughing-stocks and, to top it all, Areco lost the presidency to the equally incompetent Juan Maria Bordaberry.[24]

By then Beau Serge was long gone.

Notes

1. L. Durand: *Le Caid* (Denoel, 1976).
2. J. Sarazin: *Dossier M... comme Milieu* (Alain Moreau, 1977).
3. P. Galante and L. Sapin: *The Marseilles Mafia* (W.H. Allen, 1979).
4. R. Barberot: *A Bras le Coeur* (Robert Laffont, 1972); D. Ponchardier: *La Mort du Condor* (Gallimard, 1976); P. Chairoff: *Dossier B... comme Barbouzes* (Alain Moreau, 1975).
5. *L'Aurore*, 31 May 1976.
6. Galante and Sapin, *op. cit.*
7. A. Jaubert: *Dossier D... comme Drogue* (Alain Moreau, 1974).
8. *France-Soir*, 5 February 1973.
9. R. Peyrefitte: *La Vie Extraordinaire de Fernand Legros* (Albin Michel, 1976).
10. Jaubert, *op. cit.*
11. *Ibid.*
12. M. Acosta: "Smukke Serge," *Kriminal-Journalen*, March 1978.
13. Sarazin, *op. cit.*
14. See chapter ten.
15. Chairoff, *op. cit.*
16. According to Manuel Hevia Cosculluela, a Cuban-born CIA operative who worked with Mitrione in Uruguay's police program before returning to his homeland, Mitrione's instructions on torture included the following:

"When you receive a subject, the first thing to do is determine his physical state, his degree of resistance, through a medical examination. A premature death means a failure by the technician.

"Another important thing to know is exactly how far you can go given the political situation and the personality of the prisoner. It is very important to know beforehand whether we have the luxury of letting the subject die...

"Before all else, you must be efficient. You must cause only the damage that is strictly necessary, not a bit more. We must control our tempers in any case. You have to act with the efficiency and cleanliness of a surgeon and with the perfection of an artist..." (A.J. Langguth, *New York Times*, 11 June 1979).
17. Chairoff, *op. cit.*
18. Recently, Maurice Delaunay — France's ambassador to Gabon in 1965-72 and again in 1975-79 — was named the president of the Compagnie des mines d'uranium de Franceville, and Maurice Robert — a former SDECE officer and

chief of security for the oil company Elf-Aquitane, which controls Elf-Gabon—was named the new French ambassador to Gabon. Journalist Elie Ramaro (*Afrique-Asie*, 7 January 1980) sees the appointments of the two close collaborators in Jacques Foccart's African network, as the mother country's way of reassuring Gabon's president Omar Bongo. The French had recently engineered a coup d'état that toppled another of their African puppets, Emperor Bokassa, from the throne of the Central African Republic. (He had become expendable after revelations of his payoffs to French President Giscard D'Estaing). President Bongo, incidentally, purchased a house recently in the Beverly Hills movie colony largely populated by Arab sheiks and Iranian exiles, for the sum of $2.2 million, which was $300,000 above the asking price (*New York Times*, 15 October 1979).

19. According to certain sources it was in fact a French diplomatic passport; see Sarazin, *op. cit.*

20. Acosta, *op. cit.*

21. *Granma*, 12 September 1971.

22. Sendic was eventually recaptured and subjected to severe torture. He remains a political prisoner in Uruguay; see J. Da Veiga in *Afrique-Asie*, 29 October 1979.

23. UPI and Reuters, 7 September 1971.

24. According to journalist Warren Hoge: "Juan Maria Bordaberry, the last elected Uruguayan President, dissolved Congress in 1973 under military prodding and then was replaced himself by the armed forces three years later. The Uruguayan military, until then relatively aloof from politics, had consolidated power through its campaign to crush the Tupamaro guerillas." (*New York Times*, 14 November 1979). U.S. military aid to Uruguay between 1946 and 1975 totalled $86 million. Between 1950 and 1975 2537 Uruguayan military personnel were trained by the United States; see N. Chomsky and E.S. Herman: *The Washington Connection and Third World Fascism* (South End Press, 1979). The Carter administration resumed military aid to Uruguay in the fall of 1979, reversing a 1977 halt in the name of human rights.

EIGHT
WITH "THE OLD MAN" IN PARAGUAY

Auguste Ricord and his gang of heroin merchants were riding high when they were joined by Christian David in the latter half of the sixties. Each year they transported hundreds of kilos to the huge U.S. market, and without the noticeable losses that narcotics traffickers must normally contend with. Its street value, depending on competition, lay somewhere between $1 and $2 billion annually.

At the end of World War II Ricord fled from France and a death sentence for collaboration with the Gestapo. He wandered for several years in search of an underworld niche. By the end of the second year three of his companions in exile had been murdered. In 1947 Ricord arrived in Buenos Aires with the name Lucien Dargelles. Some say he had with him the millions he'd pocketed during the war, others say he had to start all over. What's certain is that he opened an exclusive restaurant in Argentina at the close of the fifties and soon had a chain of restaurants and motels throughout Argentina, Paraguay and Bolivia, each with the name "Paris-Nice" and an Eiffel Tower prominently out front. The motels evolved into a high-class brothel chain, and Ricord quietly began trafficking in narcotics.[1]

At the start of the sixties Ricord moved his headquarters from Buenos Aires to Asunción, Paraguay. There he could feel at home among the old Nazi luminaries, who had found safe haven under President Alfredo Stroessner. Ricord also regained contact with an old acquaintance then residing in neighboring Bolivia, former Gestapo chief Klaus Barbie, the "Killer of Lyons."[2] Ricord had much in common with Barbie, alias Klaus Altmann, inasmuch as the former had assisted the Gestapo at torture and the rounding up of French jews.

83

Since the disclosure of Barbie's whereabouts, French and German authorities alike have vainly sought his extradition for the murder of hundreds.

In 1966 Old Man Ricord enlarged his already immense narcotics network upon discovering how easily he could smuggle heroin into the U.S. via Latin America. For some reason, the U.S. Bureau of Narcotics and Dangerous Drugs (BNDD) largely overlooked the danger from the south until the seventies. It eventually grew wiser, estimating that 50-60 percent of the Marseilles-produced heroin on the U.S. market entered via Latin America, which generally meant by way of Ricord and company.

The old man surrounded himself with hard-core thugs. By 1970 the Mob's leaders were Ricord, sentenced to death *in absentia* for treason, torture and murder; Lucien Sarti, wanted for the murder of a Belgian policeman; Christian David, sentenced to death *in absentia*; André Condemine, wanted for the murder of a policeman; Jean Lunardi, wanted for murder; Francois Chiappe, wanted for two murders; and French gangster and former SAC agent, Michel Nicoli. They also had a network of henchmen encompassing nearly every metropolis in Latin America.

The money poured in, some of it to be reinvested in restaurants and night clubs in Buenos Aires, Sao Paulo, and Caracas. But Ricord lost his grip on the reins. Before long David, Condemine and Sarti took over, reducing the old man to a figurehead who drank foaming Münchnerbrau with "Die Alte Kamaraden" in one of Asunción's many German bars.

Marseilles heroin was transported to Paraguay from embarkation points in Barcelona, Lisbon, and Brussels. In charge of transportation were Condemine, as well as Chiappe, who often travelled between his Buenos Aires base and Barcelona, where his suppliers were the Orsini brothers of the Corsican mafia.

The heroin was transported by air and by sea. Part of it went via Brazil, then either overland to Paraguay or directly to the U.S.A. Some of it sailed up the Paraña River to Asunción. The greater part of the heroin sent north arrived aboard small planes known as Mau-Maus, which generally refueled in Panama before flying on to either Florida or Mexico. There they were unloaded and shipment was continued overland.

Paraguay had long been one of the great smuggling centers of the world. With 200 private landing strips scattered among the haciendas, it was impossible to monitor the enormous number of private flights. And no one seriously bothered to try, since numerous government officials pocketed shares of the take. According to Jack Anderson, Ricord's accomplices included some of Paraguay's highest-ranking officers: Pastor Coronel, the intelligence chief; General Andres Rodriguez, leader of an elite 3000-man force especially trained by the Americans; and General Vincente Quinonez, the Air Force chief-of-staff, who was responsible for Asunción airport and other landing fields.[3]

Soldiers from an elite corps, according to Anderson, were stationed to guard the contraband stores for Ricord and other big-time smugglers. Worse still, in the wake of Anderson's sensational revelations came rumors that Paraguayan Air Force officers had even flown Ricord's heroin to the United States in military aircraft.

Unlike Ricord, David didn't simply rake in the money. He thrived on danger. According to U.S. narks, in at least three instances Beau Serge himself transported large quantities of heroin into the United States, using the pseudonym "Jean-Pierre," by which he was known exclusively among friends in the Ricord Mob.

David also maintained the organization's good relations with police and spooks in Latin America. He took on assignments for Argentina's terrorist organization, the Argentine Anticommunist Alliance (AAA), and probably did the same for Brazil's notorious Death Squad. Grupo Francés, as Ricord's network was known in Latin America, had found a prize in Christian David because of his connections to SAC and French intelligence. Through him there grew new branches in the narcotics network, including one centered about the Felix Lesca gang and the Lyons SAC chief Jean Auge, and another about Jo Attia's gang, SAC leader Ange Simonpieri, and the Swiss banker André Hirsch.[4]

Notes

1. As early as 1947 Ricord is alleged to have made contact with America's future narcotics king, Santo Trafficante, jr., who was then running several Havana casinos for the Mafia. Ricord alias Dargelles reportedly headed that year to Cuba, where he sat in on a meeting with, among other notables, Ralph (brother of Al) Capone, Frank Costello, Albert Anastasia, Trafficante and Lucky Luciano; see V. Alexandrov: *La Mafia des SS* (Stock, 1978).

2. A Jaubert: *Dossier D . . .come Drogue* (Alain Moreau, 1974). As of 1974, Barbie was the president of the state shipbuilding monopoly, Transmaritima

Bolivia (*Der Spiegel*, 3 June 1974). Bolivia has few ships and no harbor, but had been negotiating with General Augusto Pinochet's Chile for a corridor to the Pacific, until recently when diplomatic relations between the two nations were severed. However, Bolivia's quest has the backing of the UN's Third World Group of 77, the non-aligned nations, and the Organization of American States; see E.Z. Gibson, *New York Times*, 28 October 1979.

3. *Washington Post*, 24 May 1972.

4. At the start of the seventies Lesca built up a large inter-European gangster network known as Eurogang and headquartered in Frankfurt, West Germany. Members of the gang were rounded up by West German police in 1975, but Lesca himself moved the operation to Tessin (*Der Spiegel*, 11 August 1975; see also Jaubert, *op. cit.*).

NINE
THE HEROIN TRAILS

As the 1970s began the French were the undisputed kingpins of the international narcotics traffic. Opium, the raw material, was extracted from the poppy harvest by the Turks, who either converted it themselves into morphine base, or sent it to refineries in Syria and Lebanon. Essentially all morphine base made from Turkish opium went to Marseilles' heroin laboratories. Until around 1966 it went by sea. But Marseilles' harbor was too easily patrolled, and so after 1966 roughly 70 percent of the morphine base went via Bulgaria and Yugoslavia to Munich.

For the first half of this century, most Marseilles heroin was sent to Tangiers, Morocco, the main embarkation point for drugs bound for the United States. Tangiers eventually gave way to such European ports as Barcelona, Lisbon, and Antwerp. In addition some of the heroin went by air.

At the close of the sixties there began what at first resembled a routine adjustment in the narcotics traffic. As time would show, however, this one involved such a colossal upheaval, that it might better be described as a tremendous political coup—yet a coup that apparently went unnoticed. At its source lay shifts in international politics, and friction between the CIA and the French SDECE. Later I will support this claim with a myriad of circumstantial evidence.

The United States, during the first presidential administration of Richard Nixon, began cracking down on Turkish opium cultivation. While it slowed the delivery of morphine base to Marseilles, the Corsicans then—and now—had other sources to tap. They had long been connected closely with the Chinese Mafia. The latter organized the production of enormous quantities of opium on the rugged hillsides of the Burma-Laos-Thailand junction known as the Golden Triangle.[1]

The sale of harvested opium is in the hands of well-organized Chiu Chao Chinese from the region between Canton and Fukien in southeast China. Hundreds of thousands of these Chinese emigrated to Southeast Asia, where they have resisted assimilation and control by local authorities.

The Golden Triangle accounted, until very recently, for some two-thirds of the world's illicit opium production, or 1300 tons of opium annually – enough to produce 130 tons of heroin at a retail value on the U.S. market of between 50 and 120 billion dollars. Conservative estimates place the yearly heroin consumption of U.S. addicts between twelve and twenty tons. The New York street price lies in the neighborhood of $300,000/kilo (1 kilo = 2.2 pounds), but many pushers dilute the heroin up to three or four times. The same kilo can then bring in close to $1 million.

A major slice of the profits of organized crime in the U.S. derives from the wholesaling of illegal drugs. The trafficking of heroin, cocaine, morphine base, etc., along with marijuana, hash, LSD and other hallucinogens, yields an annual turnover estimated as high as $75 billion.[2] That is an enormous sum, even in the context of the U.S. economy.

A very large portion of the U.S. market can be covered by derivatives of Southeast Asian opium. However, as late as 1969 only Marseilles Frenchmen produced snow-white heroin in quantities large enough to satisfy the American market. Obtaining absolutely pure white no. 4 heroin is no easy matter. The chemist generally ends with slighly brownish no. 3 heroin, or "brown sugar." Though the Chinese Mafia had ample opium, they could not produce no. 4 heroin in sufficient quantities. Excluding them from direct entry onto the U.S. scene, it limited the Chinese to delivery of raw materials to Marseilles and sale of second-rate products elsewhere.

In the golden era that culminated, at the start of 1970, with Christian David joining the Ricord gang hierarchy, Marcel Francisci and Dominique Venturi led the Corsican Mafia, and Jo Cesari was the wizard of the Marseilles labs. They were but the visible portion of the iceberg. The other 99 percent was comprised of politicians and men of responsibility and influence in French intelligence.

"Mr. Heroin" Francisci was the man with the international perspective, with direct connections to politicians and the capos of the Italian Mafia. When international agreements were to be made,

Francisci usually did the negotiating. Venturi and Joseph Orsini were in charge of effectively all drug import and export.

There were five main heroin export routes to the U.S.A., two by air and three by sea. The shipping lanes emanated from Barcelona, Lisbon, and Antwerp and either ended in Brazil/Paraguay, Haiti and the French West Indies, or went directly to the east coast of the United States. Heroin smuggled into the U.S. from the French Antilles and Haiti, like that from Paraguay, went via Florida or Mexico.

The busiest air lanes were from Luxembourg and Madrid to either Montreal or Nassau.[3] Dominique Venturi's brother Jean received the shipments in Montreal, but was obliged to pass them on to the Cotroni family. Led by brothers Giuseppe, Vincent and Frank, the latter clan transported the heroin to the U.S.A., and distributed it to the big time pushers in New York.

Heroin leaving Haiti, the Antilles, Nassau, and the Paraguay-based Ricord Mob wound up in Florida, where Santo Trafficante, jr. and the Cuban Mafia controlled the drug business in an axis that became the U.S.A.'s most powerful narcotics organization.

For years the Corsicans had tried setting up their own U.S. network, but were repeatedly foiled. It might have been easier for them to get around the Italians and Cubans by way of Mexico, had the Cotroni and Trafficante organizations not also decided to enter the picture there. At a grand assembly of mobsters from Marseilles, Montreal, New York and Miami, the rules were fixed for smuggling via Mexico. The site of the meeting was Acapulco, the time was early 1970. Representing the French were Jean Venturi, Jean-Baptiste Croce and Paul Mondolini. Croce and Mondolini became the Corsicans' permanent men in Mexico.

The tight control over the U.S. market wielded by the Cotronis of Montreal and Trafficante of Tampa was a legacy of Meyer Lansky and Lucky Luciano's reorganization of the U.S. heroin market. Lansky built himself a fantastic empire headquartered in Havana, and literally governed Cuba over the head of the dictator Fulgencio Batista. Lansky became the world's uncrowned narcotics king. His decisions affected everyone, including the bigwigs in France and Italy. He invested in the Marseilles labs and had the Corsicans reorganize themselves more efficiently. When Castro drove him from Cuba, Lansky created a similar gambling paradise in Nassau.

Nassau became a focal point in more ways than one. Besides the gambling take, the greater part of the incredible bonanza from U.S. narcotics deals – the Corsicans' share included – was laundered via

Lansky's Miami National Bank, to Nassau, and on to numbered accounts in Switzerland and Lebanon.

The Lansky fortune is estimated at $2 billion. Unable to reenter the U.S. in 1970, Lansky took temporary refuge in Israel, which eventually refused him citizenship. It is difficult to say how much of his power he retains. His operation has apparently been taken over by former subordinates. In narcotics they are the Montreal Cotroni family and, above all, Santo Trafficante, jr. in Florida, the man to whom the Ricord/David Mob consigned enormous quantities of heroin.

Notes

1. In the 30 August 1963 issue of *Life*, Stanley Karnow named Bonaventure Francisci the kingpin of opium smuggling from Laos. According to Alain Jaubert (*Dossier D . . . comme Drogue*, Alain Moreau, 1974), it was impossible to determine whether Bonaventure and Marcel Francisci were related.

2. F.A.J. Ianni: *Black Mafia* (Simon and Schuster, 1974). Ianni's estimate is the highest I have seen. The wide range of estimates demonstrates that no one really knows, or is even close to knowing, how great the narcotics handle is.

3. It was often little things which made a smuggling route especially attractive. For example, former French heroin smuggler Richard Berdin recalls his colleague André Labay's description of the important role played by the men's room at Nassau airport: "It's a small airport, and there's a common waiting room, which means that after I've gone through English customs I go straight to the American side, armed with a piece of hand luggage containing nothing but toiletries and the usual knick-knacks. There I check my baggage through to Miami. Assuming they check my hand bag, they'll wrap some kind of self-adhesive ticket around the handle to show it's been OK'd. I'll arrange my flight schedule so that my plane for Miami doesn't leave for at least an hour after our arrival in Nassau. So now I go back to the passenger lounge to wait for my flight. We meet in the men's room, where we exchange the contents of our hand luggage. Now I've got the merchandise, safely stashed in a piece of luggage bearing the customs seal of approval. When my flight is called, I climb aboard the last leg of the trip without a worry in the world. I don't see how it could miss." (R. Berdin: *Code Named Richard*, Dutton, 1974).

TEN
THE PURSUIT OF THE CORSICANS BEGINS

When Charles de Gaulle retired and Georges Pompidou was elected president of France in 1969, improvement of Franco-American relations was high on Pompidou's agenda. In early 1970 he flew to Washington. There he met with President Nixon and, on several occasions, publicly cautioned against U.S. withdrawal from Europe. Upon returning to France he went straight to work eliminating the greatest obstacle to Franco-American partnership. He appointed Alexandre de Marenches head of the SDECE and told him to clean it up. De Marenches responded by firing 815 men throughout the intelligence agency. He then chose Colonel Paul Ferrer alias Fournier as his right-hand man, and the two began to reorganize.

Pompidou himself despised several longtime espionage figures, primarily because of their role in a ruthless smear campaign waged against him prior to the 1969 election. In the course of the campaign tampered photos were circulated showing Madame Pompidou in the company of film star Alain Delon's bodyguard, Stefan Markovic – who had been murdered in 1968 – and in compromising positions with men and women alike. Names that turned up repeatedly throughout the scandal included Colonel Roger Barberot and SDECE agents Captain Paul Santenac and Roger Delouette, three arch-Gallists from Jacques Foccart's inner circle.[1] Santenac had promoted the presidential candidacy of de Gaulle's son, Real Admiral Philippe de Gaulle, who eventually refused the nomination. Barberot, who had returned from Uruguay in 1968 to help smother the May student insurrection, directed the Bureau pour le Développement de la Production Agricole (BDPA), a front for Foccart's secret financial transactions.[2]

Pompidou had to watch his step while eliminating powerful enemies because most of them enjoyed the support of a large segment of the Gaullist party. Still, with U.S. help, he used the next couple of years to choke off the worst of the resistance. The SDECE was ordered to cooperate with the CIA; SAC was cut back severely, the brunt borne by its criminal contingent; and the Corsican Mafia's power was systematically reduced.

Foccart himself was too formidable to take on frontally. His economic power, great influence, and dossiers on other politicians made him effectively untouchable. Nevertheless, he apparently compromised and went along with Pompidou on several counts.

Pompidou struck at the gangsters and shadier elements of the SDECE and SAC through their most vulnerable point – their wallets. One subject Pompidou had discussed with Nixon on his U.S. tour was the war on drugs. Nixon had described the dimensions of the problem and asked for Pompidou's assistance in stopping the heroin flow from Marseilles. Since it suited his plans perfectly, Pompidou had agreed. Reducing the Corsican Mafia's profits would also limit its political influence. But a project of that magnitude could not be accomplished overnight. Preparations had to be made.

Had Pompidou suspected what really lay in store internationally, he would certainly have had second thoughts. The outcome of that pact slowly began to emerge in 1970. In the two years that followed it struck home with the force of an avalanche.

Auguste Ricord

On 18 October 1970 a Cessna four-seater landed at Miami International airport. Registered in Argentina, the plane was one of hundreds of Paraguayan "contrabandistas" smuggling goods to and from eighty landing strips in Florida. U.S. customs agents, tipped off that the plane would be worth inspecting, emerged from hiding as the pilot crawled from the cockpit.

"No bandito!" screamed the pilot, Cesar Bianchi.

But he was just that, as the agents discovered three cases containing a total of forty-five kilos of heroin in the tail of the plane. To save his skin, Bianchi agreed to cooperate. He continued on his normal route, but with agents now on his tail. First he met his Miami contact, Felix Becker. Then Bianchi, Becker and a third man, Aron Muravnik, flew to New York to meet Pierre Gahou of the Ricord network, and finally the U.S. wholesalers.

By October 27 the heroin deal was closed and Gahou was about to fly to Paraguay with the money. But before he could depart, agents moved in and caught six men in their net. The catch was better than anticipated. Bianchi shot off at the mouth like a machine-gun as wide-eyed customs agents heard the story of Ricord's elaborate narcotics ring.

In the ensuing four months stacks of proof were assembled against Ricord. Finally, in March 1971 the United States demanded his extradition. But a military plane dispatched to Asunción for the gangster kingpin returned without its prize. Paraguayan President Stroessner had decided that if Ricord were imprisoned it would be in Paraguay. "El Viejo" Ricord was then set up in a comfortable cell containing a spring mattress, radio and TV, and was allowed visits any time night or day. Waiters brought food from his own restaurant, and he continued managing his businesses in the quiet of prison.

Stroessner only capitulated in the summer of 1972 when the United States threatened a sharp cutback in aid to Paraguay. On September 3, Ricord was extradited. The man who put the pressure on Stroessner had been Henry Kissinger. According to international spook Luis Gonzalez-Mata, himself a party to the affair, the pressure began in late 1968, a year in which one of Kissinger's friends also happened to be in Paraguay on a "weapons deal."[3] The man was CIA agent/double agent Fernand Legros, a close acquaintance of several members of the Ricord gang.[4]

Roger Delouette

The case of Roger "French Connection" Delouette involved the greatest international fireworks and was recreated in print and on screen.

On 5 April 1971 a U.S. customs agent discovered eighty-nine packets of heroin hidden in a Volkswagen van on board the *Atlantic Cognac*, a freighter docked in Port Elizabeth, New Jersey. They contained forty-five kilos of the white gold. Delouette was arrested that same day when he came for the car.

Under interrogation Delouette claimed to be working for French intelligence agency SDECE, and that his journey with the heroin had been ordered by Colonel Ferrer alias Fournier, de Marenches' right-hand man in the SDECE. Furthermore, he had been instructed to contact SDECE agent Donald McNabb, who was working at the French consulate in New York.[5] While that was sensational in itself, the scandal was far greater than press and public could know. What really inflamed the Americans was that they had agreed with French authorities to cooperate against narcotics trafficking, and a key link was the supposedly reorganized and cooperative SDECE. If Delouette's story were true, then the SDECE had not only broken its agreement, it had also pulled the rug from under Pompidou, and much of the Americans' preliminary work would have been wasted.

French Defense Minister Michel Debré, under whose auspices the SDECE operated, officially denounced Delouette's claim as a fabrication. While he admitted that Delouette had earlier taken on occasional assignments, he was no longer attached to the SDECE.

The Americans subjected Delouette to two lie detector tests, both of which he passed with honor. Prosecutor Herbert Stern's request to interrogate Fournier was then refused. As for the French, their three-day investigation of Fournier absolved him of all suspicion.

At this stage Delouette's past becomes of interest.

He began working for French intelligence in 1946 at age twenty-three. His first assignment was keeping tabs on a Greek election, under the supervision of Colonel Roger Barberot. Although their paths appeared to split, the two stuck together. While Delouette remained with the SDECE, Barberot shuttled about on various jobs according to the needs of de Gaulle and Foccart. They were reunited in Algeria, with Delouette an agent and Barberot the leader of the Black Commandos. They again crossed paths in the Central African Republic, where Barberot served as French ambassador from 1961 to 1965. When Barberot became the head of the BDPA after the May 1968 riots, he immediately hired Delouette, who proceeded to marry his boss's secretary.

In the fall of 1968 Delouette and Barberot went on a mysterious trip to Cuba, during which Delouette was approached by the SDECE and asked to become its agent on the island. He agreed and remained an SDECE agent for nearly one year, after which he and Barberot journeyed once again to Africa.[6] In late 1969 Delouette suddenly contacted the SDECE's Colonel Fournier to demand back pay and request reinstatement. Both requests were filled.[7]

Following Delouette's arrest in the United States and official refutation of his statement, Barberot surprisingly told Radio Luxembourg that he believed the operation to have been led by Paris SDECE figures seeking to do away with both Delouette and his troublesome past. The Americans evidently believed Delouette and Barberot more than they did Defense Minister Debré and Colonel Fournier. For a crime punishable by twenty years imprisonment, Delouette got off with five.

At the close of 1972 a new chapter was added to the Delouette saga. Claude-André Pastou of Christian David's Latin American organization was arrested and began to sing for the CIA and U.S. narcotics agents. Pastou claimed David had ordered him to New York at the beginning of April 1971. On April 4 he was supposed to meet Roger Delouette at the Park Sheraton Hotel to discuss Delouette's delivery of the forty-five kilos of heroin to Pastou, who would then pass them on to the wholesalers.[8]

Pastou said he met Delouette as planned and that the two agreed on a delivery the following evening. When Delouette, with good reason, did not appear, Pastou got the jitters and returned to Latin America.[9]

It's also possible that the above-mentioned forces were aware of the Nixon-Pompidou narcotics agreement and saw their own financial stakes in jeopardy. They might have sought to thwart its implementation by splitting the SDECE and its CIA colleagues.

Finally, Fournier, who was "old school" SDECE, might also have been running drugs and, therefore, not been keen on carrying through the policies of his boss de Marenches.

Michel-Victor Mertz

On 5 July 1971 a Paris court sentenced two men to five years imprisonment for trafficking in narcotics. They were Michel-Victor Mertz, fifty-one, and Achilles Cecchini, forty-nine. Considering that since 1960 they had smuggled some $3 billion (street value) worth of heroin into the U.S.A., their sentences were mild to say the least. Moreover, their trial would never have taken place had French authorities not been under intense American pressure in the wake of Roger Delouette's exposé.

Since 1961, in fact, U.S. authorities had known that Mertz and Cecchini were smuggling large quantities into the country. Several times the U.S. had asked the French to act, but to no avail. There were very special reasons for French resistance.

Michel-Victor Mertz was born in the Mosel region's French community. In 1941 he was drafted into the German army. Two years later he deserted to join the French resistance. A man who cherished no great love for the Germans, Mertz soon became an underground legend as "Commandante Baptiste." His squad became famous for its daring, Mertz himself killing 20 Gestapo agents, freeing 400 prisoners and escaping 4 times in all from the Axis powers.

In 1945 General de Gaulle awarded him the Legion of Honor, which was soon joined by a Resistance medal and War Cross. Mertz was a hero. After the war he entered French intelligence with the rank of captain and was stationed abroad.

In 1960, while in the employ of the SDECE, Mertz began smuggling heroin from France to the U.S. together with Achilles Cecchini, a Marseilles gangster tied to the Francisci-Venturi clan. In 1961 the trade was interrupted when nearly all of France's top gangsters joined de Gaulle's forces in Algeria. Mertz was among them.

The SDECE sent him on a spy mission to infiltrate the OAS in Algeria. His mission proved a great success, even though he was mistakenly arrested by his own side and placed in a detention camp for OAS ringleaders in July 1961. On July 14 SDECE chiefs were notified that Mertz had important information. He was brought before Jacques Foccart himself. He informed Foccart that the OAS was planning to blow up the president's car near Pont-sur-Seine, a bridge across which de Gaulle was driven each day. Mertz was returned to the camp to determine the exact time of assassination.

At the last moment he succeeded. De Gaulle's car drove over Pont-sur-Seine as usual, but swerved into another lane, just as the bomb exploded in the lane normally taken. De Gaulle owed Mertz his life. Following the mission, with both the president and Foccart indebted to him, Mertz returned to the trafficking of narcotics.

On 12 January 1962 he shipped an automobile to New York loaded with 100 kilos of pure heroin. The procedure he followed was a standard one. A sheet-metal worker opened up the chassis, placed the heroin beyond the scrutiny of customs officials, and then rewelded the plates. The car was sent to the U.S. under a fictitious name and picked up by a man with a forged passport in that name.

Over the next eight or nine years Mertz and Cecchini operated without interruption and bagged a huge fortune. Their bankroller, a man of high standing, remained anonymous.

Through the years, Cecchini, like Mertz, had been of great service to the Gaullist party, UDR, in the SO du RPF as well as SAC, which explains the reluctance to prosecute them. Despite his five year sentence, Cecchini was deemed too ill for imprisonment and remained a free man. Mertz first began serving time in July 1972, but appears to have been secretly released shortly thereafter.[10]

Ange Simonpieri

On 13 September 1971 the fifty-six year old Ange Simonpieri was arrested at a private clinic in Ajaccio, Corsica, for smuggling large quantities of heroin into the U.S. between 1960 and 1970. His partner in crime was the Swiss banker André Hirsch.

Simonpieri had worked for both the SDECE and SAC. Like Christian David, he had been a barbouze in Algeria directly under Pierre Lemarchand. He became so close to Lemarchand that, as a local SAC leader, he managed the "physical" part of Lemarchand's 1963 Parliamentary campaign. Because of his political connections Simonpieri was known in his birthplace Corsica, and among Marseilles gangsters, as "The Untouchable."

On 31 August 1967 the freighter *Frederico C* docked in Miami. Customs agent John Wroth spotted a hunchback on his way down the gangplank. Finding the hunch suspicious, Wroth slapped it and jokingly asked if it was a burden. The man stiffened and sprang towards a taxi in which a sunglassed woman was waiting. But the cabby refused to depart and Wroth nabbed the couple.

The man was the Swiss banker William Lambert and the woman was Josette Bauer, an escapee from a Swiss prison where she had been serving time for murdering her rich father. Customs agents discovered twelve kilos of heroin in Lambert's hunchback and the couple was slapped with seven-year sentences by a Miami court. Both claimed to be couriers for a Corsican known to them as Monsieur Small. They were to have taken the heroin to Boston and handed it to one Robert Mori of Switzerland. The trail led from Mori to the Swiss banker André Hirsch, but U.S. narks lacked the evidence to nail him.

After this episode, Hirsch and his partner Monsieur Small started the Panamanian Food and Chemical Company, which exported canned paella to the U.S.A. – only some of the cans were filled with heroin. Hirsch was finally trapped in 1969 when U.S. customs agents opened the wrong cans. He was brought before a Geneva court, but it wasn't until 29 April 1971 that he was sentenced to six and a half years in prison. On that day his lawyer, the famous Raymond Nicolet, announced that Monsieur Small was the Corsican Ange Simonpieri.

The court in Geneva had been pestering French police to question Simonpieri since 1970, but had been told Simonpieri was in a clinic with a bad heart and could not take the questioning. When Nicolet's assertion hit French newsstands, Simonpieri was quickly readmitted into the Grandval clinic with severe heart pains.

But Simonpieri's number was up. After four months of haggling, on 8 September 1971, with full press coverage, French Interior Minister Raymond Marcellin ordered court-appointed doctors to examine the patient. Five days later police put Simonpieri under arrest. In July 1972 a French court sentenced him to five years imprisonment—a penalty, like those of Mertz and Cecchini, that bore no relation to the crime. Hirsch and Simonpieri each got less time than their hapless couriers, Lambert and Bauer.

Once again there was the scent of CIA agent Fernand Legros, an acquaintance of the Hirsch family, who was seen with Madame Hirsch in Geneva after her husband had been put away.[11]

André Labay

On Sunday, 26 September 1971 U.S. customs agents arrested the Frenchman Richard Berdin on his way out of the Abbey Victoria Hotel on Fifty-First Street in New York City. His arrest grew out of the discovery of eighty-two kilos of heroin aboard the Italian liner *Rafaello* in New York harbor. Though Berdin was a small fish in the drug ring they were tracking, the customs agents had followed him for five days to several of his contacts.

In fact the arrest was a slip caused by fierce rivalry between agents of customs and the BNDD. For half a year the BNDD had been cooperating with French narks in search of Berdin's bankrollers and New York customers. Much to the narks' chagrin, customs agents struck without warning their rivals. However, luck was with customs. Weeks later Berdin, seeking a reduced sentence, fingered a French all-star drug ring that included gangsters Laurent Fiocconi, Jo Signoli, Jean-Claude Kella, Alexandre Salles, Jean Dumerain, Felix Rosso, Jean Demeester, Raymond Moulin, Patrick Lorenz, Jacky Martin, Francois Scapula, and André Andréani; plus U.S. mafiosi including Louis Cirillo, Lorenco d'Aloisio, Frank Rappa, and Giuseppe Ciacomazzo.[12]

Their sentences ranged from five to twenty-five years, while Berdin got away with three and served only one and a half. Today he's living in the U.S.A. with a new name and a new face, but still fearful of underworld revenge.

On 5 October 1971 one André Labay visited the Paris BNDD office, said he was working for the SDECE, and offered to help bring 100 kilos of heroin into the United States. He would then make another trip with the same quantity and lead the BNDD to the wholesalers. As the BNDD well knew, Labay was a ringleader of the gang on which Berdin had stooled. After telling him to return the next day, they phoned the French narcotics police. On October 6, French police arrested Labay and three other heroin traffickers, and found 106 kilos of heroin in Labay's Volkswagen.

Why did Labay show up at the U.S. narcotics office, and what did he really propose? There has been no lack of answers. Some say Labay was employed on the same side as Delouette, by forces seeking either to discredit the new SDECE leadership or to destroy the trans-Atlantic drug crusade. Others believe the contrary – that Labay was a CIA-SDECE double agent made into a scapegoat when Berdin sang.

André Labay had been another of Pierre Lemarchand's barbouzes in Algeria. Not known for his fighting, he was sent to spy behind OAS terrorist lines. In late 1961 Jacques Foccart sent him to Kinshasa (in the Congo), the Ivory Coast and Gabon. Back in France he immediately joined SAC as a fund-raiser.

For reasons unknown Labay began going his own route in the mid-sixties. With his close friends, CIA agent Fernand Legros and Thierry de Bonnay, he had his fling in the international art trade. He got involved with a Belgian insurance company that collapsed with $6 million in debts, and, like Legros, he also produced several movies.

Labay and de Bonnay ran the Parisian hotel at which the Moroccan Colonel Dlimi stayed in the aftermath of the Ben Barka affair. It was also the hotel that doubled as a mercenary recruiting station for the Katangese army of Moise Tshombé, whom the Labay/Legros/de Bonnay threesome helped abduct to Algeria. And in his Geneva apartment, Labay once hid the Algerian revolutionary, Belkassem Krim, who was later murdered.[13]

In 1968 Labay went to Haiti, where he made a small fortune from a factory. He was often visited there by Legros, and the two became personal friends of the Haitian dictator Francois "Papa Doc" Duvalier. Labay ingratiated himself with Duvalier's daughter Marie-Denise, leading some to suspect he was her lover. In Haiti he served as an SDECE-CIA double agent. He stayed in close touch with U.S. gangsters Joe Bonnano and Max Intrattor, and one of his Geneva contacts was the Lansky syndicate's financial brain, John Pullman.[14]

Marcel Boucan

Late in the evening of 29 February 1972 the sixty-ton shrimpboat *Caprice de Temps* sailed out of the cozy harbor of Villefrance on

France's Mediterranean coast. The ship was registered in Guadeloupe. Its skipper was the fifty-eight-year-old former parachutist Marcel Boucan, a Hemingway type in more ways than one.

Boucan was a charming old soldier. Since the war he had smuggled alcohol and cigarettes from Tangiers to France, and weapons the other way, first on board *l'Oiseau des Iles* and later the *Caprice de Temps*. To strangers he was just another shrimp fisherman. In fact, until 1957 he was the chairman of the Cagnes fisherman's union, and was also an extraordinarily well-read and clever man whose cabin featured the works of Kafka, Balzac, Camus, and Kant. He was married to a woman from Guadeloupe and in his later years he often sailed through the French West Indies.

As he was steaming out of Villefrance on 28 February 1972 the customs cruiser *Sirocco* was leaving Nice. Hours later customs agents hailed down the *Caprice de Temps*. Boucan ordered full steam ahead, but changed his mind when the *Sirocco* fired a salvo. Aboard the shrimpboat the agents found 425 kilos of heroin, the largest single shipment ever confiscated. The size of the load suggested desperation among smugglers following the 1971 roundup of several narcotics rings. The heroin had been destined for Santo Trafficante, jr.'s Florida-based Cuban Mob.[15]

Boucan was slapped with a fifteen-year sentence on 5 January 1973. His courtroom arrogance and noble coolness irked judges so much, that his appeal brought three more years. Such severity was unheard of in France. A dozen Marseilles gangsters were also locked up in the aftermath. They were all from the same circle of crooks that had participated in the Labay affair, which made it likely that the men upstairs, who needless to say went untouched, were also from the same political faction.

The Laboratories

In August 1971 John Cusack, the head of the U.S. Bureau of Narcotics and Dangerous Drugs (BNDD), declared in Paris that eight Marseilles heroin laboratories, financed by influential backers, were operating with complete immunity from prosecution. In return for his frankness Cusack became *persona non grata* in France and was recalled to the U.S.A. But his words sank in. Pressure was put on French authorities by the Americans, who wondered what good it did to round up narcotics rings when the heroin production itself went on unabated.

On 27 January 1972 French police stormed a heroin lab in Marseilles' Montolivet quarter. The laboratory, which produced forty kilos of good quality heroin each week, was run by Marius and Marie-Antoinette Pastore. Marius got fifteen years on 29 September 1972 while Marie-Antoinette got five.

On 16 March 1972 the police made an impressive arrest that broke the heart of many a politician, bankroller, and cop. The catch was heroin's grand old man, Jo Cesari, reputedly the best heroin chemist in the world.

Born in Bastia, Corsica in 1915, Cesari was first a sailor, then a grocer, bartender, and farmer. In the early fifties he apprenticed himself to his half-brother Dominique Albertini, the manager of several Marseilles heroin labs. In 1962 Cesari purchased a luxurious Aubagne estate, La Roseraie, that included an enormous mansion, a park, a swimming pool and a tennis court. No one could figure out where the old sailor had gotten his money.

Cesari would leave his estate for long stretches of time. In 1964 narcotics police shadowed him for several months, and converged on Clos Saint Antoine, an abandoned estate where he had set up two heroin labs and put four assistants to work. Police stormed the estate, arresting Cesari and his staff. They also made an interesting discovery in one of the back rooms: the nephew of Marcel Francisci.[16] Months earlier the boy's father, on an unannounced trip back to Corsica, had discovered his wife with a lover, whom he proceeded to shoot through the throat before returning to France with his son Jean-Francois.

As head of the family, Marcel Francisci looked after his nephew. He placed him under the wings of a Cesari laboratory worker and his wife. This is the same Francisci who denies any involvement with heroin.

Cesari was sentenced to seven years in prison, but was released a lot sooner. As soon as he was out he returned to the synthesis of his favorite organic compound, and consulted for several laboratories besides his own. His 1971 production was estimated at twenty kilos of heroin daily, which means large lots were shipped to the United States. Cesari most probably produced the huge cargos that, according to narcotics police, reached Miami via Marcel Boucan and the *Caprice de Temps*.

In March 1972, as Cesari was setting up a lab in the Suzanne building in Aubagne, police traced him through an assistant and arrested him. Their prisoner was a haunched, sickly old figure, ruined by years of acid gas inhalation. Cesari was only fifty-eight. On March 22 he hanged himself in his Baumettes prison cell, overcome, no doubt, by the spectre of a long sentence. He knew he'd never come out alive.

Cesari left behind letters making it clear he had planned to settle down in Latin America and experiment with cocaine, most likely in partnership with Christian David, whose ring survived as one of the larger remnants of the once great French narcotics empire. Cesari's death was a hard blow to Marseilles' heroin industry. No one could fill his shoes.[17] French and American police alike tried in vain to duplicate his process for producing pure heroin.

On 15 July 1972 French narks closed out a series of raids leading to the closing of three labs, all belonging to the Long brothers.

A few days later President Nixon telegrammed congratulations to Pompidou for the great strides he had made.

Marseilles has never been the same.

Notes

1. The same threesome turns up in several other circumstances, including Barberot's mysterious trip to Cuba in 1968. He was joined then by Santenac, Delouette and Gilbert Beaujolin, a well-known financier closely tied to Jacques Foccart.

2. P. Chairoff: *Dossier B . . . comme Barbouzes* (Alain Moreau, 1975).

3. L. Gonzalez-Mata: *Cygne* (Grasset, 1976).

4. R. Peyrefitte: *La Vie Extraordinaire de Fernand Legros* (Albin Michel, 1976).

5. The Newsday Staff: *The Heroin Trail* (Souvenir Press, 1974).

6. P. Galante and L. Sapin: *The Marseilles Mafia* (W.H. Allen, 1979).

7. There is doubt as to whether Fournier ever knew Delouette was formally readmitted into the SDECE. In 1972 *Newsday* reporters got hold of a 27 October 1969 letter from Defense Minister Debré to Colonel Barberot in which Debré, vowing to take care of the matter, asked that Delouette's application and demand not be discussed with other SDECE leaders.

8. A. Jaubert: *Dossier D . . . comme Drogue* (Alain Moreau, 1974).

9. If Pastou's testimony is correct, then Delouette lied about delivering heroin to an SDECE agent named McNabb, and there's no truth to Colonel Fournier's alleged involvement. What remains are one man's word against anothers and several possible explanations. First, Fournier might not have wanted Delouette back in the SDECE because he knew him to be Barberot's man and, therefore, tied to forces purged from the SDECE. Fournier could

also have been pressured from above to rehire Delouette, and then seen the heroin affair as an opportunity to get rid of him.

That seems rather farfetched, since SDECE narcotics network with the CIA and BNDD was Pompidou's pet idea. Fournier would hardly have risked his job to get rid of a single agent. Another possibility is that Barberot, or forces he represents, welcomed the opportunity to compromise their opposition within the SDECE – above all Fournier and chief-of-staff de Marenches. That Fournier later made amends with the Americans is suggested by his opening a restaurant in New York in 1978.

10. The Newsday Staff, *op. cit.*

11. Peyrefitte, *op. cit.*

12. R. Berdin: *Code Name Richard* (Dutton, 1974).

13. The exiled Algerian politician Belkassem Krim was a former leader of the revolutionary movement, FLN. After Algeria won its independence, he came into conflict with the country's first chief-of-state, Ahmed Ben Bella. Together with the latter's minister of finance, Mohammed Khider, Krim fled Algeria, while refusing to hand over the FLN's $20 million war chest to the Algerian regime. Khider had deposited the money in his own name at Geneva's Banque Commerciale Arabe, and only he and Krim knew the account number. On 3 January 1967 Khider was shot down in Madrid. Krim was murdered in a Frankfurt hotel room on 20 October 1970. Both had been closely connected with Morocco's interior minister Oufkir.

14. E. Gerdan: *Dossier A . . . comme Armes* (Alain Moreau, 1974). The Mafia's activities in Cuba were controlled by Joe Bonnano, whose close partners today in the so-called Southern Rim Mafia are Santo Trafficante, jr. and Carlos Marcello. Labay was also closely tied to Intra-Bank founder Yussef Beidas.

15. Jaubert, *op. cit.*

16. *L'Express*, 14 October 1968.

17. 1979 was the year of the rumor. Not only was Christian David alleged to be back in France, it was also said that the old French Connection was about to resume the shipment of heroin from Marseilles to the U.S.A. When the heroin chemist Jacques Masia was arrested in August 1979, French newspapers went so far as to speculate that he was a revitalized version of Jo Cesari himself! The latter, it was explained, had not really committed suicide, but had been "sheepdipped" and used as an undercover agent by the DEA and French narcotics police (*Politiken*, 28 August 1979).

ELEVEN
THE CAPTURE OF BEAU SERGE
IN BRAZIL

Auguste Ricord's March 1971 imprisonment in Paraguay taught Christian David and Lucien Sarti that it was time to move on. Their choice of location was Brazil, in particular Ilha Bella, an island off the coast north of Santos, conveniently only two hours from Sao Paulo and five from Rio de Janeiro. It also provided a small harbor and landing strip. The two holed up in the Bordelao, a small hotel run by Haide Arantez and Claudio Rodriguez, friends of Sarti's Brazilian mistress, Helena Ferreira.

Beau Serge was by then the undisputed boss of "The Brazilian Connection." Its other leaders were Sarti, Michel Nicoli, André Condemine, Francois Canazzi, Jean Lunardi, Francois Chiappe, Robert Bourdoulous, and Francois ("Fan Fan") Orsini. Most had known David through SAC. Some had been with Ricord in Paraguay. Newcomers Orsini and Canazzi were wanted in France for attempted murder.

Not all the capos lived on Ilha Bella. Some were strategically placed elsewhere – Chiappe in Buenos Aires, Pastou in Sao Paulo, Sans in Barcelona. Loosely connected to the permanent core was a long string of collaborators. The organization was solid. Heroin flowed steadily from Marseilles to Ilha Bella and on to Miami or New York. But Beau Serge ran into a major obstacle: the Italian Mafia.

Tomasso Buscetta, one of the Sicilians' most notorious thugs, was ordered to Brazil in 1970 to prepare a takeover of the narcotics traffic – a logical step in a larger plan to be described later. Buscetta was wanted in Italy for murdering twelve people, including seven policemen, in the Cisculli massacre in Sicily.[1] He's also alleged to have been responsible for the disappearance of reporter Mauro de Mauro,

who had stuck his nose into the murder of the Italian oil magnate
Enrico Mattei.[2]

Within a year of his arrival in Sao Paulo, Buscetta had his
legitimate cover: 250 taxis, a chain of snack bars, and an aluminum
plant. It was all a front, and when Ricord was put away Buscetta
decided the hour had arrived to move in on the multi-million dollar
dope business. However, he hadn't reckoned with Beau Serge.
Following an extended struggle that ended with David still on top,
Buscetta was forced to play ball like anyone else, and brought with
him into the organization his son Benedetto, Paulo Lilio Gigante, and
Guglielmo Casalini.

Life, though, was not all hard work for David and company. They
also found time for night life in Rio and Sao Paulo, threw lavish
parties, and mixed with film stars, singers and other international
celebrities. And still there was time for politics. David and others took
part in the Argentine Anticommunist Alliance's (AAA) massacres in
Argentina, and remained on good footing with the Brazilian Death
Squad. At the same time SAC agents from David's coterie lent their
expertise to the torture chamber of Sergio Fleury, head of Sao Paulo's
infamous Death Squad.[3]

However, like all other good things David's came to an end. For
Beau Serge and his Brazilian Connection, 1972 was a fateful year in
more ways than one. It began with the arrest in January of Sarti and
his girl friend Helena on suspicion of passing counterfeit money. That
proved to be only a police calling card, as the couple was soon back on
the streets.

The late-1971 plugging of French drug smuggling routes had
made things difficult for their U.S. buyers. Aware that Franco-
American forces were bent on crushing the entire French network,
New York and Miami Mafia dons treaded cautiously. Moreover, the
arrest of several dealers left the Brazilian Connection short of
customers in early 1972.

In February, shortly before carnival in Rio, David, Sarti,
Buscetta and Nicoli spent three days with Carlo Zippo, a Mafia
emissary from New York.[4] At the meeting, which transpired at Rio's
plush Copacabana Palace hotel, the mobsters developed a new
network and buyer system. Sarti, jittery after his arrest, would move
to Mexico City, the new transit point.

In March Sarti went to Mexico City, where he was joined by his
wife Liliane in an attractive residential district apartment. Sarti had
no notion that the police had been trailing him ever since his entry into

Mexico. Somebody had tipped them off. The Guatemalan authorities were after him for an armed attack on a bank; he was also wanted by the Bolivian police; and Interpol had issued descriptions of him everywhere. In the evening of April 17, Sarti and Liliane left their hideout to go to the movies. Before they got to their car, they were surrounded by police. Sarti was unarmed, but the police shot and killed him, and arrested Liliane.[5]

The next day the Mexican Minister of Justice declared that the international drug trafficker had been killed in a confrontation with the police. A couple of months later, French newspapers added that Christian David had been in Mexico City at the time of Sarti's death, but that he had escaped and made it all the way back to Brazil.[6]

On 7 May 1972 Brazilian police found the body of a young woman washed ashore on an Ilha Bella beach. It was Haide Arantez, owner of the Bordelao, the David gang hideout. Examination revealed the cause of death as strangulation. Another body appeared in the same place the next day. This time it was Haide's boy friend and partner, Claudio Rodriguez, who'd had his head busted in. The double-murder suspect was naturally Beau Serge, who was believed to have knocked off the hotel owners for disclosing the Mexican locale.

Sarti's mistress Helena Ferriera was jailed for her own safety while Brazilian police, egged on strongly by U.S. narcotics agents, hunted after the David gang. Besides entertaining the police with stories of the gang's escapades, Ms. Ferreira also claimed they met frequently with the French millionaire/playboy/art dealer Fernand Legros.

Whether because of corruption in Brazilian police ranks or an agreement involving the CIA and BNDD, David's gang remained at large for the time being, notwithstanding the police manhunt. If he was to be extradited, they would have to catch him in the act. David, in the meantime, was ensconced in a Rio villa where he'd set up his mistress Simone Delamare.

In early October 1972 the CIA and BNDD were finally ready to strike when, in Rio de Janeiro harbor, they discovered sixty kilos of heroin about to be shipped by the gang to Miami aboard the freighter *Mormac Altair*. Police picked up Michel Nicoli in Sao Paulo, and nabbed most of the other members within days. On October 17, a large police force was dispatched to Simone Delamare's house, where David's presence was no longer a secret. But Beau Serge was tipped off and managed to slip away one more time.

On October 21, two alert policemen noticed an obviously nervous young woman shopping in Salvador, in the Brazilian state of Bahia. They followed her to a third class hotel in the seedier side of town. She looked too well-dressed and sophisticated to stay at such a dive, so the two officers brought her in. At headquarters they soon determined she was David's girl friend Simone.

Shortly thereafter Beau Serge was packing up when six policemen smashed through the door to his room. He lunged for a pistol, but was grabbed before he could fire a shot. What followed was a tussle the officers won't forget.

"He was a master of karate," one of them later reported. "He threw us around like balls. If there had only been four of us, I don't see how we could have handled him."

Handcuffs and foot chains were needed to restrain Beau Serge. Nor did he relent as he lay on the floor, battered and exhausted, but rather tried bribing the Brazilian officers to release him. He offered each $100,000 plus tickets anywhere for their entire families. Leaving the hotel room, he managed, handcuffs and all, to grab a drinking glass, smash it and cut deeply into his wrist. His goal was a hospital where opportunities for escape were numerous. But his hospital stay was too short. Guards kept close watch as he was sewn up in an emergency room before being thrown into a cell. By the next day he was in a prison in Sao Paulo.

In Beau Serge's valise police found one 9 mm Browning, one silenced Beretta, one short-barreled Smith and Weson revolver, three cartridges of a crippling poison, ninety bullet cartridges of various caliber,[7] and a Uruguayan diplomatic passport in the name of Edouard Davrieux, with a photo of Christian David.

The arrest was greeted with mixed reactions in France. Worry, anger, and anxiety were aroused in certain circles, joy in others. At least one person was delighted: police lieutenant Bellemin-Noel, who looked forward to finally settling the score with the murderer of his predecessor Galibert—or so he thought.

Just how great an effort the French made to have David extradited remains in doubt. Certainly some wanted him back to stand trial. Others preferred that he never again have the opportunity to talk. There were representatives of each persuasion in the highest political echelons. Since international law placed France in the driver's seat, its efforts at extradition must have been meek at best. Many were dumbfounded when Brazil extradited Christian David to the U.S.A. without first notifying the French government.

Before extradition to the U.S.A., however, David shocked the world by "admitting" his complicity in the Ben Barka affair. He also cut the artery in his wrist a second time, and on the day before his transfer to the U.S.A., he got hold of a light bulb, crushed it, and swallowed the fragments. However, he received no medical treatment before arriving in the United States. According to his own later testimony, he was unaware of his destination when U.S. narks came for him. Presuming it was France, he resisted violently. The Americans, he claimed, pumped him so full of drugs he didn't know what was happening.

During the trial that began within days of his arrival in Brooklyn, newspapers reported he had been a victim of torture. David himself said: "I was tortured by Brazilian police for thirty days and fed nothing for twenty-six. They stole all my money. Today I can't afford a lawyer, I haven't a cent."

David and Michel Nicoli – who, with Claude-André Pastou, had been extradited to the U.S. before David – each claimed they had been hung head down over a steam-puffing pipe as the Brazilians administered electric shocks to their genitals. While David looked awful in court from his self-inflicted wounds, not a trace of the alleged torture could be seen on Nicoli. The story of torture certainly doesn't fit David's later desire to return to prison in Brazil.

On December 1 the court handed down its sentences. Auguste Ricord, extradited from Paraguay two months earlier, had gotten twenty-seven years. David and Nicoli now got twenty. Pastou, who gave the Americans important information on the Delouette affair, got seven. Other Frenchmen in David's gang were extradited back to France, where they were wanted for murder and other capital crimes. The only one to avoid arrest was André Condemine, who went underground only to be murdered. Francois Chiappe avoided extradition until 1976, when he was sentenced in New York to twenty years. Tomasso Buscetta and the gang's three other Italians were nabbed on 5 November 1972, nearly two weeks after David, and were shipped off to Italy.

Fernand Legros, the mystery man in this and earlier intrigues, was apparently placed under protective confinement in Rio shortly after David's sentencing in the United States. Officially he was arrested in connection with art frauds.[8] Each day, though, he was brought lavish meals including lobster, champagne, cognac, and fat Havana cigars. The big French underworld shakedown began just as Legros was "imprisoned." If Legros had aided the CIA in the David affair, he must have been high on the list of those to be taken care of on the other side of the Atlantic.

In 1974 SAC agents kidnapped Legros in Brazil, flew him back to France and locked him up.[9] Somebody was interested in the part he had played in certain affairs. However, Legros' friend Henry Kissinger, then secretary of state, came to his aid. Kissinger demanded his release, protesting sharply the kidnaping of a U.S. citizen.[10]

Legros still fears for his life. As recently as the spring of 1976 a nervous Legros, surrounded by bodyguards, said he had been threatened by Christian David's barbouze colleagues and had demanded police protection.

Notes

1. The Newsday Staff: *The Heroin Trail* (Souvenir Press, 1974).

2. J. Sarazin: *Dossier M . . . comme Milieu* (Alain Moreau, 1977).

3. P. Chairoff: *Dossier B . . . comme Barbouzes* (Alain Moreau, 1975).

4. Zippo was a member of the New York Gambino family (Newsday, *op. cit.*), which is interesting insofar as the prime customers of the David/Ricord organization were Santo Trafficante, jr. and his Cuban Mafia; it is especially interesting in light of the apparent rift between the so-called Southern Rim or Sunbelt Mafia—an alliance mainly of Joseph Bonnano, Trafficante and Carlos Marcello—and the New York families; see D. Moldea: *The Hoffa Wars* (Charter Books, 1978). Bonnano, 75, and his nephew Jack DeFillipi, recently went on trial on federal conspiracy charges involving the laundering of Mafia money.

5. P. Galante and L. Sapin: *The Marseilles Mafia* (W.H. Allen, 1979).

6. *L'Aurore*, 27 July 1972.

7. *Le Nouvel Observateur*, 13 November 1972.

8. *L'Aurore*, 31 May 1976.

9. French newspapers published varying conjectures as to the grounds for Legros' arrest. Most guessed he had been implicated in narcotics smuggling by association with David's gang. None supposed Legros might have helped lay a trap for Beau Serge, and therefore was in jail for his own protection.

10. Legros had become an American citizen while working for the CIA.

TWELVE:
THE LIQUIDATION

With Christian David behind bars in Illinois' Marion prison, only one important French narcotics ring remained active, and that was run by the Francisci-Venturi mob. Their network consisted of such pillars of the Marseilles underworld as Paul Mondolini, Jean-Baptiste Croce, Albert Bistoni and, until mid-1972, Etienne Mosca. Intelligent, experienced gangsters who left nothing to chance, they were considered untouchable. Mondolini, the most highly respected of all, is considered Marcel Francisci's crown prince.

On 7 July 1972 Mosca was arrested in Lyons, stunning the entire French underworld. Were the untouchables really to be hit? But when there was no follow-up, all sighed in relief.

Lightning struck six months later on 19 January 1973. French narks shadowed Croce and Bistoni to the Gondolier bar in Marseilles' old harbor quarter. Both were arrested on the way out of the bar, police having blocked the main road. Disbelief gave way to suspicion when Bistoni was released shortly thereafter. Had he talked?

Croce's arrest proved to be the trigger for a desperate, ruthless gangland war that measured up to prohibition Chicago. In the first half of 1973, thirty French mobsters were murdered – primarily in Paris, Marseilles, and Lyons.[1]

On March 31, Bistoni was at Marseilles' Tanagre restaurant with two of his strongmen. The door opened and in walked three men, pistols drawn. Seconds later Bistoni, his thugs and the restauranteur were goners. The killings were common knowledge by the time police arrived.

Among the many sensational shootouts of early 1973, several were connected to Christian David.

Police fished a drifting trunk from the Seine on 28 July 1973. Inside was the corpse of a man with bullets in his heart and neck. It was André Condemine, the David gang's minister of transportation and its only member to avoid arrest. Police investigation established he had been dead since February. Perhaps Condemine had had something to do with the arrest of Jean-Baptiste Croce. It was no secret that Condemine had sought to reconstruct a Latin American narcotics network and had settled on Mexico, Croce's territory.

Among David's other friends who were knocked off in those hectic months, the first to go was Roger Dadoun. A former member of both Felix Lesca's gang and the international gunrunning Mob David had joined upon arrival in Latin America, Dadoun was shot down in the Paris suburb of Neuilly on 13 March 1973. Dadoun's best friend (and a close one of Beau Serge's as well) was Louis Nesmoz. He had sheltered Georges Figon during the Ben Barka affair and later helped the Orsini brothers smuggle heroin via Barcelona to David in Brazil. Nesmoz avenged Dadoun's death by shooting Joel Arfoiulloux and Raymond Elbaz in Paris's Clemence bistro on 7 April 1973.

Next it was Nesmoz' own turn to taste lead. On May 19, as he and two of his men dined at the Gentilly restaurant in Paris, two men entered and shot the three of them.

Yet another was killed on 15 June 1973. Jean Auge, the Lyons area SAC chief and crime syndicate boss who had been in touch with Ricord in Paraguay and on good terms with David, Nesmoz, and Dadoun, was found after a slow and painful death with eight bullets in his stomach.[2]

While the gangsters were cutting each other down, the police were not exactly on vacation. On 10 April 1973 the Marseilles and Paris forces teamed up on a major drive that sent thirty mobsters behind bars.

The gang war subsided by mid-1973, but has never completely ended. With heroin no longer a viable commodity, there are more pockets than can be filled by other underworld operations, and so the murders continue at regular intervals. The 1975 toll included gangland boss William Zemmour, who was given a royal burial and escorted to his grave by anything able to walk, creep, or crawl in the Parisian underworld.

Several big names resorted to untraditional means of survival. Francois Chiappe, the David gang heavy stationed in Argentina, was arrested in Cordoba. He was imprisoned in 1972, just as the rest of the gang was being nabbed in Brazil. But Chiappe had excellent connections in right wing Peronist circles. A former OAS Commando Delta member in Algeria, he had remained in touch with other OAS figures assembled in the Paladin group, a Fascist terrorist combine founded in Spain by the Nazi war criminal Colonel Otto Skorzeny.[3] It was among the organizations to which Juan Peron's grey eminence, Jose Lopez Rega, allied himself when he formed the dreaded terrorist group, the Argentine Anticommunist Alliance (AAA).

When the Peronist Hector Campora became president of Argentina in May 1973, Chiappe was released and immediately recruited into the AAA. When Peron himself returned a month later from eighteen years of exile in Spain, an enormous crowd gathered at Ezeiza airport on June 20 to greet him. Among them was a large contingent of Montoneros and other leftists. Security police were well aware of their presence. Police and AAA terrorists led by Colonel Jorge Osinde attacked the demonstrators with machine guns and hand grenades. Some 100 were killed and 300 were badly wounded. The AAA's prisoners were dragged to the airport parking lot and tortured. Two of the more zealous hatchet men were Chiappe and former OAS colonel Jean Gardes.[4]

On August 6, Chiappe's wife visited the Argentine prison commissioner on her husband's behalf, to request that he be placed in protective confinement.[5] Chiappe had gotten the jitters after the discovery of his friend Condemine in the Seine. Besides, he was in constant danger of abduction by the Americans, who had long been demanding his extradition. The prison commissioner contacted the highest political authorities, and Buenos Aires' Villa Devote prison soon opened its doors. There Chiappe led the same charmed life as Auguste Ricord in Paraguay, and Fernand Legros in Brazil. His "cell" was outfitted with elegant furniture, TV and a radio, and first class food was brought in from town. Naturally he was "paroled" whenever Lopez Rega or Isabel Peron threw a party, and the threat of extradition ended when the new Argentine regime, on orders from Peron, said a final no to the United States. Instead cooperation between the two countries took a different form. In May 1974 the U.S. ambassador in Buenos Aires, Robert C. Hill, and Lopez Rega – with whom he had worked closely for years – publicly signed an agreement to wage common war against the drug traffickers. At the signatory ceremony, Lopez Rega declared that the drug war would automatically be an antiguerilla campaign as well, under the rationale that the Montoneros were the real traffickers. Pursuant to the agreement, the U.S. sent to Argentina a large number of narcotics agents trained at the

CIA's special school in Georgetown.[6]

One year later, a report of Argentina military intelligence revealed a giant narcotics network responsible for smuggling cocaine to the U.S. market. Its leaders were none other than Lopez Rega; his son-in-law Raul Lastiri; Senator Juan Carlos Cornejo; Robert Romero, managing editor of Argentina's largest provincial newspaper, *El Tribuno*; and Colonels Osinde and Raul Lacabanne, both of whom fled to safety in Paraguay.[7]

When a military coup deposed Isabel Peron, who had assumed the presidency on the death of her husband, power was seized by General Jorge Videla, who professed a strict, albeit selective, morality. He refused to harbor a hardened criminal like Chiappe in spite of the many leftists he had disposed of. In late April 1976 Videla extradited Chiappe to the U.S.A. to share the fates of Ricord, David, Nicoli, and Pastou.[8]

Simultaneously with the 1972-73 attrition in French underworld ranks, President Georges Pompidou took the opportunity to purge SAC of its undesirables. Though it seemed as if SAC was being eliminated altogether, such was not the case. No angel himself, Pompidou would call on the corps at election time and whenever else he saw fit. But Pompidou did eliminate those elements opposed to him personally, who had continued to make trouble for the new regime. Some 7000 men were weeded out, many of them criminals who had enjoyed SAC protection and now became easy marks for the police.

Many of the barbouzes booted from SAC fled to Spain to join the Paladin group, where they learned to work side-by-side with their former arch enemies, the OAS terrorists.

Not all SAC agents were as fortunate. Charles Lascorz, a charter member of SAC and its chief for southeastern France, was among the many hunted down by the police. Along with his SAC activities, he had also headed a large smuggling and swindling mob comprised exclusively of SAC agents, as had his colleague Jean Auge in Lyons.

Police tracked Lascorz to a Paris apartment in early 1972 and sent two officers to fetch him. Just how he did it is not known, but Lascorz managed to lure them to a cellar and lock the door behind him. He then fled to Spain, taking the SAC archives with him. But Spanish police arrested him on 23 January 1972 and put him in Carabanchel prison. They extradited him to France two months later, but not before the Spanish intelligence agency DGS had photocopied the archives. Lascorz was sentenced in France to three years in prison along with eight of his SAC cohorts.

Between mid-1971 and mid-1973 the French espionage and underworlds suffered staggering losses. A succession of untouchables bit the dust, most prominent among them Joseph Orsini, Jo Cesari, Jo Attia, Georges Boucheseiche, Julien le Ny, Pierre Dubail, André Condemine, Lucien Sarti, Albert Bistoni, Jean Auge, Louis Nesmoz, and Roger Dadoun. Between forty and fifty gangsters perished in the French heroin war during that interim, only two of them of natural causes.

In addition, a horde of French heroin smugglers, the entire elite included, was put behind bars. The big names were Auguste Ricord, Christian David, Michel Nicoli, Roger Delouette, André Labay,[9] Jean-Baptiste Croce, Jo Signoli, Ange Simonpieri, Jean Claude Kella, Jean Orsini, Roch Orsini, Martin Orsini, Laurent Fiocconi, Etienne Mosca, Marcel Boucan, and Richard Berdin.

A glance at French arrest figures reveals the magnitude of the slaughter of the French heroin Mafia. Twenty-five traffickers were arrested in 1969-70. In 1971 alone the number was 26 and in 1972 it shot up to 108. With the exception of a lone behind-the-scenes bankroller, all were active, professional smugglers. An even greater number of French traffickers were arrested in 1972 in the U.S. and elsewhere.

More than half the gangsters killed or imprisoned during those two fateful years were connected to intelligence agencies SDECE and/or SAC. Whether or not the two organizations had directly profited from heroin trafficking and actually managed and financed part of it remains a subject of speculation.

Nearly all French narcotics syndicates then in existence were smashed beyond recognition. Those that tried comebacks did not succeed very well. Dead or imprisoned smugglers could be replaced with time. More serious was the shortage of heroin labs in the aftermath of the great raids. The good chemists, like the smugglers, were either deceased or behind bars.[10] Moreover, French narcotics police placed an iron collar around Marseilles. Their force increased by more than 1000 percent between 1970 and 1973, and the French port became a stalking ground of U.S. narks.[11]

Equally disastrous, Turkey halted its illicit opium production by an agreement with the U.S. which ensured the Turks compensation. In 1973, of course, there were stocks of morphine base to be found in Turkey, Lebanon, and Marseilles. However, the frequent seizure of heroin shipments had thinned them out badly.

In 1970 Marseilles supplied roughly 80 percent of the heroin on the U.S. market. Fifteen percent came from Mexico and only five percent from Southeast Asia. By 1973 the French share had fallen below 50 percent, and in 1975 it was estimated at less than 15 percent. From the law enforcement standpoint, the French heroin Mafia was effectively crushed, and the U.S. narcotics intelligence agency, the Drug Enforcement Administration (DEA), considered moving its European headquarters from Paris to Amsterdam.[12]

The French underworld and its more "respectable" bankrollers were deprived of an annual income of some $150 million for a quantity of heroin which when cut in the U.S. could bring a street price of $20 billion.

But did the supply of heroin to the international market really fall by an amount equal to the French share? Did it fall at all?

Wasn't it true that pure heroin could only be produced in Marseilles and that the world's drug habit would be largely relieved if only one could smash the French and Turkish suppliers? Isn't that what Nixon told Pompidou?

Yes, but how often did Nixon tell the truth?

Notes

1. Various sources claim that some of these murders were "liquidations" executed by a special "assassination squad" set up by the White House and led by a former CIA agent, Lt. Col. Lucien Conein–see, for example, E.J. Epstein: *Agency of Fear* (Putnam, 1977); J. Hougan: *Spooks* (William Morrow, 1978); and chapter fifteen of this volume.

2. A fifth member of this circle, Didier Barone, was also involved in heroin trafficking with both Jean Claude Kella and Christian David. What is especially interesting about Barone is his connection to Fernand Legros, with whom he was involved in art deals.

3. P. Chairoff: *Dossier B...comme Barbouzes* (Alain Moreau, 1975).

4. *Liberation*, 19 July 1976.

5. *L'Aurore*, 31 May 1976.

6. *Counterspy, Vol. 3,* No. 2, 1976.

7. *Latin America Political Report,* 19 December 1975.

8. *L'Aurore*, 31 May 1976.

9. André Labay and Jo Signoli got thirty and twenty years respectively in a Paris court on 7 December 1973.

10. The Long brothers were sentenced on 11 October 1973. Armand and Marcel each got eighteen years and Louis got twelve. Another "lab-owner," Louis Ambrosiono, was sentenced to twenty on November 30.

11. The Newsday Staff: *The Heroin Trail* (Souvenir Press, 1974).

12. John Cusack in *Drug Enforcement*, Spring, 1976. The last two major trials of Corsicans were held in Marseilles. In July 1974, twenty-seven men and two women were sentenced. They were the remnants of the Francisci empire run by Jean-Baptiste Croce. Finally on 26 May 1977, eleven men were sentenced in connection with the Marcel Boucan affair.

A key figure in the last-mentioned case was Laurent Fiocconi. With the aid of a prison chaplain he fled from Manhattan's Federal House of Detention in 1974 together with six other major narcotics traffickers – Ernest Malizia, Enrique Barrera, Gilbert Fornsztejn, Mario Perna, Nelson Garzia, and Amado Lopez. Fiocconi was arrested in Bogotá, Colombia in 1975 only to escape once more (*New York Times*, 14 April 1977).

The last of the Ricord organization to be arrested was Dominique Orsini. In 1975 he was tracked down in Senegal, Africa by DEA agents and brought back to the U.S. On 12 April 1978 he was found murdered in his isolation cell in the Federal pen in Atlanta (*France Soir*, 13 April 1978). Months earlier his cellmate Vincent Papa had been murdered, as had their lawyer, Gino Gallina. Like Orsini, Papa had been mixed up in The French Connection. He was the key to the theft of 398 pounds of heroin from the New York City Police Department's property room (*Boston Globe*, 10 August 1978). Orsini and Papa had allegedly been negotiating with the FBI via Gallina for reduced sentences in return for information (*France Soir*, 13 April 1978). Perhaps the information concerned policemen involved in the theft. Ironically, all three men were rubbed out shortly before the publication of P. Rosenberg and S. Grasso's *Point Blank* (Grosset and Dunlap, 1978), in which Papa's name has clearly been changed to "Larry Boston."

PART II
THE GREAT HEROIN COUP

THIRTEEN
THE FATEFUL DAYS:
A CHRONOLOGY OF THE HEROIN COUP

"We have turned the corner on heroin," declared a proud Richard Nixon after the massacre of the Corsican Mafia. But shutting off the pipeline of heroin from Marseilles did not produce the shortage he predicted. Except for a brief period in 1973, the supply increased, tremendously. By 1975 the heroin glut far surpassed even that of the Corsican heyday of the late sixties. According to a 1977 report of the House Select Committee on Narcotics Abuse, heroin addiction had doubled in four years. One year later New York's special narcotics prosecutor, Sterling Johnson, Jr. stated: "There is more dope on the streets now than at any time since the late sixties and early seventies, when we had an epidemic going. We've got another epidemic, and more critical."[1]

When the heroin flow from Marseilles was shut off in 1972-73, two new sources of supply immediately filled the vacuum. Southeast Asia –Laos, Burma and Thailand–suddenly produced vast amounts of white no. 4 heroin, the type that supposedly could only be produced by Marseilles chemists. The high quality heroin went primarily to the 40 percent of all U.S. heroin addicts who were living in New York, and who were accustomed to Marseilles heroin. The other new source was Mexico. But its product, the less pure "brown sugar," served mainly to regulate the market and to generate new customers.

The remarkable switch from Turkey-Marseilles-U.S.A. to Southeast Asia-Mexico-U.S.A. shifted billions of dollars and the power that comes with it. Such a market revolution could not have happened without astute planning and direction, which demanded political savvy and political cooperation. The plans for this tremendous heroin coup were on somebody's drawing board before Nixon and Georges

121

Pompidou met in early 1970. They were made long before Attorney General John Mitchell and French Justice Minister Raymond Marcellin met in Paris on 26 February 1971, when they signed the anti-narcotics agreement that led to the eradication of the Corsican drug Mafia. Most probably they were in place by 1968.

The occurrence of such a conspiratorial heroin coup is, of course, a hypothesis. In the following chapters I will trace the logic and the likelihood of its having transpired.

Involved in one way or another in the planning, the execution, or both, were: President Nixon and part of the White House staff; Meyer Lansky's corporate gangster syndicate—in particular its Cuban exile wing run by Florida capo Santo Trafficante, Jr.; the Cuba/China lobby; ultrareactionary forces in Southeast Asia, primarily the Kuomintang Chinese on Taiwan and in the Golden Triangle; and intelligence and law enforcement factions of the CIA and BNDD/DEA.

It was, needless to say, *not* a willful conspiracy of *all* the above. But we can assert with reasonable certainty that the CIA, Trafficante, and other mafiosi, certain Southeast Asians, and *some* people in the White House must have been in the know.

The plan took three years to execute. Though the major maneuvers began in 1970, one could detect the opening skirmishes soon after Nixon's election victory in 1968:

–Henry Kissinger put pressure on Paraguay to extradite Auguste Ricord, the main Corsican supplier of narcotics to the U.S. market.[2] Paraguay's President Alfredo Stroessner at first chose to ignore that pressure.[3]

–In 1968 the Mafia's premier heroin importer, Santo Trafficante, Jr., travelled to Southeast Asia to check out possibilities for a new supply network involving Chinese opium merchants.[4] When he made the trip, the Corsican Mafia was supplying Trafficante with all the no. 4 heroin he could sell.

–Nixon and Pompidou met in January 1970 to restore close Franco-American partnership. It was a crucial step in the destruction of the French narcotics apparatus that controlled 80 percent of the heroin trade.

–At the start of July 1970, White House staffer Egil Krogh proposed Operation Heroin, a major action against the narcotics smugglers. His idea was approved.

–U.S. Mafia capos held a summit July 4-16 at the Hotel Sole in Palermo, Sicily. There they decided to pour money into Southeast

Asia and transform it into the main source of heroin.[5]

– On 23 July 1970 Richard Nixon approved the Huston Plan to establish an espionage group that would supercede existing intelligence and enforcement agencies. The super-group was to be steered from the White House, thus giving the president effective control over all intelligence – including domestic spying on U.S. citizens. The plan fell through, mostly due to the opposition of J. Edgar Hoover. However, the White House continued to develop the plan under cover of its fast-growing, media-hyped narcotics campaign.

– In August 1970 the Corsicans, apparently informed of the outcome of the Palermo meeting weeks earlier, called their Southeast Asian connections to an emergency meeting at Saigon's Continental Hotel. Thereafter two loads of morphine base would be sent to Marseilles each month.[6] However, the shipments were continually sabotaged, and rarely arrived at their destination.

– Another major development in 1970 was the implementation of Nixon's Vietnamization program, through which the controls in Vietnam were returned to the CIA. The program pumped a fortune into South Vietnam, much of it pocketed by officials. Investigations of endemic corruption among non-coms and senior U.S. Army personnel led to a Hong Kong office run by a lieutenant of drug czar Trafficante.[7]

– Pure no. 4 heroin appeared in Saigon in 1970, creating an epidemic of addiction among GIs. All previously available heroin had been of the coarse form that could only be smoked. The new heroin wave was hushed up.

There were two other significant developments in 1970: (1) to end persistent rivalry among customs, the Internal Revenue Service (IRS) and the Bureau of Narcotics and Dangerous Drugs (BNDD), Nixon named the BNDD the sole U.S. representative on drug matters; and (2) the Mafia dispatched the notorious Tomasso Buscetta to Brazil to prepare a takeover of narcotics smuggling upon Auguste Ricord's extradition to the U.S.

– On 26 February 1971 France and the United States signed the definitive agreement for a combined assault on heroin. Within days Ricord was sentenced *in absentia*. On April 6 Roger Delouette was picked up in New York. As detailed in chapter ten, after that the Corsican network collapsed quickly.

– On 27 May 1971 Congressmen Morgan Murphy and Robert Steele issued their report, *The World Heroin Problem.* Among their sensational findings was that some 15 percent of the GIs in Vietnam

were addicted to heroin. The causes were easy to identify. Most
obvious was the sudden appearance of enormous quantities of no. 4
heroin. Fourteen-year old girls sold 90 percent pure heroin for peanuts. Pushers stuffed it into soldiers' pockets free of charge. Add to
that the crackdown that effectively eliminated marijuana and hash
from the barracks.

– On the day the Murphy-Steele report was issued, Nixon, John
Erlichman, and Krogh agreed to secretly budget $100 million for a
covert BNDD kidnaping and assassination program. Before that the
White House had asked BNDD director John Ingersoll to draft a plan
for "clandestine law enforcement" that would include assassination of
major traffickers.[8]

– Days later Nixon set up a special narcotics action and intelligence group right in the White House. In the same period the Special
Investigation Unit (the infamous Plumbers) set up shop in Room 16 of
the Executive Office Building. The two groups overlapped, and several of their members were associates of Mafia kingpin Trafficante.

– On 17 June 1971 Nixon, on television, declared war on narcotics:
"If we cannot destroy the drug menace in America, then it will destroy
us. I am not prepared to accept this alternative."

– On 30 June 1971 the United States and Turkey signed an agreement that would halt Turkish opium cultivation. In return the U.S.
handed the Turkish government $30 million.

– On 1 July 1971 Nixon advisor Charles Colson recruited former
CIA agent Howard Hunt as a White House consultant.[9] Hunt and
Gordon Liddy would work out of Room 16 on narcotics intelligence,
one of Hunt's specialties.

– On 25 July 1971 the Asian Peoples Anti-Communist League
(APACL) and World Anti-Communist League (WACL) met in Manila.
The two international lobbies for the Nationalist Chinese, prime
bankrollers of international opium and heroin smuggling, angrily
attacked Nixon for his approaching trip to Peking.[10]

In August 1971 the BNDD announced the location in Southeast
Asia of twenty-nine drug refineries, fifteen of them allegedly producing heroin. Among the largest was one in Vientiane, Laos, which
was camouflaged as a Pepsi Cola plant. Nixon, representing Pepsi's
interests in 1965, had promoted its construction. Though the plant
never capped a bottle, it continued to be subsidized by U.S.A.I.D.[11]

In October 1971 top BNDD analyst John Warner told an interviewer that the continued flooding of the U.S. heroin market, despite
the shutdown of French supply routes, indicated that more than the

previously assumed 5 percent of U.S. heroin was originating in Southeast Asia.

–On 1 November 1971 BNDD agents arrested a diplomat attached to the Philippine embassy in Laos, and a Chinese journalist from Thailand, attempting to smuggle forty kilos of heroin into the U.S.A. That same year BNDD agents at JFK airport arrested the son of Panama's ambassador to Taiwan with fifty kilos of heroin. Finally, and most dramatically, Parisian police nabbed the Laotian Prince Chao Sopsaisana attempting to smuggle in sixty kilos. Sopsaisana, the head Laotian delegate to the APACL, was about to become Laos' emissary in Paris.[12]

The focus nevertheless remained on the French narcotics traffickers. Nixon could also produce results in the newly arisen Southeast Asian danger zone, but those amounted to the smashing of the remnants of the Corsican Mafia and their Southeast Asian supply network.

Through it all the U.S. supported Marshall Nguyen Cao Ky and other South Vietnamese politicians known to be making immense profits from the heroin traffic. When U.S. reporters exposed Ky's narcotics airlift, the CIA station and U.S. embassy in Saigon issued blanket denials.[13]

In late 1971 BNDD director Ingersoll issued the following statement: "The CIA has for some time been this Bureau's strongest partner in identifying foreign sources and routes of illegal trade in narcotics. Liaison between our two agencies is close and constant in matters of mutual interest. Much of the progress we are now making in identifying overseas narcotics traffic can, in fact, be attributed to CIA cooperation."[14]

The catch was that BNDD "progress" and CIA "cooperation" went only as far as the French Mafia. CIA cooperation on Southeast Asia was another matter. The agency hindered BNDD agents and kept the press in the dark, while itself smuggling large quantities of opium via Air America.[15] A notable discrepancy arose in 1972 between CIA and BNDD estimates of the heroin traffic. CIA reports had 25 percent of the heroin coming from Mexico, the rest from Marseilles. The BNDD estimated that Southeast Asia already supplied 30 percent of the heroin on the U.S. market.[16]

–In January 1972 Nixon created, again by decree, the Office for Drug Abuse Law Enforcement (ODALE) to flush out pushers in thirty-eight cities. Simultaneously, New York's police narcotics squad was reorganized following revelations of blatant corruption. ODALE ceased to exist on 1 July 1973 when it, the BNDD and the narcotics intelligence branches of the Justice Department and Customs Bureau were merged to become the Drug Enforcement Administration (DEA), which now operates in the U.S. and worldwide.

– On 17 July 1972 James McCord, Frank Sturgis, Bernard Barker, Eugenio Rolando Martinez, and Virgilio Gonzalez, led by Hunt and Liddy, broke into the Democrats' Watergate offices in Washington. Of these seven men, four were from Miami, four were active or former agents of the CIA, four had been involved in the Bay of Pigs invasion, and three were closely linked to the Cuban narcotics Mafia.

– The same day Nixon telegrammed Pompidou his congratulations. Two days earlier, France had closed out a series of raids against the Marseilles heroin labs. The great heroin coup was well on its way to completion.

On 9 August 1972 Nixon made William C. Sullivan the director of the Office of National Narcotics Intelligence (ONNI), which would coordinate domestic drug intelligence. Sullivan had been the president's choice to head the Huston Plan's aborted super-intelligence agency.[17]

With Egil Krogh executive director of the Cabinet Committee on International Narcotics Control, covering foreign narcotics intelligence,[18] complete control over narcotics management was in the president's hands.

– In August 1972 U.S. troops were withdrawn from South Vietnam. The country was turned over to the CIA and a narcotics trafficking South Vietnamese government.

In late August, in the midst of Nixon's reelection campaign, the BNDD announced the first noticeable heroin shortage on the streets of America. Nixon's battle with the French Mafia had borne fruit. Soon he would rid the U.S.A. entirely of the White Death. However, someone had forgotten to mention that returning GIs had helped triple the U.S. addict population from the 1969 figure of 250,000. In reality, then, the total heroin supply was appreciably *greater* than that prevailing prior to Nixon's campaign against the French. Americans, however, would reelect Nixon, who cited apparent gains in foreign affairs and the struggle against the drug plague.

– On 12 August 1972 New York crime families decided at a Staten Island summit to resume the drug traffic they had supposedly abandoned in the fifties.[19] Citing "social responsibility," they decried the Cuban and Black Mafias' sale of heroin in the suburbs to children of "decent people," and vowed that the drugs would thereafter remain in the ghetto. But the importance of the families had waned. Others, especially Trafficante's Cuban organization, had become too strong.

The heroin coup was complete by 1973. The French were out, and new labs, routes, and buyer networks were in place, with Southeast Asia the main supplier. That year the U.S. heroin supply did fall noticeably, largely because part of the plan was about to fall through. South Vietnam, Laos, and Cambodia were slipping out of U.S. hands, forcing traffickers and bankrollers to regroup in safer surroundings, above all in Thailand.[20]

A final item of interest in 1973 was the appearance before a Senate committee of the international speculator and smuggler Frank Peroff, who had served as an undercover agent for the DEA against the Cotroni brothers of Montreal. He testified that the renegade international businessman, Robert Vesco – a major supporter of Richard Nixon – and his associate Norman Leblanc, were bankrollers of international heroin trafficking.[21]

Notes

1. B. Herbert: "The Fleetwood Kids," *Penthouse*, August 1978.

2. L. Gonzalez-Mata: *Cygne* (Grasset, 1976).

3. Interestingly, CIA agent Fernand Legros arrived that year in Paraguay and negotiated a weapons deal with the regime of dictator Stroessner – see R. Peyrefitte: *La Vie Extraordinaire de Fernand Legros* (Albin Michel, 1976).

4. A. McCoy: *The Politics of Heroin in Southeast Asia* (Harper & Row, 1972). Prior to the publication of this book on 20 August 1972, Cord Meyer, Jr., a CIA covert operations division leader, visited Harper & Row to demand the galleys. The publisher refused, subject to receipt of an official CIA request. When that came the proofs were delivered over McCoy's objections. The agency returned them with corrections, but the publisher rejected them and the book was published unaltered.

5. F. Wulff in the Danish *Rapport*, 14 April 1975.

6. C. Lamour and M.R. Lamberti: *Les Grandes Maneuvres de l'Opium* (Éditions de Seuil, 1972).

7. McCoy, *op. cit.*

8. E.J. Epstein: *Agency of Fear* (Putnam, 1977).

9. E.H. Hunt: *Undercover* (Berkeley-Putnam, 1974).

10. Documents of the 5th WACL and 17th APACL Conference, Taiwan, November 1971.

11. *N.A.C.L.A. Report*, October 1972.

12. P.D. Scott: "From Dallas to Watergate," *Ramparts*, November 1973.

13. McCoy, *op. cit.*

14. The Committee of Concerned Asian Scholars: *The Opium Trail* (New England Free Press, 1971).

15. P.D. Scott: *The War Conspiracy* (Bobbs-Merrill, 1972).

16. McCoy, *op. cit.*

17. S. Blumental: "How the FBI Tried to Destroy the Black Panthers," in *Government by Gunplay*, S. Blumental and H. Yazijian, Eds. (New American Library, 1976).

18. P.D. Scott: "From Dallas to Watergate," *op. cit.*

19. The Newsday Staff: *The Heroin Trail* (Souvenir Press, 1974).

20. The heroin entrepreneurs had also been unduly optimistic about their supply. By the start of 1973 they began investing in a new, European market, while still supplying the U.S. Nonetheless, the slight hitch in Southeast Asia was rapidly dealt with, and soon the flood of heroin hit Europe like a tidal wave.

21. L.H. Whittemore: *Peroff* (Ballantine Books, 1975).

FOURTEEN
HEROIN IN SOUTHEAST ASIA

The place was Kunming in the South China province of Yunnan. The time was the end of World War II. Amid the chaos of war, opium and gold became the primary media of exchange, and cult-like bonds were forged among a small staff of Americans and high-ranking Chinese. Yunnan was a center of Chinese opium cultivation and Kunming was the hotbed of military operations, among them Claire Chennault's 14th Air Force and Detachment 202 of the Office of Strategic Services (OSS).

Among Detachment 202's notorious collection of special agents, one in particular – E. Howard Hunt – has needed no introduction since the Watergate break-in. In Kunming, the spy novelist who later became a comrade of Cuban exiles and China Lobbyists befriended an equally intriguing character, the French Foreign Legionnaire turned OSS agent, Captain Lucien Conein.[1] Although not part of Detachment 202 proper, Conein frequented Kunming while awaiting parachuting over Indochina.[2]

Indochina remained Conein's base of operation after World War II, when, like Hunt, he slid over from the OSS to its successor, the CIA. He then operated throughout South and North Vietnam, Cambodia, and Burma, and became the top U.S. expert on the area – as well as on the opium-smuggling Corsican Mafia. He was Ambassador Henry Cabot Lodge's middle man in the 1963 plot to overthrow South Vietnam's President Ngo Dinh Diem (who was assassinated along with his brother Ngo Dinh Nhu, the Corsicans' partner in the drug traffic). A decade later, Conein and Hunt, working for the Nixon White House Plumbers, would attempt to make it appear that the plot had been ordered by JFK. Both Conein and William Colby, mastermind of the CIA's Phoenix assassination program, were recalled to the U.S. at the start of the seventies.

After Mao Tse-tung's rise to power in China, OSS veterans formed a number of firms that would be linked both to the CIA and to its reactionary client regimes in the Far East. With financial assistance from his friends in Asia, OSS China hand C.V. Starr gained control of several U.S. insurance companies. As brought to light during the McClellan hearings, Jimmy Hoffa awarded one of them, U.S. Life, and a smaller company, Union Casualty–whose agents Paul and Allen Dorfman were among Hoffa's links to the underworld[3]–a Teamsters Union contract despite a lower bid from a larger, more reputable insurance firm.[4]

Starr's attorney was the powerful Washington-based Tommy "The Cork" Corcoran. Corcoran's law partner, William Youngman, was a director of U.S. Life. Corcoran's other clients included the United Fruit Company, Chiang Kai-shek's influential brother-in-law T.V. Soong, and the mysterious airline, Civil Air Transport (CAT), of which 60 percent was owned by the Taiwan regime and 40 percent by the CIA.[5] On behalf of United Fruit, Corcoran triggered a CIA plot– in which E. Howard Hunt was the agency's chief political action officer–to overthrow Guatemala's President Jacobo Arbenz in 1954.[6]

OSS China hand Willis Bird settled in Bangkok, Thailand to head an office of Sea Supply, Inc., a CIA proprietary headquartered in Miami, which furnished weapons to opium-smuggling Nationalist Chinese (KMT) troops in Burma. One William Bird, representing CAT in Bangkok, coordinated CAT airdrops to KMT troops and ran an engineering firm that constructed short airstrips used for the collection of Laotian opium.[7]

Sea Supply also provided arms and aid to Phao Sriyanonda, the head of Thailand's 45,000-man paramilitary police force and reputedly one of the most corrupt men in the history of that corruption-ridden nation. For years his troops protected KMT opium smugglers and directed the drug trade from Thailand.[8]

When President John F. Kennedy in 1962 attempted a crackdown on the most hawkish CIA elements in Indochina, he sought the prosecution of Willis Bird, who had been charged with the bribery of an aid official in Vientiane. But Bird never returned to the U.S. to stand trial.

Upon returning to Miami, the OSS Chief of Special Intelligence and head of Detachment 202 in Kunming, Colonel Paul Helliwell, was a busy man. In Miami offices of the American Bankers Insurance Co.

he functioned simultaneously as the Thai consul, and the counsel for Sea Supply as well as for insurance companies run by his former subordinate C.V. Starr.[9] American Bankers Insurance was itself a most unusual firm; one of its directors, James L. King, was also a director of the Miami National Bank through which the Lansky syndicate reportedly passed millions en route to Geneva's Swiss Exchange and Investment Bank. One of the Swiss bank's directors, Lou Poller, also sat on the board of King's Miami National Bank.[10]

Moreover, in the fifties and sixties, Thai and Nationalist Chinese capital was invested in Florida's explosive development, much of it by way of the General Development Corporation controlled by associates of Meyer Lansky.[11] It's important to note the dubious alliance of Southeast Asian power groups with those concerned with Florida and Cuba. This early mutuality of business interests is the key to all that follows, and Miami is the nerve center to which we will continually return.

The alliance was comprised of the China Lobby, OSS China hands, Cuban exiles, the Lansky syndicate, and CIA hawks pushing for all-out involvement in Indochina and against Castro's Cuba. It coalesced between 1961 and 1963, and its members had three things in common: a right wing political outlook, an interest in Asian opium, and a thirst for political might. The last factor led to another common denominator in which the alliance invested heavily: Richard M. Nixon.

Some people effectively overlap the entire spectrum of the alliance. Among them are Howard Hunt and Tommy Corcoran, the man behind United Fruit's dirty work. United Fruit was a client of the Miami-based Double-Chek Corp., a CIA front that supplied planes for the Bay of Pigs invasion.[12] Corcoran was the Washington escort of General Chennault's widow Anna Chen Chennault, erstwhile head of the China Lobby, the key to Southeast Asian opium.[13]

Another key figure in the China Lobby was weapons dealer/financier William Pawley, the American cofounder of Chennault's Flying Tigers.[14] Pawley's name was the password to intrigue: OSS China, Tommy Corcoran,[15] CIA cover firms,[16] and arms shipments to KMT Chinese on Taiwan in defiance of a State Department refusal of authorization.[17] All were either directly or indirectly connected to Pawley. He also rubbed elbows with the U.S. heroin Mafia when, in 1963, he, Santo Trafficante, Jr. and Cuban exiles took part in one of the countless boat raids on Cuba.[18]

The China Lobby's Southeast Asian connection naturally went via the Taiwan regime, which controlled the opium-growing Chinese in the Golden Triangle and, with the CIA, owned the opium-running CAT airlines. As Ross Y. Koen wrote in 1964:

"There is considerable evidence that a number of Nationalist Chinese officials are engaged in the illegal smuggling of narcotics into the United States with the full knowledge and connivance of the Nationalist Chinese government. The evidence indicates that several prominent Americans have participated in and profited from these transactions. It indicates further that the narcotics business has been an important factor in the activities and permutations of the China Lobby."[19]

British writer Frank Robertson went one step further in 1977:

"Taiwan is a major link in the Far East narcotics route, and a heroin producer. Much of the acetic anhydride – the chemical necessary for the transformation of morphine into heroin – smuggled into Hong Kong and Thailand, comes from this island, a dictatorship under the iron rule of the late Chiang Kai-shek's son, Chiang Ching-kuo."[20]

When the Communists routed Chiang Kai-shek's forces in 1949, some 10,000 KMT troops fled to Southeast Asia and settled in a remote part of Burma. Heavily armed, they soon assumed control of the area and intermarried with the local population. Under General Li Mi they continued to infiltrate China proper, but each time they were repulsed. While awaiting Chiang's signal for a final, two-front onslaught, Burma's KMT army needed a source of income. Many had grown opium in Yunnan and so the poppies, which flourished on the hillsides, became the force's cash crop.

Around 1950 the CIA became interested in the KMT troops. With General Douglas MacArthur pushing to arm them for an attack on Red China, the agency secretly flew them weapons in CAT airplanes. But when the KMT instead used the weapons against the Burmese army, Burma protested before the UN, where it was decided that 2000 KMT troops would be flown by CAT to Taiwan by 1954. Those who eventually made the trip, however, were only farmers and mountain people in KMT uniforms, and the weapons they took out were obsolete.[21] Nonetheless, with help from the Red Chinese army, Burma drove most of the KMT forces into Thailand and Laos, though many later returned. The Kuomintang and their kin now number over 50,000. Though only a fraction are soldiers, the KMT still controls hundreds of thousands of Chinese occupying the region, especially in Thailand.

The junction of Burma, Thailand, and Laos, the Golden Triangle, is the site of the bulk of the world's opium production and thereby the source of enormous fortunes for the French and later the Americans. The French held effective control over the Southeast Asian opium traffic until 1965. Between 1946 and 1955 the Mixed Airborne Commando Group (MACG) and the French Air Force managed the shipment of opium from Burma to Laos. A guerilla corps comprised mostly of Laotian Meo tribesmen and led by Colonel Roger Trinquier, MACG remained unusually independent despite its direct connections to the SDECE and Deuxieme (Second) Bureau. To finance their secret Indochina operations, these organizations turned to the smuggling of gold and opium, with MACG in charge of the latter. Large quantities of opium were shipped to French Saigon headquarters and passed on to the Corsican Mafia, who in turn smuggled the drug to Marseilles.

When the French withdrew from Indochina in 1955 after their defeat by the Vietminh, and after the CIA pushed aside the SDECE, MACG leaders communicating through CIA agent Lucien Conein offered the Americans their entire guerilla force. Against Conein's advice they refused.[22] History would cast doubt on the wisdom of that decision.

In 1955 CIA agent General Edward Lansdale began a war to liquidate the Corsican supply network. While Lansdale was cracking down on the French infrastructure, his employer the CIA was running proprietaries, like Sea Supply and CAT, that worked hand-in-hand with the opium-smuggling Nationalist Chinese of the Golden Triangle, and with the corrupt Thai border police.[23]

The Lansdale/Corsican vendetta lasted several years, during which many attempts were made on Lansdale's life. Oddly enough, his principal informant on Corsican drug routes and connections was the former French Foreign Legionnaire, Lucien Conein, then of the CIA. Conein knew just about every opium field, smuggler, trail, airstrip, and Corsican in Southeast Asia. He spent his free time with the Corsicans, who considered him one of their own. Apparently they never realized it was he who was turning them in.[24]

When Lansdale returned from Vietnam in the late fifties, the Corsicans recouped some of their losses, chartering aging aircraft to establish Air Opium, which functioned until around 1965. That year, the Corsicans' nemesis Lansdale returned to Vietnam as an advisor to Amabassador Lodge. There was also an upheaval in the narcotics traffic, and perhaps the two were connected. CIA-backed South Viet-

namese and Laotian generals began taking over the opium traffic –
and as they did so, increasing amounts of morphine and low-quality
heroin began showing up on the Saigon market.

The first heroin refineries sprang up in Laos under the control of
General Ouane Rattikone. President Ky in Saigon was initially in
charge of smuggling from the Laotian refineries to the South Vietnamese; and Lansdale's office, it is to be remembered, was working
closely with Ky. Lansdale himself was one of Ky's heartiest supporters, and Conein went along with whatever Lansdale said.[25]

One result of the smuggling takeover by the generals was the end
of the Corsicans' Air Opium. The KMT Chinese and Meo tribesmen
who cultivated raw opium either transported it themselves to the
refineries or had it flown there by the CIA via CAT and its successor,
Air America, another agency proprietary. Though the Corsicans still
sent drugs to Marseilles, the price was becoming prohibitive, since
they were forced to buy opium and morphine in Saigon and Vientiane
rather than pick up the opium for peanuts in the mountains.

In 1967 a three-sided opium war broke out in Laos between a
Burmese Shan State warlord, KMT Chinese and General Rattikone's
Laotian army. Rattikone emerged victorious, capturing the opium
shipment with the help of U.S.-supplied aircraft. The KMT, for its
part, managed to reassert its dominance over the warlord. The smuggling picture was becoming simplified, with Southeast Asian opium
divided among fewer hands, and most of the Corsicans out of the way.

General Lansdale returned to the U.S. in 1967, leaving Conein in
Vietnam. The next year Conein greeted a new boss, William Colby.
Since 1962 Colby had run the agency's special division for covert
operations in Southeast Asia, where his responsibilities included the
"secret" CIA war in Laos with its 30,000-man Meo army. He shared
that responsibility with the U.S. amabassador in Laos, William H.
Sullivan, who would later preside over the Tehran embassy during the
fall of the Shah.

Many of the agents who ran the CIA's war in Laos had earlier
trained Cuban exiles for the Bay of Pigs invasion, and afterward had
taken part in the agency's continued secret operations against Cuba.[26]
Since exiles were furnished by the Trafficante mob,[27] intelligence
agents had intermingled with representatives of America's number
one narcotics organization. The same agents would now become involved with the extensive opium smuggling from Meo tribesmen
camps to Vientiane.[28]

In 1967 Colby devised a plan of terror for the "pacification" of

Vietnam. Operation Phoenix organized the torture and murder of any Vietnamese suspected of the slightest association with Vietcong. Just as Lansdale was travelling home, Colby was sent to South Vietnam to put his brainchild to work. According to Colby's own testimony before a Senate committee, 20,857 Vietcong were murdered in Phoenix's first two years. The figure of the South Vietnamese government for the same period was over 40,000.[29]

It was during Colby's tour in Vietnam that the heroin turned out by General Ouane Rattikone's labs appeared in quantity, and with unusually high quality. The great heroin wave brought on a GI addiction epidemic in 1970; Congressional reports indicated that some 22 percent of all U.S. soldiers sampled the drugs and 15 percent became hooked.[30]

Former Air Marshal, then Vice President, Nguyen Cao Ky (now alive and well in the United States) and his underlings still controlled most of the traffic. President Nguyen Van Thieu and his faction, comprised mostly of army and navy officers, were also in it up to their necks. According to NBC's Saigon correspondent, Thieu's closest advisor, General Dang Van Quang, was the man most responsible for the monkey on the U.S. Army's back. But the U.S. Saigon embassy, where Colby was second in command, found no substance to the accusations, Ky's record notwithstanding: Ky had been removed from U.S. Operation Haylift, which flew commando units into Laos, for loading his aircraft with opium on the return trips.

In the face of skyrocketing GI heroin abuse, the Army Criminal Investigation Division (CID) looked into General Ngo Dzu's complicity in the heroin traffic and filed a lengthy report at the U.S. embassy.[31] The embassy ignored the report and chose not to forward it to Washington.[32] The BNDD also investigated the roots of the heroin epidemic, but was impeded in its work by the CIA and U.S. embassy. In 1971, however, a string of heroin labs were uncovered in Thailand, and a number were closed down.

In 1971, furthermore, Colby and Conein were recalled to the United States. Colby became the Deputy Director of Operations, the man in charge of the CIA's covert operations. More remarkable, though, was Conein's homecoming after twenty-four years of periodic service to the CIA in Indochina, raising the question of why the U.S.'s foremost expert on Indochina had been brought back to Washington just as the crucial phase of Vietnamization was about to begin.[33] Ironically, Corsican friends still around for Conein's departure presented him with a farewell gold medallion bearing the seal of the Corsican Union.

At the war's cataclysmic end, the CIA admitted that "certain elements in the organization" had been involved in opium smuggling and that the illegal activities of U.S. allies had been overlooked to retain their loyalties. In reality, the agency had been forced to confess because of its inability to refute the tales of returning GIs, among them that of Green Beret Paul Withers, a recipient of nine Purple Hearts, the Distinguished Service Cross and Silver and Bronze Stars:

"After completing basic training at Fort Dix in the fall of 1965 [Withers] was sent to Nha Trang, South Vietnam. Although he was ostensibly stationed there, he was placed on 'loan' to the CIA in January 1966 and sent to Pak Seng, Laos. Before going there he and his companions were stripped of their uniforms and all American credentials. They were issued Czechoslovakian guns and Korean uniforms. Paul even signed blank sheets of paper at the bottom and the CIA later typed out letters and sent them to his parents and wife. All this was done to hide the fact that there were American troops operating in Laos.

"The mission in Laos was to make friends with the Meo people and organize and train them to fight the Pathet Lao. One of the main tasks was to buy up the entire local crop of opium. About twice a week an Air America plane would arrive with supplies and kilo bags of opium which were loaded on the plane. Each bag was marked with the symbol of the tribe."[34]

The CIA, reportedly, did not support any form of smuggling after 1968. Del Rosario, a former CIA operative, had something to say about that:

"In 1971 I was an operations assistant for Continental Air Service, which flew for the CIA in Laos. The company's transport planes shipped large quantities of rice. However, when the freight invoice was marked 'Diverse' I knew it was opium. As a rule an office telephone with a special number would ring and a voice would say 'The customer here'–that was the code designation for the CIA agents who had hired us. 'Keep an eye on the planes from Ban Houai Sai. We're sending some goods and someone's going to take care of it. Nobody's allowed to touch anything, and nothing can be unloaded,' was a typical message. These shipments were always top priority. Sometimes the opium was unloaded in Vientiane and stored in Air America depots. At other times it went on to Bangkok or Saigon."[35]

Even while the CIA trafficked in opium, President Nixon ranted on TV against drug abuse and lauded the crackdown against French smuggling networks.

Notes

1. E.H. Hunt: *Undercover* (Berkeley-Putnam, 1974).

2. Another of Conein's OSS sidekicks, Mitchell WerBell III, was years later indicted in a major drug conspiracy case (T. Dunkin: "The Great Pot Plot," *Soldier of Fortune, Vol. 2*, No. 1, 1977), and now runs an antiterrorist training school in Georgia (T. Dunkin: "WerBell's Cobray School," *Soldier of Fortune, Vol. 5*, No. 1, 1980).

3. D. Moldea: *The Hoffa Wars* (Charter Books, 1978).

4. U.S. Congress, Senate, Select Committee on Improper Activities in the Labor or Management Field, *Hearings*, 85th Cong., 2nd Sess. (cited in P.D. Scott: *The War Conspiracy*, Bobbs-Merrill, 1972).

5. CAT, which became Air America, was also identical with the "CATCL" that emerged from Claire Chennault's Flying Tigers.

6. D. Wise and T.B. Ross: *The Invisible Government* (Random House, 1964); Hunt, *op. cit.*

7. Scott, *op. cit.*

8. F. Robertson: *Triangle of Death* (Routledge and Keagen Paul, 1977); A. McCoy: *The Politics of Heroin in Southeast Asia* (Harper & Row, 1972).

9. Scott, *op. cit.*

10. *New York Times*, 1 December 1969; H. Messick: *Lansky* (Berkeley, 1971).

11. Carl O. Hoffmann, the former OSS agent and general counsel of the Thai king in New York in 1945-50, later became the chairman of Lansky associates' First Florida Resource Corp.

12. L. Gonzalez-Mata: *Cygne* (Grasset, 1976).

13. R.Y. Koen: *The China Lobby in American Politics* (Harper & Row, 1974).

14. Pawley, the ultraconservative former Pan Am executive and Assistant Secretary of both State and Defense, set up the Flying Tigers under a secret order of President Franklin D. Roosevelt exempting him from U.S. neutrality provisions; see A. Chan Chennault: *Chennault's Flying Tigers* (Eriksson, 1963).

15. Corcoran assisted in the establishment of the Flying Tigers and later Civil Air Transport; see Scott, *op. cit.*

16. Lindsey Hopkins, Jr., whose sizable investments included Miami Beach hotels, was an officer of the CIA proprietary, Zenith Technical Enterprises of Bay of Pigs note. He was also an officer of the Sperry Corp., through whose subsidiary, the Intercontinental Corp., Pawley helped found the Flying Tigers in 1941. Pawley was Intercontinental's president. See Scott, *op. cit.*

17. U.S. Congress, Senate, Committee on Judiciary, *Communist Threat to the United States through the Caribbean, Hearings*, 86th Cong., 2nd Sess. (cited in Scott, *op. cit.*).

18. See chapter fifteen; it has also been revealed that a prominent Chinese American, Dr. Margaret Chung of San Francisco, who was a major supporter of the Flying Tigers, trafficked in narcotics together with the Syndicate; see

P.D. Scott: "Opium and Empire," *Bulletin of Concerned Asian Scholars*, September 1973.

19. Koen, *op. cit.*

20. Robertson, *op. cit.*. After a one-year suspension, the U.S. State Department recently approved the sale of $280 million in military weaponry to the repressive Taiwan regime (*New York Times*, 20 January 1980), the same regime whose disdain for human rights was most recently expressed by the preparation of cases of sedition against sixty-five opposition demonstrators (*New York Times*, 24 January 1980). The CIA's Taiwan station chief in the late fifties and early sixties, when the unholy alliances were forged, was Ray S. Cline. Closely associated with the China Lobby, Cline became famous for his drunken binges with Chiang Ching-kuo, currently the president of Taiwan (see V. Marchetti and J.D. Marks: *CIA and Cult of Intelligence*, Jonathan Cape, 1974). A CIA hawk, Cline also helped a gigantic Bay of Pigs-style invasion of the Chinese mainland which was rejected by President Kennedy. Cline is currently the "director of world power studies" at Georgetown's Center for Strategic and International Studies (CSIS), which, according to writer Fred Landis ("Georgetown's Ivory Tower for Spooks," *Inquiry*, 30 September 1979), "is rapidly becoming the New Right's most sophisticated propaganda mill." In testimony before the House Select Committee on Intelligence, Cline defended CIA manipulation of the press, saying "You know that first amendment is only an amendment."

21. McCoy, *op. cit.*

22. D. Warner: *The Last Confucian* (Angus & Robertson, 1964).

23. McCoy, *op. cit.*

24. Conein told writer McCoy: "The Corsicans are smarter, tougher and better organized than the Sicilians. They are absolutely ruthless and are the equal of anything we know about the Sicilians, but they hide their internal fighting better." (McCoy, *op. cit.*).

25. McCoy, *op. cit.*

26. T. Branch and G. Crile III: "The Kennedy Vendetta," *Harper's*, August 1975.

27. U.S. Congress, Senate, Select Committee to Study Governmental Operations with respect to Intelligence Activities, *Alleged Assassination Plots Involving Foreign Leaders*, Interim Report, 94th Cong., 1st Sess. Senate Report No. 94-463, 1975.

28. C. Lamour and M.R. Lamberti: *Les Grandes Maneuvres de l'Opium* (Éditions du Seuil, 1972); McCoy, *op. cit.*; Committee of Concerned Asian Scholars: *The Opium Trail* (New England Free Press, 1971).

29. Marchetti and Marks, *op. cit.*

30. Congressman M.F. Murphy and R.H. Steele: *The World Heroin Problem* (U.S. Govt. Printing Office, 1971).

31. Like Nguyen Cao Ky, Ngo Dzu came to the U.S. as a refugee after the final debacle in South Vietnam. Though accused by Rep. Steele of responsibility for the addiction of thousands of GIs to heroin, Dzu went about as a free man until his 13 February 1977 death in Sacramento of apparent heart failure.

32. McCoy, *op. cit.*

33. Conein's summons home coincided with Howard Hunt's recruitment by the White House and the creation of the special narcotics and Plumbers groups.
34. Committee of Concerned Asian Scholars, *op. cit.*
35. Lamour and Lamberti, *op. cit.* (quote retranslated from the French).

FIFTEEN
THE CUBANS OF FLORIDA

Meyer Lansky, the Syndicate's financial wizard and its chairman from around 1947, began building his Cuban empire in the early forties. When free elections chased his close friend and dictator Fulgencio Batista from office in 1944, Lansky also left the island, entrusting his empire to the Trafficante family headed by Santo, Sr. Lansky and Batista settled in Hollywood, Florida, just north of Miami. Before long, Lansky was running an illegal casino empire on the coast, and in 1947 he eliminated Bugsy Siegel and moved into Las Vegas.

All the while Lansky expanded the narcotics trade founded by Lucky Luciano. The older Mafia dons deemed the trade taboo, so Lansky's wing of the Syndicate cornered the market, with Trafficante's eldest son, Santo, Jr., overseeing the heroin traffic.[1]

When Florida's illegal casinos were shut down in 1950, Lansky promoted Batista's return to power in Cuba. The drive bore fruit in 1952. With Trafficante, Sr.'s death in 1954, Santo, Jr. became Lansky's right-hand man and manager of his Cuban interests. Until then, he had managed the Sans Souci Casino, a base for running Havana's tourist trade and keeping tabs on heroin shipments from Marseilles to New York via Florida and Cuba.[2]

Trafficante, Jr. has proven more talented than his father. Extraordinarily intelligent and energetic, he has handled the most acute crises with detached calm. Luciano characterized him as "...a guy who always managed to hug the background, but he is rough and reliable. In fact, he's one of the few guys in the whole country that Meyer Lansky would never tangle with."[3]

In no time, Trafficante, Jr. ingratiated himself with dictator Batista, while remaining loyal to Lansky, who appointed him manager of his own Florida interests in addition to those in Cuba. Lansky needed to spend increasing amounts of time in New York, between travels to Las Vegas, Rome, Marseilles, Beirut, and Geneva.

Many envied Lansky's ever-increasing power and wealth, among them Murder, Inc. chairman of the board Albert Anastasia. In 1957 the latter tried enlisting Trafficante's aid in removing Lansky from the Havana scene. It was one of Anastasia's last moves. Trafficante arranged a "friendly" meeting in New York's Sheraton Hotel. An hour after Trafficante had checked out, Anastasia was murdered in the hotel's barber shop, shaving cream still on his face.[4]

According to Peter Dale Scott, "certain U.S. business interests collaborated with the narcotics-linked American Mafia in Cuba – as they did with similar networks in China and later in Vietnam – for the Mafia supplied the necessary local intelligence, cash and muscle against the threat of communist takeover."[5] As Scott wrote those words in 1973, Cuban-Americans recruited by the CIA were suspected by federal and city authorities to be "involved in everything from narcotics to extortion rackets and bombings."[6] The Church committee and other Senate and law enforcement reports would confirm these allegations.

Again we observe the Cuba/Southeast Asia/CIA triangle, and it's no secret who managed the Cuban side. There Trafficante, Jr. hired the fast-learning natives, while dictator Batista's men made the empire safe for organized crime, often appearing more loyal to Trafficante than to Batista himself. In return the Cubans learned the business.

With Fidel Castro's 1 January 1959 ouster of Batista, Lansky and Trafficante were in trouble. Though they were expelled from their Cuban kingdom, nearly a year elapsed before the Syndicate departed and the casinos were closed. Along with Trafficante and Lansky, half a million Cubans left the island in the years following Castro's takeover. Some 100,000 settled in the New York City area, especially Manhattan's Washington Heights and New Jersey's Hudson County. Another 100,000 headed to Spain, others to Latin America, and a quarter of a million made their new home in Florida, the site of Trafficante's new headquarters.

Out of the Trafficante-trained corps of Cuban officers, security staffers and politicians, a Cuban Mafia emerged under the mobster's control. It specialized in narcotics, first Latin American cocaine, then

Marseilles heroin. With his Cubans Trafficante also grabbed control of La Bolita, the numbers game that took Florida by storm and became a Syndicate gold mine.[7]

Besides the Cubans, who comprised the main wing of his organization, Trafficante also worked closely with the non-Italian Harlan Blackburn mob, a break with Mafia tradition.[8] But the core of the Trafficante family remained Italian, and the Italians also dealt in drugs. In 1960 his man Benedetto "Beni the Cringe" Indiviglio negotiated the opening of a narcotics route with Jacques l'Americain, the representative of Corsican boss Joseph Orsini.[9] Benedetto and his brothers Romano, Arnold, Charles and Frederick eventually ran Trafficante's Montreal-bound smuggling network, and were later joined by the notorious New York wholesaler Louis Cirillo.[10]

Trafficante settled in Tampa, but continued to run some of his activities from Jimmy Hoffa's Teamster Local 320 in Miami. Trafficante and David Yaras of Sam Giancana's Chicago mob were instrumental in founding Local 320, which, according to the McClellan hearings, was a front for Syndicate narcotics activities.[11]

After losing his Havana paradise, far-sighted Meyer Lansky used straw men to buy up much of Grand Bahama Island and erected a new gambling center around the city of Nassau. But though Lansky and Trafficante each survived in style, neither they nor the Cuban exiles relinquished hope of a return to Cuba. Moreover, they were not alone in dreaming of overthrowing Castro. The CIA in particular let its imagination run wild to this end. Its covert operations expert, General Edward Lansdale, seriously planned to send a submarine to the shore outside Havana, where it would create an inferno of light. At the same time, Cuba-based agents would warn the religious natives of the second coming of Christ and the Savior's distaste for Fidel Castro. However, "Elimination by Illumination" was shelved in favor of less fantastic suggestions for Castro's assassination. The latter brought together the CIA, Cuban exiles, and the Syndicate in the person of Santo Trafficante.

In 1960 the CIA asked its contract agent Robert Maheu to contact the mobster John Roselli. Roselli introduced Maheu to Trafficante and Sam Giancana, the Chicago capo, and the strange bedfellows arranged an attempt on the life of Castro.[12] The agency had previously stationed an agent on Cuba who was to flash the green light when assassination opportunities arose. He was Frank Angelo Fiorini, a one-time smuggler of weapons to Castro's revolutionary army, to whom Castro had entrusted the liquidation of the gambling casinos.[13]

Through the latter assignment Fiorini had made the acquaintance of Trafficante.

In February 1961 Maheu, Trafficante and Roselli met at Miami's Fountainebleu Hotel. There Maheu gave the hoods untraceable poison capsules for delivery to a Cuban exile connected with the Trafficante mob.[14] Other Cubans were to smuggle them to the island and poison Castro; but the attempt failed. Trafficante engineered more attempts, including one in September 1962,[15] and his organization also provided Cubans for the Bay of Pigs invasion.[16]

Never before had there existed a more remarkable, fanatical group of conspirators than that assembled to create, finance, and train the Bay of Pigs invasion force. The top CIA figures were Lansdale protégé Napoleon Valeriano, the mysterious Frank Bender, and E. Howard Hunt, who was himself involved in at least one of the attempts on Fidel Castro's life. They were supported by a small army of CIA operatives from four of its Miami cover firms.[17]

Runner-up to Hunt for the Most Intriguing CIA Conspirator award is Bender, a German refugee whose true identity remains a matter of speculation. Some contend that he had been an agent of the West German Gehlen espionage network under the name Drecher; others contend it was Droller.[18] The former security chief for Dominican Republic dictator Rafael Trujillo claims that Bender was in fact one Fritz Swend, a Gehlen collaborator and leader of ex-Nazis in Peru. Prior to the Bay of Pigs invasion Swend was allegedly the CIA's man in the Dominican Republic as Don Frederico. There he purportedly planned the invasion along with mobster Frank Costello and ex-Cuban dictator Batista.[19]

The invasion's moral and financial supporters included many leading China Lobbyists. Most important was the multi-millionaire behind Claire Chennault's Flying Tigers, William Pawley.[20] Pawley had been involved in the CIA's 1954 overthrow of Guatemala's democratically elected Arbenz regime. Like Lansky and Trafficante, Pawley had had a big stake in Cuba. Prior to Castro's takeover he had owned the Havana bus system and sugar refineries. He met with President Eisenhower several times in 1959 to persuade the president to assist Cuban exiles in overthrowing Castro. Pawley then helped the CIA recruit anti-Castro Cubans.[21]

The key Cuban exile conspirators in the Bay of Pigs operation and the ensuing attacks on Cuba and Castro included Manuel Artime, Orlando Bosch, Felipe de Diego, and Rolando Martinez – the first a close friend of Howard Hunt's, the last two future Watergate burglars. The name of Bosch was to become synonymous with terrorism.

Distinguishing the noncriminal element among the Bay of Pigs' anti-Castro Cubans is no easy matter, since so many emerged from Trafficante's Cuban Mafia. According to agents of the BNDD, nearly 10 percent of the 1500-man force had been or eventually were arrested for narcotics violations.[22] Its recruiters included Syndicate gangsters like Richard Cain, the former Chicago policeman who became a lieutenant for Sam Giancana.

The Dominican Republic, a focal point in the invasion scheme, also became a transit point for Trafficante's narcotics traffic. Furthermore, the CIA, according to agents of the BNDD, helped organize the drug route by providing IDs and speedboats to former Batista officers in the Dominican Republic in charge of narcotics shipments to Florida.[23]

It is of paramount importance to note the close CIA cooperation with Trafficante's Cuban Mafia, whose overriding source of income was the smuggling of drugs.

One of Trafficante's personal CIA contacts for the Bay of Pigs was Frank Fiorini, Castro's liquidator of Mob casinos, who now preferred the name Frank Sturgis.[24] In late 1960 Sturgis ran the Miami-based International Anti-Communist Brigade (IACB), said to be financed by the Syndicate.[25] According to Richard Whattley, a brigade member hired for the invasion, "Trafficante would order Sturgis to move his men and he'd do it. Our ultimate conclusion was that Trafficante was our backer. He was our money man."[26]

Another detail from Sturgis's past is especially interesting in light of Frank Bender's alleged ties to the Gehlen organization. For a period in the early fifties Sturgis was involved in espionage activities in Berlin, serving as a courier between various nations' intelligence agencies, and was thereby inevitably in contact with the Gehlen network.[27]

The Bay of Pigs invasion was, of course, a fiasco. But that hardly stopped the CIA, the Syndicate, or their Cuban exile troops. Wheels were soon turning on new assassination attempts under CIA agent William Harvey, who again collaborated with the underworld. Within months, the Miami CIA station JM/Wave was again in full swing. It sponsored a series of hit-and-run attacks on strategic Cuban targets that spanned three years and involved greater manpower and expenditures than the Bay of Pigs invasion itself.

To head the JM/Wave station, the CIA chose one of its up-and-coming agents, the thirty-four year old Theodore Shackley, who came direct from Berlin. His closest Cuban exile associates were Joaquín Sangenis and Rolando (Watergate burglary) Martinez.[28] Some 300 agents and 4-6000 Cuban exile operatives took part in the actions of JM/Wave. As later revealed, one of its last operations was closed down because one of its aircraft was caught smuggling narcotics into the United States.[29]

Shackley is another contender for the Most Intriguing CIA Conspirator award. After years of collaboration with Trafficante organization Cubans, he and part of his Miami staff were transferred to Laos,[30] where he joined Lucien Conein.[31] There they helped organize the CIA's secret Meo tribesmen army, the second such army drummed up by Shackley that was up to its ears in the drug traffic.

Vientiane, where Shackley was the station chief, became the new center of the heroin trade. Later he ran the station in Saigon, where the traffic flowed under the profiteering administration of Premier Nguyen Cao Ky. When the agency prepared its coup against the Chilean President Salvador Allende, Shackley was its chief of covert operations in the Western Hemisphere. When William Colby became the director of the CIA in 1973, Shackley took over his job as chief of covert operations in the Far East. Eventually he was booted out of the agency as part of the shakeup ordered by its current director Stansfield Turner.[32]

In the JM/Wave period a great expansion in China Lobby-Trafficante-Cuban exile-CIA connections occurred. William Pawley financed a mysterious summer 1963 boat raid against Cuba in his own yacht, the Flying Tiger II. Besides Pawley himself, the crew included mafioso John Martino, who had operated roulette wheels in one of Trafficante's Havana casinos; CIA agents code-named Rip, Mike, and Ken; the ubiquitous Rolando Martinez; and a dozen other Cuban exiles led by Eddie Bayo and Eduardo Perez, many of whom eventually disappeared mysteriously.[33] Loren Hall, another former Trafficante casino employee, claimed that both his boss and Sam Giancana had helped plan the raid.[34] Claire Boothe Luce, a queenpin of the China Lobby, testified during Senate hearings on the CIA that she had financed an exile gunboat raid on Cuba after JFK had ordered the agency to halt such raids.

I will not wander deeply into the quagmire of circumstances surrounding the murder of President John F. Kennedy. However, it is worth repeating a few lines from the final report of the House Select Committee on Assassinations: "The Committee's extensive investigation led to the conclusion that the most likely family bosses of organized crime to have participated in such a unilateral assassination plan were Carlos Marcello and Santo Trafficante."[35]

Of the many connections between Trafficante and Dallas the most important are his association with Jack Ruby, who visited him in a Havana prison in 1959; his statement to Cuban exile financier José Aleman that Kennedy "is going to be hit"; and his close association with fellow Mafia capo Carlos Marcello. The Cuban exiles, drug racketeers, and the CIA had no shortage of anti-Kennedy motives, which were all the more intensified as the three forces gradually welded together.

The anti-Cuba actions continued well into 1965, at which time a crucial three-year turnabout for the Lansky Syndicate began. Its money had been invested in the unsuccessful attempts at toppling Castro and in its new casino complex in Nassau, which was threatened by local antigambling forces. So when Southeast Asia began emerging as a new heroin export center, Lansky sent his financial expert John Pullman to check out the opportunities for investment. Close on his heels went Frank Furci, the son of a Trafficante lieutenant.[36]

From 1968 on, Trafficante's Cubans were in effective control of the traffic in heroin and cocaine throughout the United States.[37] The Florida capo's only gangland partner of significance was the Cotroni family in Montreal.

Trafficante carried out his business in a cool and collected manner. Never out of line with the national Syndicate, he enjoyed relative anonymity while other, less prominent gangsters wrote their names in history with blood. His organization was so airtight that when narcotics investigators finally realized how big a fish he was, they had to admit he was untouchable. The BNDD tried nabbing him in its 1969-70 Operation Eagle, then the most extensive action ever directed against a single narcotics network. The Bureau arrested over 120 traffickers, wholesalers, and pushers, but made no real dent. Within days, well-trained Cubans moved into the vacated slots.[38]

To the BNDD's surprise, a very large number of those arrested in Operation Eagle were CIA-trained veterans of the Bay of Pigs and Operation 40. Among them were Juan Cesar Restoy, a former Cuban senator under Batista, Allen Eric Rudd-Marrero, a pilot, and Mario Escandar.[39] Their fates were most unusual. Escandar and Restoy, alleged leaders of the narcotics network, were arrested in June 1970 but fled from Miami City Jail in August. Escandar turned himself in, but was released soon afterward when it was established that Attorney General John Mitchell had neglected to sign the authorization for the wiretap that incriminated Escandar. He returned to narcotics and was arrested in 1978 for kidnapping, a crime punishable by life, but for which he got only six months.[40] As this book went to press the FBI was investigating Escandar's relationship with the Dade County (Miami) police force.

Juan Restoy, on the other hand, turned to blackmail. He threatened to expose a close friend of President Nixon's as a narcotics trafficker, if not given his freedom and $350,000.[41] Restoy was shot and killed by narcotics agents, as was Rudd-Marrero.

In late 1970, in the wake of Operation Eagle, Bay of Pigs veteran Guillermo Hernandez-Cartaya set up the World Finance Corporation (WFC), a large company alleged to be a conduit for Trafficante investments and for the income from his narcotics activities.[42] Duney Perez-Alamo, a CIA-trained explosives expert involved with several Cuban exile terrorist groups, was a building manager for the WFC. Juan Romanach, a close Trafficante associate, was a WFC bank director.[43] As Hank Messick put it:

"Escandar, of course, was a friend of Hernandez-Cartaya, who was a friend of Dick Fincher, who was a friend of Bebe Rebozo, who was a friend of Richard Nixon, who once told John Dean he could get a million dollars in cash."[44]

In 1968 Trafficante himself went on an extended business trip to the Far East, beginning in Hong Kong, where he had located his emissary Frank Furci.[45] After a slow 1965-66 start, Furci had made great headway. Through his own Maradem, Ltd. he had cornered the market on Saigon's night spots catering to GIs.[46] He even ran officer and soldier mess halls, and he had set up a chain of heroin labs in Hong Kong to serve the GI market.

From Hong Kong, Trafficante journeyed to Saigon, registering at the Continental Palace hotel owned by the Corsican Franchini family. His last stop was in Singapore, where he contacted a branch of the splintered Chinese Mafia.

Several doors had to be opened to gain access to the opium treasure. The first led to the CIA-controlled Taiwan regime, the second to the Golden Triangle's KMT Chinese and Laotian Meo tribesmen. The latter door had already been opened by the CIA. Still another led to the Triads (Chinese gangster organizations) in Hong Kong. Trafficante opened that door with the help of Furci, who gave him access to Southeast Asia's overseas Chinese. There was no way around the Nationalist Chinese suppliers and middle men. The world had long been told that the narcotics came from Red China, but the facts belied that propaganda claim.[47]

Trafficante liked what he saw in his Southeast Asian tour. With enough trained chemists, his Mob could be supplied with heroin at a fraction of what it was then paying out to the Corsicans. But first the smuggling networks had to be worked out and the Corsicans had to be eliminated.

So Santo Trafficante began his war against the Corsicans.[48] His major foe, Auguste Ricord in Paraguay, wasn't about to roll over and die. Ricord got hold of his own Hong Kong connection, Ng Sik-ho,[49] also known as "Limpy Ho," a major Nationalist Chinese heroin smuggler well-connected to the Taiwan regime.[50] After Ricord's emissaries had travelled twice in 1970 to Japan, where they met with Mr. Ho,[51] heroin shipments began going to Paraguay via, among other transit points, Chile.[52] When in 1972 Ricord was extradited to the U.S., Limpy Ho tried establishing his own smuggling route to the U.S. via Vancouver. But that failed when two of his lieutenants, Sammy Cho and Chang Yu Ching, were arrested in the U.S. with fifty pounds of pure heroin.

By early 1970, Southeast Asian-produced heroin was ready to be tested on GI guinea pigs. Meyer Lansky, facing charges of business illegalities, turned over control to Trafficante and fled to Israel. On July 4 Lansky narcotics associates reportedly made their investment plans for Southeast Asia at a twelve-day meeting with representatives of several Mafia families at the Hotel Sole in Palermo, Sicily.[53]

Weeks later the Corsican Mafia contemplated counter-moves in a meeting at Philippe Franchini's suite in Saigon's Continental Palace Hotel. Turkish opium production was already waning and could no longer be relied upon. Unrest in the Middle East was destabilizing the production of morphine base. The Corsicans had to do something to regain control over their longtime Southeast Asian domain, a task made all but impossible by the U.S. presence. But the Corsicans still had large stocks of morphine, their Marseilles labs, and a smoothly functioning smuggling network. Trafficante and company could agree that if the Corsicans were to be neutralized, it had to be done totally and effectively. That was a job for President Nixon and his White House staff, the BNDD/White House Death Squad, and the Central Intelligence Agency.

Notes

1. Santo Trafficante, Jr.'s first important appearance in his role as overseer of the heroin traffic might have been at a 1947 summit in Havana reportedly attended by Auguste Ricord, alias Lucien Dargelles, the French Nazi collaborator who became Latin America's narcotics czar; see V. Alexandrov: *La Mafia des SS* (Stock, 1978).

2. A. McCoy: *The Politics of Heroin in Southeast Asia* (Harper & Row, 1972).

3. M. Gosch and R. Hammer: *The Last Testament of Lucky Luciano* (Little, Brown & Co., 1974).

4. Lansky was not then entirely sure of Trafficante's loyalty. He had the latter swear a "holy" oath, witnessed by Vincent Alo: "With an ancient Spanish dagger – none from Sicily was available – Trafficante cut his left wrist, allowed the blood to flow, and wet his right hand in the crimson stream. Then he held up the bloody hand: 'So long as the blood flows in my body,' he intoned solemnly, 'do I, Santo Trafficante, swear allegiance to the will of Meyer Lansky and the organization he represents. If I violate this oath, may I burn in Hell forever.' " – H. Messick: *Lansky* (Berkeley, 1971).

5. P.D. Scott: "From Dallas to Watergate," *Ramparts*, November 1973.

6. *New York Times*, 3 June 1973.

7. E. Reid: *The Grim Reapers* (Bantam, 1970).

8. *Ibid.*

9. P. Galante and L. Sapin: *The Marseilles Mafia* (W.H. Allen, 1979).

10. The Newsday Staff: *The Heroin Trail* (Souvenir Press, 1974).

11. D. Moldea: *The Hoffa Wars* (Charter Books, 1978).

12. U.S. Congress, Senate, Select Committee to Study Governmental Operations with respect to Intelligence Activities, *Alleged Assassination Plots Involving Foreign Leaders*, Interim Report, 94th Cong., 1st Sess., Senate Report No. 94-463, 1975. (Henceforth referred to as *Assassination Report*).

13. P. Meskill: "Mannen som Ville Myrde Fidel Castro," *Vi Menn*, 1976.

14. *Assassination Report, op. cit.*

15. *Ibid.*

16. *Ibid.*

17. D. Wise and T.B. Ross: *The Invisible Government* (Random House, 1964); P.D. Scott: *The War Conspiracy* (Bobbs-Merrill, 1972).

18. The name Drecher appears in T. Szulc: *Compulsive Spy* (Viking, 1974); Droller is used in P. Wyden: *The Bay of Pigs* (Simon & Schuster, 1979).

19. L. Gonzalez-Mata: *Cygne* (Grasset, 1976). According to this source (the author was the chief of security for the Dominican Republic's dictator, Rafael Trujillo), Howard Hunt went to the Dominican Republic with the mobster John Roselli in March 1961.

20. Pawley eventually built five large airplane factories around the world. It is also likely that he was involved in the CIA's Double Chek Corp. in Miami, as he had similarly been in the Flying Tigers. The CIA's air proprietaries are said to

stick together. When in 1958, CIA pilot Allen Pope was shot down and taken prisoner in Indonesia, he was flying for CAT. When he was released in 1962 he began flying for Southern Air Transport, another agency proprietary, which operated as late as 1973 out of offices in Miami and Taiwan. Southern's attorney in 1962 was Alex E. Carlson, who a year before had represented Double Chek when it furnished pilots for the Bay of Pigs invasion; see V. Marchetti and J.D. Marks: *CIA and the Cult of Intelligence* (Jonathan Cape, 1974).

On 23 March 1980, just as Iran's revolutionary government was about to request that Panama extradite Shah Reza Palevi, the ex-dictator who had been installed on his throne in 1953 by a CIA coup, he was flown off to Cairo on an Evergreen International Airlines charter. As reported by Ben Bradlee of the *Boston Globe*, (20 April 1980), in 1975 Evergreen had assumed control over Intermountain Aviation, Inc., a CIA proprietary. George Deele, Jr., a paid consultant for Evergreen, controlled the CIA's worldwide network of secret airlines for nearly two decades.

21. M. Acoca and R.K. Brown: "The Bayo-Pawley Affair," *Soldier of Fortune, Vol. 1*, No. 2, 1976.

22. The Newsday Staff, *op. cit.*

23. H. Kohn: "Strange Bedfellows," *Rolling Stone*, 20 May 1976.

24. The main character in Howard Hunt's 1949 spy novel, *Bimini Run*, was "Hank Sturgis."

25. H. Tanner: *Counter-Revolutionary Agent* (G.T. Foules, 1972).

26. Kohn, *op. cit.*

27. Meskill, *op. cit.*

28. Shackley was also indirectly responsible for Martinez's participation in the 17 June 1972 Watergate breakin; see T. Branch and G. Crile III: "'The Kennedy Vendetta," *Harper's*, August 1975.

29. *New York Times*, 4 January 1975.

30. Branch and Crile, *op. cit.*

31. J. Hougan: *Spooks* (William Morrow, 1978).

32. Shackley might also have been responsible for the CIA's tapping of all telephone converstions to and from Latin America in the first half of 1973 "in connection with narcotics operations" (see *Newsweek*, 23 June 1975). According to Branch and Crile, *op. cit.*, Shackley, as chief of the CIA's Western Hemisphere Division of Clandestine Services, "had overall responsibility for the agency's efforts to overthrow the Allende regime in Chile."

In a recent article in which he refers to Shackley as one of "the CIA's most esteemed officers," journalist Michael Ledeen claims that Shackley left the agency voluntarily when "forced to choose between retirement and accepting a post that would have represented a de facto demotion." (*New York*, 3 March 1980). Ledeen, incidentally, is a colleague of Ray S. Cline at Georgetown's rightwing propaganda mill, the Center for Strategic and International Studies (see chapter 14, footnote 20).

33. Acoca and Brown, *op. cit.*

34. D. Russell: "Loren Hall and the Politics of Assassination," *Village Voice*, 3 October 1977.

35. The *New York Times*, ed.: *The Final Assassinations Report* (Bantam,

1979). In early 1980 the Justice Department was investigating allegations that Marcello had offered Mario T. Noto, the Deputy Commissioner of Immigration, a guaranteed "plush job" after retirement, in return for Noto's help in lifting Marcello's travel restrictions. Noto's attorney, ironically, is Myles Ambrose, who stepped down from his job at the head of the BNDD in the wake of corruption allegations. (*New York Times*, 11 February 1980).

36. McCoy, *op. cit.*

37. H. Messick: *The Mobs and the Mafia* (Spring Books, 1972).

38. The Newsday Staff, *op. cit.*

39. H. Messick: *Of Grass and Snow* (Prentice-Hall, 1979); The Newsday Staff, *op. cit.*

40. *Miami Herald*, 30 March 1978.

41. Messick: *Of Grass and Snow, op. cit.*

42. *Ibid.*

43. *Ibid.*

44. *Ibid.*

45. McCoy, *op. cit.*

46. *Ibid.*

47. In the early seventies the opium bankrollers in Taiwan sent out, through their international lobby, the WACL, propaganda charging Red China with "the drugging of the world." The propaganda was directed at Nixon's rapprochement with mainland China. A 1972 BNDD report stated, however, that "not one investigation into heroin traffic in the area in the past two years indicates Chinese Communist involvement."

48. The existence of such a drug war is also mentioned in A. Jaubert: *Dossier D...comme Drogue* (Alain Moreau, 1974).

49. S. O'Callaghan: *The Triads* (W.H. Allen, 1978).

50. F. Robertson: *Triangle of Death* (Routledge and Keagen Paul, 1977).

51. O'Callaghan, *op. cit.*

52. McCoy, *op. cit.*

53. F. Wulff in the Danish *Rapport*, 14 April 1975. A BNDD agent on the scene was reportedly discovered and liquidated. Apparently he hadn't known that the code words were "baccio la mano" – I kiss your hand. Subject number one of the meeting was Southeast Asia, which the conferees decided would replace Turkey and Marseilles as the main source of opium and heroin. Mexico, to which Sam Giancana was sent, would be a safety valve. On one thing they were uananimous: the Corsicans had to be eliminated. To begin with, $300 million was to be invested in the bribery of politicians, as well as of military and police officers in Thailand, Burma, Laos, South Vietnam, and Hong Kong. Another nine-figure sum was set aside to maximize opium production in the Golden Triangle.

SIXTEEN
THE FRIENDS OF RICHARD NIXON

Richard Nixon's connections to the Syndicate and its stooges are a matter of record. The only question is when they began. Some say it was 1946, when Nixon ran for Congress in California and Murray Chotiner, a top Syndicate defense attorney, ran his campaign with support from the gangster Mickey Cohen.[1]

Others place the Nixon-underworld wedding as early as 1943, when Nixon was working in the Office of Price Administration, at a desk responsible for controlling the market in rubber goods. There he allegedly met his future pals George "The Senator from Cuba" Smathers and the Cuban-American Bebe Rebozo who later struck it rich in real estate. The two were then small time: Smathers a lawyer for a Syndicate front smuggling auto tires from Cuba, Rebozo the owner of a gas station that sold the tires.[2]

The Florida clique was a happy family. Nixon liked to take fishing jaunts with the likes of Rebozo, Meyer Lansky's associate Tatum "Chubby" Wofford,[3] and Richard Danner, who would later manage the Sands casino in Las Vegas for Howard Hughes.[4] He also got to know people even closer to the Syndicate, who had extensive interests in Cuba. In 1952, one short month after the dictator Batista's comeback, Nixon and Danner joined throngs of tourists who unloaded their savings at one of the Syndicate's Cuban casinos.[5] Nixon would return frequently. He, Rebozo, and Smathers allegedly invested in the island during the fifties,[6] and in 1955, as vice president of the United States, Nixon would pin an award on Batista, with whom he was photographed in the dictator's palace.

Nixon also helped plan the Bay of Pigs invasion in 1959. Chairing the 54/12 Group, a National Security Council subcommittee in charge of covert actions, the vice president pushed for the plan's approval before his 1960 presidential race against John F. Kennedy.[7] According to Howard Hunt, Nixon was the invasion's "secret action officer" in the White House.[8] President Eisenhower, who would later plead ignorance of the plan's extent, assumed it was limited to support for anti-Castro guerillas in the mountains.[9] When JFK took over the oval office, he was presented with a *fait accompli.*

If Eisenhower was really left out in the cold on the plan's magnitude, then William Pawley must have been among Nixon's co-conspirators. As mentioned earlier, Pawley talked Eisenhower into arming the anti-Communist Cubans.[10] Pawley was and would remain one of Nixon's most ardent supporters.[11]

When the invasion proved a bust, Nixon's voice was among the loudest accusing Kennedy of undermining it by refusing reinforcements. In the years that followed he continued to cultivate support among the Cuban exiles and other right wing constituencies. Cubans for Nixon and Asians for Nixon touted him as a man who would not forsake the cause of anticommunism. The Nixon of near-hysterical anticommunism would win additional allies in the Syndicate and in powerful business circles tied in with the military and espionge.

Fortunately for Nixon, forces behind the above lobbies were also influential in organized labor, especially the Teamsters Union. Teamster boss Jimmy Hoffa became a pawn of the Lansky syndicate, which borrowed millions from the union's pension fund. However, Hoffa's obsequiousness towards the Mob was dampened by Attorney General Robert Kennedy's aggressive investigation of Teamster policies. In 1967, prior to Nixon's decisive electoral campaign, Hoffa landed in jail with a thirteen-year sentence for misuse of union funds. The new Teamster strongmen, Frank Fitzsimmons and Anthony "Tony Pro" Provenzano, were friends of Nixon and in the hands of the Syndicate.[12] When Nixon pardoned Hoffa just prior to Christmas 1971, Hoffa had to promise to stay out of organized labor.

In the sixties Nixon grew even closer to his friends in Miami, who by then had made millions in land speculation. Dade County north of Miami became known as "Lanskyville," as a string of seemingly legitimate real estate firms handled the Lansky Mob's enormous holdings. Among the more prominent firms were:[13]

1) The Cape Florida Development Co., run by Donald Berg and Nixon's pal Rebozo. The two worked closely with Al Polizzi, the

former head of the Syndicate's Mayfield Road Gang in Cleveland, then in charge of the Syndicate's Florida contractors. An investigation into the placement of stolen securities at Rebozo's bank was nipped in the bud.

2) The Mary Carter Paint Co., which in 1967 became Resorts International, that now runs the world's most profitable casino in Atlantic City, New Jersey, and was purportedly the brainchild of Mr. Lansky. Resorts' Paradise Island casino in the Bahamas was managed by Ed Cellini, a longtime Lansky casino operator.

3) The General Development Corp., run by two Lansky strawmen, Wallace Groves and Lou Chesler. Its board of directors included Lansky broker Max Orovitz and the gangster Trigger Mike Coppola. Groves bought up half of Grand Bahama Island for the Syndicate and contracted with Nixon's law client, National Bulk Carriers, to construct a harbor there.

4) The Major Realty Co., whose controlling shareholders were Senator Smathers and Lansky's men Orovitz and Ben Siegelbaum.

Through his friends, Nixon acquired land on Key Biscayne and Fisher's Island, off the Florida coast. In return he readily made himself available for personal appearances. When Mary Carter in 1967 opened the Nassau Bay Club casino on Grand Bahama Island, Nixon was the guest of honor. One year later he was there when Resorts International opened its casino on Paradise Island.

Nixon also expressed his friendship in other ways. Hoffa was not the only one who did not have to pay his full debt to society. Neither did Leonard Bursten, Carl Kovens, or Morris Shenker, all Syndicate associates, the last two solid Nixon campaign supporters.[14] Robert Morgenthau, the federal attorney for the southern district of New York, became interested in some of Nixon's friends in 1968. He proved Max Orovitz guilty of willful violation of stock registration laws, and was investigating Syndicate money transfers to Switzerland. The latter threatened to lead to an indictment of Nixon's friend John M. King of Investor's Overseas Service (IOS).[15] Morgenthau, however, was removed from office.

Glancing at major contributors to Nixon's 1968 and 1972 campaign chests, one finds the names of Miami straw men Lou Chesler and Richard Pistell, Resorts' president James Crosby and John M. King, the Texas billionaire Howard Hughes, master swindler Robert Vesco, and the California millionaire C. Arnholdt Smith, a close associate of the gangster John Alessio and later convicted of misuse of bank funds.

The list of Nixon's major personal and political supporters starts with Rebozo, Smathers, Dewey, Hoffa, and Frank Fitzsimmons, all with their Syndicate associations; and goes on to include William Pawley and the China Lobby's Madame Anna Chan Chennault.

Nearly all of Nixon's major supporters in Florida were involved in one way or another in the Bay of Pigs operation. The same can be said of the top Syndicate figures, four of whom escorted the invasion force in a yacht for part of the voyage, while Trafficante's lieutenants in Miami and the Dominican Republic stood ready to seize the casinos.

Moreover, one cannot overlook Nixon's particular connection to IOS-multimillionaire Vesco, who until recently was in exile in Costa Rica, where he allegedly financed the smuggling of narcotics.[16] Vesco provided covert financial aid to Nixon's reelection campaign, and was closely associated with Nixon's brother Edward and nephew Donald, Jr. Richard Nixon himself is alleged to have met secretly with Vesco in Salzburg, Austria.[17] The White House, finally, came to Vesco's aid in a case brought against him by the Securities and Exchange Commission,[18] just as an investigation of his narcotics activities was similarly choked off.[19]

Notes

1. H. Kohn: "Strange Bedfellows," *Rolling Stone*, 20 May 1976.
2. C. Oglesby: "Presidential Assassinations and the Closing of the Frontier," in *Government by Gunplay*, S. Blumenthal and H. Yazijian, eds. (New American Library, 1976).
3. The 1950 Kefauver investigation discovered that one of Lansky's largest back room casinos in Miami was set up in the Wofford Hotel run by Tatum "Chubby" Wofford.
4. Howard Hughes helped Nixon out as early as 1956 with a secret $100,000 donation, as well as a $205,000 loan to his brother Donald.
5. J. Gerth: "Richard Nixon and Organized Crime," in *Government by Gunplay, op. cit.*
6. Kohn, *op. cit.*
7. H.G. Klein in the *San Diego Union*, 25 March 1962.
8. Kohn, *op. cit.*

9. Oglesby, *op. cit.*

10. M. Acoca and R.K. Brown: "The Bayo-Pawley Affair," *Soldier of Fortune, Vol. 1,* No. 2, 1976.

11. J. Hougan: *Spooks* (William Morrow, 1978).

12. *Time,* 18 August 1975. Six months after an 88-count indictment, Frank Fitzsimmons' son Richard, a Teamsters organizer, was recently sentenced to thirty months and a $10,000 fine for accepting bribes from trucking company officials (*Boston Globe,* 16 February 1980).

13. Information on the four firms is from the October 1972 *NACLA Report.*

14. Bursten, a friend of Hoffa's who was at one time a director of the Miami National Bank, saw his fifteen-year sentence, in connection with the bankruptcy of a Beverly Hills housing development that had received a $12 million Teamster pension fund loan, reduced to probation after the intervention of Murray Chotiner. Kovens, another leading Florida Teamster official, was convicted in the same pension fraud case as Hoffa, but released from federal prison with the help of Senator Smathers and then went on to collect $50,000 for Nixon's 1972 reelection campaign. Shenker, whom *Life* magazine in 1971 called the "foremost mob attorney," saw the Justice Department's multi-year investigation of his tax violations turned down by Nixon's Attorney General Richard Kleindienst on the basis of "insufficient evidence," after which the files on Shenker at the offices of the U.S. Attorney at St. Louis disappeared; see Gerth, *op. cit.*

15. *NACLA Report, op. cit.*

16. Hougan, *op. cit.*

17. *Ibid.*

18. *Time,* 6 May 1974.

19. L.H. Whittemore: *Peroff* (Ballantine, 1975). As of November 1979, a federal grand jury in New York City was investigating Vesco's masterminding an alleged scheme whereby Libyan government officials were to pay off members of the Carter administration to facilitate Libya's purchase of American C-130 transport planes; see the *New York Times,* 4 November 1979. Five months later, in the midst of Jimmy Carter's reelection campaign, an assistant U.S. attorney announced that a second federal grand jury in Washington had returned no indictments following its investigation of allegations that Vesco had attempted to bribe Carter administration officials to fix his long-standing legal problems. The grand jury's foreman, Ralph Ulmer, immediately criticized the incompleteness of the announcement, charging that "the statement is incomplete and thus misleading, which is about par for the course for the Justice Department." (*New York Times,* 2 April 1980).

Ulmer had earlier charged that "cover-up activities are being orchestrated within the Justice Department under the concept that the Administration must be protected at all costs... Among other things information was withheld from the grand jury... a witness was encouraged to be less than candid with the FBI." (*Boston Globe,* 30 August 1979.)

SEVENTEEN
WHITE HOUSE HANKY PANKY

Never had Richard Nixon's White House staff been so preoccupied with narcotics matters as in the summer of 1971. They were obsessed with two projects: a new White House intelligence and enforcement unit as envisioned by the Huston Plan, and a comprehensive narcotics control apparatus, similarly under direct presidential control. The two *idées fixes* converged in a conspiratorial and political-criminal network of hitherto unimagined dimensions.

That summer the White House set up the Special Action Office for Drug Abuse Prevention alongside the Special Investigation Unit, otherwise known as the Plumbers. Several of the Plumbers also worked on narcotics affairs. The groups' key figures included:

Egil Krogh (chief Plumber) – who followed John Erlichman (for whose law firm he had worked part time) to the White House in 1968 within months of his graduation from the University of Washington Law School. He was named deputy assistant to the president for law enforcement, and within three years found himself in charge both of Nixon's narcotics and law enforcement campaign, and of the Plumbers squad. His single-minded ambition surfaced in a declaration to the noted psychiatrist and narcotics expert, Dr. Daniel S. Freedman, when the latter refused to support one of Krogh's programs: "Well, don't worry. Anyone who opposes us we'll destroy. As a matter of fact, anyone who doesn't support us, we'll destroy."[1] Krogh would wind up in jail for the break-in at the office of Daniel Ellsberg's psychiatrist, Dr. Lewis Fielding.

Walter Minnick (temporary Plumber) – a young graduate of Harvard Business School and former agent of the CIA, who joined

159

Krogh's narcotics staff in spring 1971 and later helped draft the reorganization plan that created the DEA.

John Caulfield (Plumber) – a former agent of the New York City Police Department's Bureau of Special Services (BOSS), which specialized in narcotics and "monitoring the activities of terrorist organizations." In the 1960 presidential campaign he had been assigned to protect candidate Nixon in New York City. That and his close relationship with Nixon's personal secretary, Rose Mary Woods (of eighteen and one-half minute tape gap fame), gained him a foot in the door of the White House.[2]

Myles Ambrose – the former Customs Commissioner, who was named head of the narcotics campaign's domestic strike force. He would later leave government service in disgrace.

G. Gordon Liddy (Plumber) – a former FBI agent whose narcotics intelligence job at the Treasury Department had been terminated, only weeks prior to his recruitment by the White House, for his outspoken lobbying against gun-control legislation. Eventually, he would get six-to-twenty for his role in the break-in at the Watergate complex and one-to-three for the job at Fielding's office.

Howard Hunt (Plumber) – a former CIA agent closely connected to the agency-trained Cuban exiles, many of whom had emerged from Santo Trafficante's Cuban narcotics Mafia. Hunt was employed as a special advisor on narcotics problems in Southeast Asia. In November 1973 Judge John Sirica would sentence him to two-and-a-half to eight years – reduced from an initial thirty-five – for the Watergate break-in.

Lucien Conein – a CIA agent, Ed Lansdale's right-hand man in Vietnam, and an expert on Southeast Asian narcotics centers and the Corsican Mafia. He was brought into the White House by his old buddy Hunt.

David Young – a young lawyer who put up a sign outside his office, "Mr. Young, Plumber," when apprised that he would be plugging leaks and that the trade had run in his family. He came to Krogh's staff from Henry Kissinger's National Security Council.

It was a strange mix of novices and experienced agents with the most intriguing pasts.

Hunt and Liddy were located in Room 16 of the Executive Office Building, headquarters for the Plumbers group's secret narcotics missions and other, crooked operations on behalf of the Committee to Re-Elect the President (CREEP). The Plumbers' first assignment was the break-in at the office of Daniel Ellsberg's psychiatrist.[3] For the break-in dirty work, Hunt enlisted Bernard Barker, Eugenio Rolando Martinez and Felipe de Diego, three of his Cuban friends who had been involved in the Bay of Pigs invasion. Martinez and de Diego also took part in the CIA's follow-up Operation 40, and the ubiquitous Martinez was in on Trafficante-masterminded boat raids on Cuba.[4]

By the summer of 1971 the White House Death Squad was well on its way. Hunt sought out Barker in Miami for what Hunt called "a new national security organization above the CIA and FBI." Barker would assemble a force of 120 CIA-trained exiles for Operation Diamond, which, under cover of narcotics enforcement, would kidnap or assassinate political enemies. Barker signed up.[5]

In the fall of 1971 Hunt asked another of his Cuban friends, Bay of Pigs veteran Manuel Artime, to set up "hit teams" for the liquidation of narcotics dealers. As later revealed, Artime's primary target was to have been the Panamanian strongman, General Omar Torrijos.[6]

Krogh and his staff, meanwhile, tightened their grip on narcotics control. After the BNDD takeover of customs' international jurisdiction, Krogh pushed Bureau chief John Ingersoll for results to feed Congress and the press. In September 1971 Krogh was named to direct the newly formed Cabinet Committee on International Narcotics Control. In collaboration with the State Department, BNDD, CIA and Henry Kissinger's office, the committee coordinated the international struggle against narcotics. State Department narcotics advisor Nelson Gross, chosen to supervise the joint actions, was later sentenced to two years for attempted bribery and income tax evasion.[7]

Egil Krogh was less than satisfied with existing narcotics efforts, especially those of the CIA, whose intelligence reports, according to Ingersoll, were decisive for the work of the BNDD. Krogh wanted the White House instead to handle the BNDD's intelligence work. Nixon's staff would then decide which drug traffickers to pursue. Krogh's dissatisfaction was expressed to Hunt, who immediately proposed an Office of National Narcotics Intelligence (ONNI) where all narcotics intelligence reports would be analyzed and follow-up actions decided.[8]

Hunt told Krogh he could enlist for the office experienced CIA figures, starting with Lucien Conein at its head.[9] Nixon, however, chose William C. Sullivan instead. Once second to J. Edgar Hoover in the FBI, Sullivan had managed Division Five, which investigated espionage, sabotage, and subversion.[10] He also directed Operation Cointelpro, the bureau's vendetta against dissident political and cultural groups (such as the Black Panthers), and had been Nixon's choice to direct the Huston Plan's elaborate surveillance of U.S. citizens.[11]

Hunt, nevertheless, found a niche for his friend. Conein was assigned to the BNDD as a "strategic intelligence officer," and came to control overseas narcotics intelligence, originally the domain of ONNI,[12] while Sullivan concentrated on domestic affairs.[13]

The White House now controlled narcotics intelligence at home and abroad. But that still wasn't enough. Nixon's staff also sought to control enforcement itself, and that required effective strike forces. In January 1972 the White House set up the Office for Drug Abuse Law Enforcement (ODALE) according to a plan conceived by Gordon Liddy. It became the domestic strike force under Myles Ambrose — whose government career ended with news of his pleasure trip to the ranch of a Texan indicted for narcotics and gun-running.[14] ODALE soon became notorious for its record of illegal raids, no-knock entries into private homes, and beatings of innocent people.[15] Some called it the American Gestapo.

Overseas, as well, the White House was dissatisfied with the BNDD's enforcement powers. Dr. J. Thomas Ungerleider, a member of the National Commission on Marijuana and Drug Abuse, noted in a record of his conversations with BNDD officials: "There was some talk about establishing hit squads (assassination teams), as they are said to have in a South American country. It was stated that with 150 key assassinations, the entire heroin refining operation can be thrown into chaos. 'Officials' say it is known exactly who is involved in these operations but can't prove it."

Hunt, Liddy and others in Room 16 did not confine themselves to narcotics campaigns and political assassinations. On behalf of CREEP they raised campaign funds from more or less shady sources and sabotaged the campaigns of George Wallace, Hubert Humphrey, Edmund Muskie, and George McGovern. Hunt's CIA colleagues are among those who suspect he spiked Muskie's lemonade with an LSD-like substance prior to the candidate's famous tearful speech.[16]

Besides Hunt's Cubans, the familiar Frank Sturgis, who had earlier taken orders from Santo Trafficante, took on narcotics work and special assignments for CREEP.[17] According to a 1972 FBI report, sources in Miami had claimed Sturgis was then associated with organized crime activities. He later told an interviewer that he had aided Hunt in a 1971 investigation of the drug traffic reaching the U.S. from Paraguay via Panama.[18] He was in on several actions connected with the investigation, which focussed exclusively on Auguste

Ricord's Grupo Francés.[19]

Sturgis was everywhere in the hectic spring of 1972. In May he was among the men who assaulted Daniel Ellsberg on the steps of the Capitol. Later that month he and Cubans including Bernard Barker arranged a Miami demonstration in support of Nixon's decision to mine Haiphong harbor. Sturgis himself was at the wheel of the truck leading the procession. He helped recruit agitators to disrupt the Democratic national convention, and in the June 17 Watergate break-in Sturgis joined CIA/Trafficante Cubans and White House narcotics conspirators.[20]

As the noted Berkeley researcher Peter Dale Scott put it in 1973: "In my opinion it is no coincidence that the key figures in Watergate – Liddy, Hunt, Sturgis, Krogh, Caulfield – had been drawn from the conspiratorial world of government narcotics enforcement, a shady realm in which operations of organized crime, counter-revolution and government intelligence have traditionally overlapped."[21]

In July 1973 Nixon's narcotics forces were essentially consolidated according to Reorganization Plan Number Two worked out by former CIA agent Walter Minnick and Egil Krogh. The Drug Enforcement Administration (DEA) was formed out of the BNDD, ODALE, ONNI and Customs Intelligence. Four thousand operatives, including fifty CIA agents (many of them Cubans from the ODALE hard core), five hundred customs agents and most of the BNDD staff made the DEA a powerful new agency.

Ingersoll of the BNDD, Ambrose of ODALE and Sullivan of ONNI all resigned as John R. Bartels became the DEA's first director. His was no small task. Earlier rivalries persisted. The strange brew of agents with widely varying backgrounds and assignments made the DEA difficult if not impossible to steer. U.S. narcotics enforcement has a history of corruption, scandal and exposure of agent collaboration with the criminals it has been assigned to police. Still, no bureau has been as plagued by scandal as the DEA has in seven years of existence. The exposés and charges run the gamut from trafficking in drugs, teamwork with the Mob and protection of major traffickers, to thievery, gunrunning, torture, and assassination of drug traffickers.[22]

When Lucien Conein became the head of the DEA's Special Operations Branch he allegedly carried out an assassination program after setting up the DEA's Special Operations Group (DEASOG), under cover of the B.R. Fox Company and housed on Connecticut Avenue in Washington.[23] DEASOG's twelve members – the Dirty

Dozen – were hard-nosed and experienced Latino CIA agents transferred over to the drug agency for the occasion. Prior to DEASOG,
Conein had set up another DEA "intelligence" operation, Deacon I,
employing Cuban exile veterans of CIA training camps, who were
supervised by thirty other Cubans, all formerly of the CIA's Clandestine Services.[24]

In response to the claim that DEASOG was a "hit team," Conein
told journalist George Crile: "That is a big ------- lie. That is bull----."
However, a DEA official had told Crile: "When you get down to it,
Conein was organizing an assassination program. He was frustrated
by the big-time operators who were just too insulated to get to." DEA
officials also told Crile that "meetings were held to decide whom to
target and what method of assassination to employ. Conein then
assigned the task to three of the former CIA operatives assigned to
the Connecticut Avenue safe house."[25]

DEASOG shared its Washington office with an old friend and
colleague of Hunt and Conein's from OSS China, the weapons dealing
soldier of fortune and specialist in assassination, Mitch WerBell III.[26]
WerBell told Crile he had been a business partner of Conein's as late
as 1974, and that he and Conein had worked together on providing the
DEA with assassination devices.[27] Among WerBell's other associates
were Frank Sturgis, Cuban exile leaders, and Robert Vesco, who, like
WerBell himself, has been charged with bankrolling narcotics smuggling.[28] Carlos Hernandez Rumbaut, the bodyguard of Vesco's close
friend and business partner, former Costa Rican President Pepé
Figueres, is a former Conein agent who fled the country to avoid imprisonment on a drug conviction.[29] He has reportedly reentered the
U.S. twice with a U.S. diplomatic passport.[30]

Assassination, it can be argued, became a *modus operandi* under
Richard Nixon. The CIA carried out assassination and extermination
campaigns in Vietnam, Guatemala, Argentina, and Brazil[31] – aided in
Latin America by the local Death Squads. The White House appears
to have sponsored a secret assassination program under cover of drug
enforcement. It was continued by the DEA, which seemingly overlapped with the CIA in political rather than drug enforcement.

Until 1974 the training of torturers and members of Latin American death squads came under the auspices of the CIA and
USAID's Office of Public Safety. Some 100,000 Brazilian policemen, for example, were trained and 523 of them were chosen for
courses in the U.S.A.[32] They were trained at the International Police
Academy in Georgetown, Washington, D.C. and at a secret CIA

center in the same city on R Street, under cover of International Police Services, Inc. When school was out the prize pupils returned home to work, beside CIA advisors, as functionaries or torturers in such effective repression apparatuses as Sao Paulo's Operacao Bandeirantes.[33] Many would moonlight with the Death Squads.

After Tupamaros guerillas kidnapped and killed U.S. police advisor Dan Mitrione in Uruguay, Washington's schools for foreign police came into the limelight and Congress cut off their funding.[34] Nonetheless, the training program and direct assistance and supervision continued. A 1976 investigation authorized by Senator James Abourezk revealed that the U.S. torture academies had not in fact been completely closed down. According to Jack Anderson, Abourezk found such a school had been in operation since 1974 in Los Fresnos, Texas at the site of a former "bomb school." Another journalist, William Hoffman, later confirmed the existence of a school for torture in Los Fresnos, which had since moved to Georgia, where it was known as the Law Enforcement Training Center.[35] Interestingly, Conein's friend WerBell runs his own large training center in Georgia, The Farm. It's used for, among other things, the training of law enforcement officers.[36]

Much of the old police support apparatus was simply transferred to AID's International Narcotics Control program (INC), which really spelled DEA. In 1974 the DEA had some 400 agents in Latin America, or roughly the number of advisors recalled from the OPS program. INC's budget for technical equipment abroad, meanwhile, jumped from $2.2 million in 1973 to $12.5 million in 1974.

The politics of the new drug effort were exposed when, in 1974, the man behind Argentina's death squad (the Argentine Anticommunist Alliance), Social Minister Lopez Rega, appeared on TV with U.S. Ambassador Robert C. Hill to publicize the two nations' antinarcotics collaboration with the words: "Guerillas are the main users of drugs in Argentina. Therefore, the anti-drug campaign will automatically be an anti-guerilla campaign as well."[37]

It's striking how close the various extermination and repression campaigns have been to the narcotics traffic. The Meo Army deployed by the CIA in Laos smuggled large quantities of opium. Lopez Rega and his Argentine AAA henchmen were eventually exposed as keys to a cocaine ring.[38] One of the chief AAA hatchet men, Francois Chiappe, was a lieutenant in the Ricord/David heroin network.[39] Paraguay's most ruthless high-ranking officers were exposed as heroin profiteers. Christian David took part in extermination campaigns in Argentina, Brazil, and Uruguay. Operacao Bandeirantes' chief, Sergio Fleury, and several of his colleagues pocketed large protection payoffs.[40] Fleury's number two man in the Sao Paulo Death Squad, Ademar Augusto de Oliveira, alias Fininho, fled to Paraguay after he was charged with murder. There, under the name Irineu Bruno da Silva, he worked for the Ricord gang.[41] When David's successor, the Brazilian narcotics dealer Milton Concalves Thiago, alias Cabecao (The Brain), was arrested in 1975, it was learned that he had been paying off the entire Rio de Janeiro Death Squad, which included four narcotics police lieutenants.[42] And finally as we go to press we learn that the dictator, Pinochet, assumed control of Chile's cocaine trade, then turned it over to his secret police, DINA, which shared the profits with its Cuban exile henchmen.[43]

The political violence set in motion by the White House narcotics offices ran smoothly. But what of actual drug enforcement? From its inception it focussed on dismantling the French narcotics network. When that was done, America would be free of the heroin plague, or so said Nixon and his staff. Reports of increasing amounts of heroin from Southeast Asia and Mexico were obscured by the great public relations campaign on the struggle against the Corsicans.

The Turkey/Marseilles/U.S. heroin pipeline was indeed shut down, and the French Corsican Mafia was almost totally decimated. But major new suppliers in Southeast Asia and South America were left untouched – despite warnings and reports – and despite the many CIA "experts" on the Latin American drug scene. Not only were most major heroin suppliers in the two regions left alone, they were protected. And they were aided by the arrest of small-time competitors.

At home the story was nearly the same. ODALE and DEA nabbed only minor distributors and sidewalk pushers.

Notes

1. L. Lurie: *The Impeachment of Richard Nixon* (Berkeley, 1973).
2. J.A. Lukas: *Nightmare* (Viking, 1976).
3. It is interesting to speculate whether Ellsberg's knowledge of top-secret operations in Vietnam touched on narcotics. His supervisors in Southeast Asia had been General Lansdale and Lieutenant Colonel Conein. Ellsberg and Conein were apparently quite close in Vietnam. Conein reportedly saved Ellsberg's life when the latter got romantically involved with the mistress of a

Corsican Mafia capo. The gangster threatened to kill Ellsberg. Conein, in turn, told the gangster it would lead to his own funeral and war between the CIA and the Corsicans – see J. Hougan: *Spooks* (William Morrow, 1978).

4. See chapter fifteen.

5. 1977 CBS interview of Bernard Barker; see also G. Crile III in the *Washington Post*, 13 June 1976.

6. J. Marshall: "The White House Death Squad," *Inquiry*, 5 March 1979.

7. E.J. Epstein: *Agency of Fear* (Putnam, 1977).

8. *Ibid.*

9. *Ibid.*

10. D. Wise and T.B. Ross: *The Invisible Government* (Random House, 1964).

11. S. Blumenthal: "How the FBI Tried to Destroy the Black Panthers," in *Government by Gunplay*, S. Blumenthal and H. Yazijian, eds. (New American Library, 1976).

12. H. Messick: *Of Grass and Snow* (Prentice-Hall, 1979).

13. A 1971 New York investigation revealed that 47 percent of the city's 300,000 addicts were Black, 27 percent Hispanic and only 15 percent White – see C. Lamour and M.R. Lamberti: *Les Grandes Maneuvres de l'Opium* (Éditions du Seuil, 1972); i.e., there were some 150,000 Black addicts in New York City alone. Still, Nixon named as director of ONNI, William C. Sullivan. The man who had planned and executed Operation Cointelpro would now battle the forces doping the potentially troublesome elements of the Ghetto. Ironically, Malcolm X and the Panthers, prime Cointelpro targets, had been the only ones to make significant headway against ghetto drug addiction.

14. T. Meldal-Johnsen and V. Young: *The Interpol Connection* (Dial, 1979).

15. Epstein, *op. cit.*

16. M. Copeland: *Beyond Cloak and Dagger* (Pinnacle Books, 1974).

17. H. Kohn: "Strange Bedfellows," *Rolling Stone*, 20 May 1976.

18. *True*, August 1974.

19. In his book *Cygne* (Grasset, 1976), intelligence agent Luis Gonzales-Mata describes being assigned a special task by CIA agent "Robert Berg." He was to convince the Paraguayan dictator Stroessner that Ricord was behind a planned coup attempt against him financed with heroin from Red China. Stroessner was in a bind, since he very well knew that the source of the heroin was not Red China but his bosom buddies in Taiwan.

20. C. Bernstein and B. Woodward: *All the President's Men* (Warner Books, 1975).

21. P.D. Scott: "From Dallas to Watergate," *Ramparts*, November 1973.

22. U.S. Justice Department DeFeo Report, 1975; the list of DEA abuses has recently been expanded to include a computerized information system covering 570,000 names (a number which may be compared with the 8000 federal drug arrests each year) – see E. Rasen: "High-Tech Fascism," *Penthouse*, March 1980.

23. Hougan, *op. cit.*

24. *Ibid.*

25. Crile, *op. cit.*

26. Another OSS China hand, Clark McGregor, replaced John Mitchell as the head of CREEP.

27. Crile, *op. cit.*

28. T. Dunkin: "The Great Pot Plot," *Soldier of Fortune, Vol. 2*, No. 1, 1977; L.H. Whittemore: *Peroff* (Ballantine, 1975).

29. Hougan, *op. cit.*

30. Crile, *op. cit.*

31. Cuban exiles took part in an extermination campaign in Guatemala between 1968 and 1971. According to Amnesty International, 30,000 people were murdered there between 1962 and 1971, most of them in the last three years. Similarly, anti-Castro Cubans had their hand in the Argentine AAA's murder campaign believed to have claimed 10,000 lives. In Brazil the Sao Paulo Death Squad alone is estimated to have assassinated 2000 between 1968 and 1972, while many others perished in the torture chambers.

32. *Skeptic*, January/February 1977.

33. A.J. Langguth: *Hidden Terrors* (Pantheon, 1978).

34. *Ibid.*

35. *Gallery*, May 1978.

36. Dunkin, *op. cit.* Among other antiterrorism trainees at WerBell's camp in Powder Springs have been several members of U.S. presidential candidate Lyndon Larouche's U.S. Labor Party. The Marxist turned extreme rightist and anti-Semitic U.S. Labor Party has voluntarily sent the FBI and local police forces "intelligence" reports on left wing movements, and regularly exchanges information with one Roy Frankhouser, the self-proclaimed Grand Dragon of the Ku Klux Klan in Pennsylvania and active member of the American Nazi Party – see the *New York Times*, 7 October 1979.

37. P. Lernoux: "Corrupting Colombia," *Inquiry*, 30 September 1979. In July 1978, DEA chief Peter Bensinger strongly recommended that Colombian authorities militarize the Guajira Peninsula, home of the marijuana/cocaine traffic. Two months later, newly elected (and current) President Julio Cesar Turbay issued a security statute empowering the military to arrest any Colombian deemed subversive, without recourse to *habeas corpus* or other constitutional guarantees. In April 1980, the Colombian Army was about to abandon its U.S.-financed multi-million dollar drug war, its failure connected, no doubt, to an estimated $110 million in protection money distributed annually by the smugglers (*New York Times*, 3 April 1980). Meanwhile, the military has assumed the dominant position in what was one of Latin America's few remaining democracies. U.S. military aid to Colombia – where, according to Amnesty International's April 1980 report, military personnel torture political prisoners in thirty-three locations throughout the country, resorting to fifty identifiable techniques – totalled $155 million between 1946 and 1975; 6200 Colombian military personnel were trained by the U.S. in the same period (N. Chomsky and E.S. Herman: *The Washington Connection and Third World Fascism*, South End Press, 1979). U.S. military aid for 1979 was $12.7 million, the highest amount in Latin America.

38. *Latin America*, 19 December 1975.

39. *L'Aurore*, 31 May 1976; *Liberation*, 19 July 1976.

40. *Le Nouvel Observateur*, 21 May 1973; A. Lopez: *L'Escadron de la Mort* (Casterman, 1973); H. Bicudo: *Meu Depoimento sobre o Esquadrao da Morte* (1976).

41. *Le Nouvel Observateur*, 21 May 1973.

42. *Diario de Noticias*, 7 May 1975.

43. See the foreword, footnote 52.

EIGHTEEN
ONE MORE COVER-UP

In early 1973 the Department of Health, Education and Welfare estimated the number of U.S. heroin addicts at 600,000. By the end of that year, Dr. Robert Egebjerg, director of the Alcohol, Drug Abuse and Health Administration, placed the number at 300,000. And in June 1974 DEA international operations chief John T. Cusack, testifying before the House Committee on International Narcotics Control, said that the addict population was down to 200,000.[1]

This giant cover-up hid the fact that Nixon's heroin war was no more than window-dressing. On 7 October 1974, six weeks after Nixon's resignation, the head of the White House Special Action Office on Drug Abuse Prevention, Dr. Robert Dupont, was pressured to release a secret report that the number of addicts had in fact *risen*, reaching even into formerly untouched middle class suburbs.[2]

On 27 April 1976 President Gerald Ford said in a message to Congress: "By mid-1973 many were convinced that we had turned the corner on the drug problem. Unfortunately, while we had won an important victory, we had not won the war on drugs. By 1975 it was clear that drug use was increasing, that the gains of prior years were being lost, that in human terms narcotics had became a national tragedy. Today, drug abuse constitutes a clear and present danger to the health and the future of our Nation."

In February 1977 the House Select Committee on Narcotics Abuse and Control reported that the addict population totalled some 800,000. And in 1978 New York City's special narcotics prosecutor, Sterling Johnson, spoke of a heroin epidemic worse than that of the late sixties and early seventies.[3] But the cover-up hadn't stopped in 1974.

From 1975 until the end of 1978 the DEA consistently maintained that between 80 and 90 percent of the heroin consumed in the U.S. was Mexican. However, the claim doesn't stand up against the following facts: 1) 80 percent of the world's heroin – exactly the figure exported from Marseilles until 1972 – was, at least until late 1976, produced from opium harvested in the Golden Triangle and distributed via Bangkok, Singapore, and Hong Kong;[4] 2) the number of arrests of couriers en route from Southeast Asia increased steadily after 1973;[5] 3) reports from New York and other big cities testified to the arrival of large shipments of white heroin from Southeast Asia; 4) the market's supply of heroin did not dwindle despite aerial destruction of an estimated 60 percent of Mexico's poppy fields in early 1976;[6] 5) an effective tidal wave of Golden Triangle heroin began flooding Europe in 1973, while many couriers en route to the U.S. and Canada were nabbed by European police; 6) the DEA was aware of Santo Trafficante's dealings in Southeast Asia, as well as the later Mafia summit in Palermo where large sums of money were set aside for investment in the Golden Triangle; 7) it was easy to verify the narcotics flow from Mexico, since the border was subject to close surveillance, but to conclude that most of the heroin on the U.S. market originated in Mexico was a stretch of logic.

Even the DEA had to admit the tenuousness of its claims. On 24 February 1976, the DEA's John Cusack admitted that his agency's estimate that only 8 percent of U.S. heroin came from Southeast Asia was surprising, considering the region's prolific opium production. He added:

"We are also concerned about our detection during 1975 of substantial quantities of white no. 4 heroin moving directly from Bangkok to the United States. In December, for example, forty-six kilograms of heroin were seized in Bangkok, concealed in the household effects shipment of a returning U.S. serviceman. Follow-up investigation in the development of an extensive conspiracy prosecution has identified twelve additional shipments entering the United States since 1974."

Twelve such shipments meant 552 kilos, or more than the entire 470 kilos confiscated in the U.S. in 1975 – and from only one of many Southeast Asian smuggling networks. Cusack went even further: "It appears almost certain that the bulk of the white heroin found during 1975 in the inner-city areas of our eastern cities has been Asian no. 4 smuggled from Bangkok."[7]

Why then did the DEA continue to overstate Mexico's role and minimize Southeast Asia – even after the publication, in 1972, of Alfred McCoy's *The Politics of Heroin in Southeast Asia*? Perhaps to justify the great expenditure in support of right wing military and police forces in Latin America. (The later boom in Colombian cocaine would also provide justification.) Southeast Asia was downplayed so as not to jeopardize relations with America's loyal, if corrupt, allies – most of all Thailand, Taiwan, and the latter's overseas agents. They were allowed to profit from opium and heroin in relative peace.

Another reason: the DEA could not expose the Southeast Asia connection without compromising the CIA. A secret 1977 House Government Operations subcommittee report accused the CIA of helping an Asian opium ring smuggle drugs into the United States and then lying about it to Congress. Puttaporn Khramkhruan, a Thai national, was arrested in 1973 for smuggling fifty-nine pounds of pure opium into the U.S. via JFK airport. Citing national security interests, the agency had the case squelched, and Khramkhruan was sent back home. However, the House subcommittee eventually established that he was a CIA operative in Thailand.[8] In fact, he was on the payroll of a CIA proprietary using the Agency for International Development (AID) as a cover for training the corrupt Thai border police.[9] Furthermore, Khramkhruan told a DEA investigator that he had been an officer in the KMT army and guarded opium mule caravans. His CIA contact was the U.S. consul in Chiang Mai, Thailand.[10] In its report, the House Committee stated: "It was ironic that the CIA should be given the responsibility of narcotics intelligence, particularly since they are supporting the prime movers."[11]

In March 1977 the DEA began to speak of "major maneuvers in the international Asian narcotics market for a share of the U.S. drug scene" and of a "coalition between the U.S. Mafia, the Corsicans and the Chiu Chao Chinese Triad."[12] The coalition had, in reality, existed at least since 1970 and perhaps as early as Trafficante's 1968 journey to the East and it had functioned effectively, shipping large amounts of heroin to the U.S., since 1972-73. The difference was that the Corsican arm of the coalition, their own umbrella oganization having been smashed, was now essentially reduced to some 100 men working with the U.S. Mafia and the Chinese, most of them as chemists in Thailand's mobile heroin labs.[13]

Who has controlled the Golden Triangle opium traffic and heroin production since the establishment of the Mafia-Chinese coalition – besides the CIA, that is? The answer is the Kuomintang (KMT)

Chinese and overseas Chiu Chao syndicate – men such as Chang Chi-fu, Lo Hsing-han, Tsai Chien Cheng and older, more familiar figures like General Li Mi.[14] Still head of what's left of the KMT forces, General Li resides in luxury outside Chiang Mai and received official visits there from the United States as recently as late 1976.[15]

In 1976-77 a minor war was about to erupt over the control of the region's opium traffic and mobile refineries. Potential combatants were Chu Chi-fu's United Shan Army (of rebels against the Burmese regime) and KMT forces under General Li. However, the opposing leaders were brought together by a senior Thai officer and an agreement was reached on the marketing of drugs and supply of arms to fight Communist forces in Burma's Shan states.[16] Again we see the connection between narcotics and anti-Communist paramilitary operations – albeit Chu Chi-fu later pulled out of the agreement, was arrested in Thailand, and eventually extradited to Burma.

The DEA's Golden Triangle unit, SNO, made many whole and half-hearted attempts to eradicate the narcotics plague. All failed. Production has been great, the world's heroin market having multiplied in the seventies. SNO won't say outright that the CIA is undermining them, nor that politics underlies their constant failures. A SNO agent, nevertheless, came close to doing so in this 1976 statement to Alfred McCoy:

"If they were selling shares in Golden Triangle Heroin, Inc. in five, ten and twenty-year bonds, I would put my money on a twenty-year bond. The only thing that would end the whole Golden Triangle business would be a communist takeover in Thailand. If that happened, I'd sell my stock."[17]

Southeast Asia was initially the sole supplier to the rapidly growing European market. Until 1972 heroin abuse was essentially an American problem. But since the heroin shift from Marseilles to Southeast Asia, the European habit has rapidly worsened. In 1972 ten kilos of Golden Triangle "brown sugar" were confiscated in Europe. By 1975 the figure was up to 227 kilos. The country hardest hit has been West Germany, where the large U.S. troop concentration serves as a magnet for heroin, where it is estimated that some 60-80,000 Germans use hard drugs, and where there were over 500 hard drug-related deaths in 1979.

In the summer of 1977, we might note, the administration of Jimmy Carter rejected a proposal by a consortium of rebel army leaders in northern Burma that the U.S. spend $36 million over a six-year period to purchase and destroy the Southeast Asia opium crop.[18]

Among the official explanations was the alleged policy of the United States to deal only with recognized local governments – a policy which in its time had found a number of exceptions, like the overseas Kuomintang Chinese.[19]

Notes

1. I. Frank and G. Richardson: "Epidemic," *Penthouse*, September 1977.

2. *Ibid*. In light of recent years' revelations of CIA mind control experimentation with LSD, it's worth noting the enormous spread of the hallucinogen in 1971-72. Behind it was the cover organization, Brotherhood of Love, whose backers, like Gulf Oil heir William Mellon Hitchcock, exploited and manipulated self-styled LSD prophets like Timothy Leary. The Brotherhood was directly connected to the Robert Vesco-controlled Fiduciary Trust Company of the Bahamas. LSD proceeds were laundered through the usual Syndicate banks in Geneva. See *Der Spiegel*, No. 39, 1974.

3. B. Herbert: "The Fleetwood Kids," *Penthouse*, August 1978.

4. A. McCoy: "The New Politics of Heroin in Southeast Asia," *Oui*, December 1976.

5. F. Robertson: *Triangle of Death* (Routledge and Keagan Paul, 1977).

6. *Politiken*, 27 March 1976.

7. *Drug Enforcement*, Spring 1976.

8. J. Anderson and L. Whitten, *Boston Globe*, 3 October 1977.

9. J. Hougan: *Spooks* (William Morrow, 1978).

10. J. Burgess: "The Thailand Connection," *Counterspy, Vol. 2*, No. 4, 1976.

11. Anderson and Whitten, *op. cit.*

12. *San Francisco Examiner*, 9 December 1977; Robertson, *op. cit.*

13. Robertson, *op. cit.*

14. Lo Hsing-han and his supporters at one time aided the Burmese government in its fight against Communist insurgents in northwest Burma. However, when the government asked him to disband his organization in 1973, Lo Hsing-han refused and signed a pact with the rebels. The Burmese army eventually pushed him and his army into Thailand where he was arrested and extradited back to Burma. In the fall of 1977 he lost his final appeal to Burma's highest court to quash a death penalty for treason. (*New York Times*, 7 November 1977).

15. McCoy, *op. cit.*

16. *Far Eastern Economic Review*, 15 April 1977.

17. McCoy, *op. cit.*

18. *New York Times*, 13 July 1977.

19. According to *High Times* magazine (April 1980), the Shan States rebels have long been subsidized by Taiwan intelligence. Moreover, the article goes on, intelligence sources in Burma have suggested that the DEA, in an about-face attempt to weld together a local force against *right* wing opium armies, has approached Burmese Communist guerillas – who, having been abandoned by the current, less revolution-minded Peking regime, had themselves taken steps toward moving in on the opium trade.

NINETEEN
THE MEXICAN CONNECTION

The exaggeration of Mexico's and the downplaying of Southeast Asia's roles as suppliers of heroin to the United States does not mean that Mexico was unimportant. But the DEA and the U.S. press compound the distortion by constantly asserting that the production and smuggling of heroin in Mexico is strictly a Mexican business. No U.S. Mafia is supposedly involved, other than customers on the other side of the border. Heroin shipments are allegedly controlled by seven large Mexican families: the Herreras, the Maciaces, the Romeros, the Favelas, the Sicilia-Falcons, the Valenzuelas, and the Aviles-Quinteros. [1] Let's take a look at one of them.

Alberto Sicilia-Falcon, leader of the Sicilia-Falcons, is not a Mexican at all; he was born in Matanzas, Cuba. He and his family left the island immediately after Castro's takeover to become part of Miami's Cuban exile milieu. After the Bay of Pigs invasion he was trained by the CIA at Fort Jackson for Operation 40. [2] From there his trail is faint for several years. However, according to Mexican police, he was in Chile helping the CIA to undermine the government of Salvadore Allende.

In mid-1973 he turned up in Mexico, where in record time he established a gigantic heroin and marijuana ring. According to DEA director Peter Bensinger, in 1975 the ring numbered more than 1600, including film stars and international businessmen. Sicilia-Falcon himself resided in villas in Tijuana and San Diego. Heroin was transported to San Diego from a warehouse in Culiacan, marijuana from a processing plant in Mexicali to a U.S. distribution center in Coronado Kays.

In late 1973 one of Sicilia-Falcon's truckers was stopped on his way back to Mexico. The truck was loaded with arms bound for Nicaragua. According to a later report of the Bureau of Alcohol, Tobacco and Firearms, one illegal weapons dealer in Brownsville, Texas alone supplied Sicilia-Falcon with 12 million rounds of ammunition in 1974.

The guns-for-drugs traffic proceeded unhindered until early 1975, when the government of then President Luis Echeverria discovered that Sicilia-Falcon's weapons shipments went to groups in Mexico. "External forces are attempting to destabilize our country," said Echeverria in a 1975 speech, in obvious reference to his neighbor to the north.

Then the Mexicans began an intense surveillance of Sicilia-Falcon, who, they learned, often met and conversed by telephone with a mystery man in Guernavaca, some ninety kilometers south of Mexico City. When a lemonade bottle bearing the man's fingerprints was sent to the FBI, the bureau informed Mexican authorities that the man was Sam Giancana, the Chicago Mafia capo, heroin trafficker, and CIA collaborator. The Mexicans agreed to a French extradition request for Giancana, but when his Paris-bound plane stopped over in Houston, Giancana was whisked away by U.S. agents. Soon thereafter he was found murdered in his Chicago mansion. Mexican interior ministry officials claimed the CIA had done all it could to prevent the mobster's extradition.

On 2 July 1975 Sicilia-Falcon was arrested. Under rough interrogation he claimed to be an agent of the CIA, and that his drug ring had been set up on orders from and with the support of the agency. Part of his profits were to go towards the purchase of weapons and ammunition for distribution throughout Central America for the destabilization of "undesirable" governments. If true, U.S. heroin addicts were again footing the bill for clandestine paramilitary operations and anti-Communist terror campaigns. And Sicilia-Falcon and his Syndicate associates were not short of funds. In his possession police found two Swiss bank books to the tune of $260 million.

Still, the strange testimony of Alberto Sicilia-Falcon did not end with his confession. His family's heroin and arms shipments continued and, on 26 April 1976, he and three of his lieutenants escaped from Lecumberri prison through an electrically lit, 100-yard long tunnel dug from outside. They were recaptured three days later, at which time Sicilia-Falcon, fearing for his life at the hands of the CIA, requested transfer to another prison and additional security.[3]

Echeverria and Sicilia-Falcon each were right about the destabilization program. FBI documents released later disclosed that between 1970 and 1976 the FBI served as a secret link between the U.S. embassy in Mexico City and the U.S. Border Patrol in California and Texas, "in order to help destabilize" the government of President Echeverria. J. Edgar Hoover had believed that Echeverria had surrounded himself with "old Communists and Communist Party sympathizers."[4] A memo from Hoover to the U.S. legal attaché praises "the detonation of strategic and effective bombs in Mexico City" and "the wave of night machine-gunnings to divide subversive leaders."[5]

Besides Echeverria's progressive attitude, another reason for U.S. hostility towards his government was the Mexican president's refusal to approve World Bank and International Monetary Fund plans for the exploitation of Mexico's newly discovered oil reserves. The first order of business of his successor Jose Lopez Portillo in 1976 was approval of the same plans. And the newspaper *El Sol de Mexico* wrote shortly after the latter's inauguration that year: "The new government is not interested in publicity regarding the Sicilia-Falcon case. It will quietly extradite him to the U.S. as soon as the new extradition agreement between the two countries comes into effect."

In the Sicilia-Falcon case the DEA and CIA struggled bitterly against one another. It was symptomatic of a split within the DEA's own ranks, a split rooted in the effective control of its narcotics intelligence division by transplanted agents of the CIA.

Since the DEA's emergence many of its agents have resigned in disgust with its *modus operandi*. Long-standing conflicts between the CIA and BNDD and between the BNDD and Customs did not evaporate when all the narcotics agents were pooled in the DEA. Moreover, the CIA seems still to be guided by political interests incompatible with drug enforcement.

A 1975 Narcotics Control Action Plan for Mexico, drafted by the DEA, CIA and State Department, opened the way for new appropriations for fighting narcotics in Mexico through INC. Thirty helicopters as well as other aircraft and computer terminals were brought in, and extensive training programs were initiated. The notorious Operation Condor began in January 1976 with an army of DEA-trained Mexican narcotics agents and their U.S. supervisors, mobilized to fight the drug traffic in the countryside. Reports of the operation reveal that U.S. taxpayers' money has in fact been used for political extermination; that DEA helicopters are used by private landowners to attack peasant revolutionaries with rockets, small-arms fire and napalm;[6] that large groups of farmers and independent narcotics dealers have been murdered or tortured while the major narcotics families have been protected.[7]

House subcommittee investigators went to Mexico in 1975 to determine how organized internal corruption and payoff rings within the DEA had made possible the monopoly of Mexican heroin by a few powerful crime families. According to writer Ron Rosenbaum: "Some critics of DEA go even further than the subcommittee investigators and charge the protection of heroin profiteers is not caused by internal corruption but is, in fact, the true function of the agency under the present narcotics laws."[8]

DEA-supervised killing and torture had not stopped as of 1978, when the Mexican Bar Association documented eighteen forms of torture applied by Mexican narcotics agents. Prisoners and Mexican agents alike affirmed that DEA agents not only knew of the torture, but at times were also present at the interrogations.[9]

Notes

1. D. Rosen: "The Mexican Connection," *Penthouse*, February 1977.
2. "Die gefahrlichen Geschafte des Alberto Sicilia," *Der Spiegel*, No. 20, 1977. Much of the following story comes from this account.
3. *Ibid.*
4. *High Times*, August 1978.
5. *Ibid.*
6. *Ibid.*
7. C. Pyes: "Legal Murders," *Village Voice*, 4 June 1979.
8. R. Rosenbaum: "The Decline and Fall of Nixon's Drug Czar," *New Times*, 5 September 1975.
9. Pyes, *op. cit.*

TWENTY
GUNS FOR DRUGS

In August 1976 Lucien Conein's chum Mitch WerBell III (whose B.R. Fox Company had shared a Washington office with Conein's DEA Special Operations Group) was brought before a Miami federal court on charges of conspiracy to smuggle 50,000 pounds of marijuana a month from Colombia to the United States. He and several co-conspirators had allegedly hatched the plot in the summer of 1975, just when Alberto Sicilia-Falcon was arrested in Mexico. Multi-ton marijuana loads were to have been flown from Colombia to an isolated ranch in the Florida Everglades near the cowtown of Okeechobee.[1]

The star prosecution witness was one of WerBell's close associates, the convicted cocaine and marijuana smuggler Kenneth Gordon Burnstine. However, weeks before his scheduled court appearance he died in the mysterious crash of his P-51 Mustang at an air show. Most of the vital tape recordings and films of meetings between Burnstine, WerBell, and other defendants were no longer producible in court.

WerBell's defense was that his role in the plot had been as an undercover agent for Conein. Both Conein and Egil Krogh were to have been witnesses on his behalf. But Krogh testified that he didn't know WerBell had worked for the DEA's Special Operations Branch, and Conein wasn't called at all. Another defense witness was the soldier of fortune Gerry Hemming, whose private army of Cuban exiles and Americans, the International Penetration Force, appears, from Hemming's description of its missions, to have played an active role in Operation 40. During the trial, Hemming would stay late into the night in WerBell's hotel room.[2]

WerBell was found innocent and released, just like the Thai opium smuggler/CIA agent Puttaporn Khramkhruan before him in 1973. He went home to Georgia to pursue his weapons business and law enforcement training camp. According to writer Hank Messick, in 1978 he was involved in far Right politics with the likes of Major General John K. Singlaub (who had been relieved of his command in Korea after outspoken criticism of President Carter) and members of the American Security Council[3] – the key U.S. link to the far Right's international umbrella organization, the World Anti-Communist League (WACL). As reported recently in the *New York Times*, the beneficiaries of his antiterrorist training have included members of the far Right, anti-Semitic U.S. Labor Party.[4]

WerBell owns eight companies, most of them dealing in firearms used by law enforcement and intelligence units. One of the firms, Studies in the Operational Negation of Insurgents and Counter-Subversion (SIONICS), specializes in the production of M10 and M11 silenced machine pistols. The latter two weapons, designed by Gordon Ingram and WerBell, are about the ultimate weapons for terror and extermination. Their sales agent was WerBell's Military Armament Corporation.[5]

Together with the anti-Castro Cuban arms dealers Anselmo Alliegro and the mercenary Gerry Hemming, WerBell founded the Parabellum Corporation in 1971 in Miami.[6] Parabellum was licensed to sell arms in Latin America. It was also the firm from which Watergate burglar Frank Sturgis planned to obtain weapons for Cuban exiles who were going to (but eventually did not) disrupt the 1972 Miami conventions.[7]

In 1974 WerBell – according to a motion filed by his own lawyer when WerBell, his son and his company Defense Services, Inc. were charged with illicit weapons sales – was involved in a "conspiracy among the CIA, Robert Vesco, and various corporations to finance clandestine guerilla activities in Latin America."[8] Vesco wanted to purchase WerBell's stock of 2000 silenced M10 machine pistols. When WerBell failed to secure an export license, he devised a plan to smuggle the weapons to Vesco. The two later negotiated the construction of a factory in Costa Rica which would be licensed to fabricate the pistols.[9]

Intriguingly, in that same period someone was negotiating with a U.S. firm for rights to fabricate, in Mexico, fully automatic weapons for clandestine guerilla actions in Latin America. That someone was Mexico's Cuban exile heroin czar, Alberto Sicilia-Falcon,[10] and among the weapons he was inspecting was the Ingram M10, 9 mm Parabellum.[11]

Although the M10 and M11 could be acquired legally only with the special permission of U.S. officials, large numbers of silenced M10s turned up in the hands of European fascist terrorists in 1976-77. When Pierluigi Concutelli, a leader of the Italian terrorist group Ordine Nuovo, was arrested in Rome in February 1977, police found in his apartment the silenced M10 which he had used to murder the Rome magistrate Vittorio Occorsio.[12] Occorsio had been shot down on the streets of Rome in July 1976 after announcing he would expose the close collaboration between Fascist terror groups and the Mafia.[13]

However, it was among *Spanish* terrorists in particular that WerBell's machine pistols appeared in quantity.[14] Most notably, a sizable consignment of M10s, sent to Spain under license from U.S. authorities, had been purchased by Spanish intelligence agency DGS,[15] which has allegedly coordinated the actions of Fascist terrorists.[16]

The fugitive IOS billionaire Vesco employed a large contingent of Cuban exiles in his Costa Rica sanctuary.[17] Moreover, his weapons negotiations coincided with the efforts of the fanatic anti-Castro Cuban leader Orlando Bosch to assemble Cuban exile groups into an army of terror, CORU, that would later carry out assassinations and other dirty work for several Latin American regimes. During Bosch's 1974-75 drive, a wave of murder struck Miami's Cuban exile haven. Most victims had been opposed to Bosch. With the obstacles to his plan removed, CORU was established in June 1976.[18]

While Vesco and WerBell were hatching their weapons deal Bosch's base of operation just happened to be Vesco's kingdom of Costa Rica – and Mafia heroin boss Santo Trafficante, Jr. was also reportedly there between January 1974 and the summer of 1975. Journalist Jim Hougan speculates in his book *Spooks* that the three might have joined forces in a CIA conspiracy to escalate anti-Communist terror in Latin America.[19]

In 1973 some of the details began to surface in a series of scandals linking these individuals. DEA undercover agent Frank Peroff charged Vesco with financing extensive heroin smuggling. For his initiative Peroff was fired summarily and his life was threatened. Before the Senate Investigations Subcommittee could probe deeply the case was squelched through the intervention of the White House. The Oval Office had already helped Vesco – a friend of the Nixon family – in his run-in with the Securities and Exchange Commission, which had sought his prosecution for the trail of swindle he had left in the world of international finance. Midway through the subcommittee investigation of the heroin charges, the DEA announced the disappearance of its Vesco file.[20]

One year later, as the subcommittee investigated WerBell's weapons deal with Vesco, it learned that Vesco had once employed government narcotics agents. In 1972 two bugging specialists from the BNDD flew from Los Angeles to New Jersey to sweep Vesco's home and office of surveillance devices. According to the subcommittee, the sweeping tour had been arranged by an admitted friend of Vesco's who was also involved in supplying the fugitive with 2000 machine guns and helping him estalish a factory for the weapons in Costa Rica.[21] Guess who.

That was not the last heard of Robert Vesco in connection with drugs. In the summer of 1977 police uncovered the smuggling of large quantities of heroin and cocaine to Rhode Island. In one of the involved ships they discovered a ledger in which it was written: "to Vesco/6 million/he picked up w. shrimper (Lansky)/'Courier' beat up."[22]

Several things point to Vesco involvement in the long-standing partnership of the CIA, the Lansky/Trafficante syndicate and the Cuban exiles, in a drugs-for-guns-for-terror deal to step up armed suppression and anti-communism in Latin America. Journalist Hougan ventures that the conspirators might have used such go-betweens and couriers as the beautiful Patricia Richardson Martinson. According to her ex-husband, the former army intelligence agent William Spector, Ms. Martinson had very close relationships with almost everyone of importance in the drug business: Yussef Beidas, the Lebanese founder and managing director of INTRA Bank, known as one of the major financiers of the heroin traffic; Paul Louis Weiller, a French financier similarly alleged to be behind the narcotics trade; Eduardo Baroudi, a big-time heroin and gun smuggler suspected of having arranged Beidas' mysterious death in Switzerland; Christian "Beau Serge" David; Conrad Bouchard, a top heroin trafficker heavily involved in Frank Peroff's Vesco heroin allegations; and Marcel Boucan, the skipper of the *Caprice du Temps*, which was seized in 1972 with 425 kilos of pure heroin.[23]

Yet another likely intermediary among the apparent conspirators is the CIA contract agent/arms dealer/art dealer Fernand Legros. In 1971 the CIA helped get Vesco released from Saint-Antoine prison in Geneva, where he had been arrested in the Bernard Cornfeld/Investors Overseas Service case. Legros was in that same prison and spoke with Vesco. In January 1973 the two were reunited in Nassau.[24]

Legros was seen in the company of Beidas in Geneva and Rio de Janeiro. His closest friend was the convicted heroin trafficker André Labay, a close associate of Haiti's Duvalier dynasty. In Geneva Legros also met frequently with Evelyne Hirsch, the wife of the imprisoned bankroller André Hirsch, whose South American heroin contact had been Christian David. Just as the U.S. put the screws on the Paraguayan government for the extradition of Auguste Ricord, Legros was in Paraguay to close out a weapons deal with President Stroessner. Later, when Legros was placed in protective confinement in Brazil, newspapers speculated on his involvement in the David Mob's narcotics deals.

Recent years' investigations into the CIA/organized crime connection have resulted in an epidemic of sudden deaths. In the CIA/DEA/Vesco/Syndicate scheme alone one can mention Kenny Burnstine; WerBell associate Colonel Robert F. Bayard, who was shot down in an Atlanta parking lot in July 1975;[25] another WerBell associate and codefendant in his marijuana case, John Nardi, who was shot in Cleveland;[26] and Vesco's security chief Bobby Hall, who was shot to death in his Los Angeles home in July 1976.

After the Senate Investigations Subcommittee's attempted probe into the Vesco heroin case was sabotaged from the highest quarters, committee chairman Henry Jackson asked: "Did the U.S. government wish to keep Vesco out of this country for some reason? Did he have some special information which he could supply to explain, in part, the national nightmare we have just lived through?" One Senate investigator offered an answer: "More than any single person, Vesco has information which, if he talked, would make Watergate look like a picnic."[27]

Notes

1. T. Dunkin: "The Great Pot Plot," *Soldier of Fortune, Vol. 2*, No. 1, 1977.

2. *Ibid.* According to an interview with Hemming published in the April 1976 issue of *Argosy* magazine, Hemming settled in Florida after contacting the CIA to tell the agency all he knew about Castro's operations. There he founded Interpen, which specialized in training anti-Castro Cuban exiles in special camps in Florida for long-range guerilla warfare against the Castro regime.

Thus began a long and friendly advisory relationship not only with the CIA, but with the Mob, the Hughes empire and other wealthy and influential Americans as well. About the financing of Interpen, Hemming said, "There were dribs and drabs from people connected with organized crime, some from the right wing, and even from some quite liberal sources." Hemming also said: "In 1961, some *Mob people* wanted my group to do a couple of jobs in Canada" – emphasis added – (against a ship with machinery for Cuba)... "John Roselli I knew – but I didn't know who he was"... and about CIA/Cuban terror in Latin America: "All this was a kind of Operation Phoenix for Latin America. There's a guy I know in Miami who worked on this more than once. Evidently he's now had a falling out with some Cubans involved in narcotics. He's a close friend of Bebe Rebozo, and Rebozo's interested in protecting him." Interpen reportedly disbanded in 1964.

3. H. Messick: *Of Grass and Snow* (Prentice-Hall, 1979).

4. *New York Times*, 7 October 1979. According to the magazine *Soldier of Fortune* (January 1980), WerBell established Cobray International, Inc., an antiterrorist school primarily for business executives, in Georgia in 1979. Its acting president, Col. Barney Cochran (USAF retired), served as "deputy commander for the Joint Unconventional Warfare Task Force EUROPE" in 1970-74, and has also been chief of the Unconventional Warfare Branch and special assistant for counterinsurgency and special activities organization of the Joint Chiefs of Staff. In the latter post he was responsible for development of "hardware" for Global Special Operations and unconventional warfare. The school's chief marksmanship instructor, Bert Waldron, holds the record for sniper killings in Vietnam – 113.

5. J. Hougan: *Spooks* (William Morrow, 1978).

6. *Ibid.*; see also Gerry Hemming's interview in *Argosy*, April 1976.

7. Argosy, *op. cit.*

8. Documents of the U.S. District Court, Northern District of Georgia, Atlanta Division, in criminal case no. CR 74-471 A (cited in Hougan, *op. cit.*).

9. Hougan, *op. cit.*

10. "Die gefahrlichen Geschafte des Alberto Sicilia," *Der Spiegel*, No. 20, 1977.

11. U.S. Congress, Senate, Committee on Government Operations, *Illicit Traffic in Weapons and Drugs Across the United States-Mexican Border, Hearings,* 95th Cong., 1st Session (1977).

12. *Time*, 2 February 1977; F. Laurent: *L'Orchestre Noir* (Stock, 1978).

13. *Time, op. cit.*

14. *Cambio 16*, 20 February 1977.

15. Laurent, *op. cit.*

16. P. Chairoff: *Dossier B...comme Barbouzes* (Alain Moreau, 1975); L. Gonzalez-Mata: *Cygne* (Grasset, 1976).

17. Hougan, *op. cit.*

18. According to the November 1977 issue of the *Dominican Republic Task Force Newsletter* (cited in the January-February 1978 *NACLA Report*), the Bonao, Dominican Republic site of the CORU founding was a club for executives of the Falconbridge Nickel Company, which is controlled by the Keck family of Houston, Texas. There is, however, some confusion about the date,

which the same source indicated was June 1975. *Counterspy, Vol. 3*, No. 2 listed the date as June 1974. The summer 1976 date, however, is that used by Bernard Cassen in *Le Monde Diplomatique* of February 1977, by an anonymous contributor to the *Nation* of 19 March 1977, and by Blake Fleetwood in *New Times* of 13 May 1977. Bosch, incidentally, like Vesco and WerBell, was associated with narcotics, insofar as his daughter and son-in-law were arrested in 1977 for smuggling cocaine.

19. Hougan, *op. cit.* Vesco had his own contact in the Lansky Syndicate – Dino Cellini, with whom he had met secretly at Rome's Fiumicino Airport in 1972.

20. L.H. Whittemore: *Peroff* (Ballantine, 1975).

21. *Ibid.*

22. Messick, *op. cit.*; *Boston Globe*, 30 September 1977.

23. Hougan, *op. cit.*

24. R. Peyrefitte: *La Vie Extraordinaire de Fernand Legros* (Albin Michel, 1976).

25. Dunkin, *op. cit.*

26. Messick, *op. cit.*

27. Whittemore, *op. cit.* Somewhere among Robert Vesco's memorabilia floats the strange affair of the Brotherhood of Love. Through it thousands of potential activists were stoned for years on LSD, and enormous profits from the sales of tablets were reinvested through the Investors Overseas Service-controlled Fiduciary Trust Company (*Der Spiegel*, No. 39, 1974). In the same connection, it is interesting to note that when, in the fall of 1978, Italian police investigated the American Ronald Stark's close involvement with Italian terrorists, they discovered he had been heavily involved in the Brotherhood of Love until 1971, and had run one of its LSD labs in California. In his terrorist period Stark was closely in touch with the U.S. embassy in London, which had opened a letter to him with "Dear Ron" (*Panorama*, 31 October 1978).

TWENTY-ONE
THE COUP

This chapter contains my personal interpretation of the great heroin coup. Errors are possible on any or all points, inasmuch as the clandestine operations treated in this book transpire in a closed world infested with lies and cover-ups. There will always be loose ends.

The coup itself, which transferred control over the heroin gold mine from one part of the world to another, I regard as a fact of life. Similarly do I regard the involvement of elements of the White House staff. Just how high up it went the reader can decide for him or her self.

Of the many heretofore mentioned details in the coup's planning and execution, I find the following essential:

1) Prior to the coup, Lansky syndicate narcotics boss Santo Trafficante, Jr. had made the necessary arrangements in Southeast Asia and Mexico, and had started a war with the Corsican Mafia.

2) Trafficante's old partner, the CIA, had long since assumed control over Southeast Asia opium smuggling, following Ed Lansdale and Lucien Conein's defeat of the local branch of the Corsican underworld.

3) In 1971, when the coup's execution was seriously under way, Cuban exiles, a group with which Trafficante enjoyed a unique rapport, appeared in the White House's mysterious narcotics operation. They were tied especially to Conein and E. Howard Hunt.

4) Through a succession of bureaucratic reorganizations the White House assumed control over narcotics intelligence and enforcement.

5) U.S. narcotics officials waged an all-out war against the Corsicans' Turkey/Marseilles/U.S.A. network, while warnings of a serious heroin threat from Southeast Asia were all but dismissed.

6) When the Corsican Mafia was neutralized the narcotics enforcement apparatus was suddenly reorganized as the DEA, and shortly thereafter heroin began flowing into the United States from Southeast Asia and Mexico.

7) The CIA-infiltrated DEA grabbed control of Latin America's political repression apparatus, was accused of protecting major narcotics dealers, and was exposed as an accomplice to gun-running financed with the profits from the narcotics traffic.

8) The White House protected Robert Vesco, who appears to be a central figure in the scheme of heroin smuggling and gun-running.

In these eight points we find the will, the power and the motives, not for the once proclaimed victory over the traffickers, but for the dramatic transfer of underworld power that suddenly became a reality in 1973.

The Syndicate was in on it. The White House, the CIA, and special lobby groups were in on it, too, at least indirectly. But we still need ask who in particular and why. We will rely on logic and guesswork, only to identify individual accomplices and their particular contributions and motives.

Let us first consider the Lansky Syndicate, represented by Santo Trafficante and his Cuban narcotics Mafia. In addition to motives he might have shared with the CIA, Trafficante had many other reasons to take part in the heroin coup. First, it meant cheaper heroin deliveries and therefore greater profits. Second, he wanted the Corsicans out because, behind his and the rest of the Syndicate's backs, they had begun setting up their own U.S. distribution network. Finally, Trafficante's drug Mob did not want to see a repeat of BNDD Operation Eagle–U.S. drug enforcement's last effective raid against his network.

What were the possibilities for Trafficante's playing an active role in the coup's execution, apart from preparation of the Southeast Asia –and Mexico–based networks? Without help from the CIA and powerful lobbies, his chances were slim. With their assistance he could infiltrate the narcotics nerve center, the White House. Here we might discuss just who in fact helped him.

If it is true that Trafficante fought the Corsicans so bitterly from 1971 on, how can it be that Marcel Boucan and his shrimpboat were seized in February 1972 with 425 kilos of pure heroin, en route to Trafficante in Florida? There is only one explanation, which Boucan himself offered in court – that Boucan was set up by his American client. How else can the unprecedented seizure by French Customs following a tip from the CIA be explained? If it was a plot to exhaust the stocks of the remaining French heroin rings, and thereby cause panic among the Corsicans, then it worked.

How guilty was Richard Nixon, who presided over the heroin coup? Personally, I believe that, under strong pressure, he was a more or less willing tool, rather than the force behind it all. Pointing to Nixon's guilt are his close association with the Cuba Lobby, with people connected to Lansky and Trafficante, and with Robert Vesco. In addition, his dirty tricks department relied heavily on Cuban exiles. The Cubans would never have supported him with dangerous criminal acts, demonstrations, donations and votes, if he had really been out to eliminate their most profitable business. Nixon would have been ruining the Cuban Mafia, and to an extent the Syndicate as well – and thereby his friends in Florida. He would have been digging his own grave. Thus Nixon tackled the drug problem as he did every political problem – he followed the path of least resistance. And that meant ignoring his criminal allies in Florida and Southeast Asia while he hounded the Corsicans – who had no constituency – to death.

That Nixon might have been involved in the heroin coup for his own personal gain is lent credence by the following quote from Dan Moldea's respected book, *The Hoffa Wars* (Charter Books, 1978): "A former Nixon aide, not privy to the Haig investigation, says that one of his associates in the White House mentioned to him sometime 'during the impeachment summer,' that someone high up, maybe [White House chief of staff, General Alexander] Haig,' was interested in Nixon's possible 'organized crime involvements.' That conversation involved 'a massive payoff' from those in 'Army service club scandals in Vietnam' during 1969 or 1970. The aide says that the service club ripoffs 'involved the Mafia and millions of dollars' and that the main focus of the interest by 'someone high up' in the White House was on whether 'the top Mafia guy' who ran 'all these things in Southeast Asia' had made payoffs to Nixon. The crime figure, he says, was 'the one who was apparently known as the so-called mastermind or architect of the Southeast Asian drug trade . . . who was very powerful and very well known as a mob leader. . . . According to government narcotics experts, the central figure in the Indochina-Golden Triangle narcotics traffic was Santos Trafficante."

In my opinion the central manipulator in the whole narcotics scheme was the CIA, or rather a faction within it. It is erroneous to treat the agency as a monolith. Various lobby groups have their own agents in the company, generating internal power struggles that reflect political polarizations external to the CIA. There are, doubtless, CIA factions wholeheartedly in favor of ending America's policeman and oppressor roles, and in favor of social democratic rather than right wing regimes. Equally certain is the fact that one should take the agency's new, outwardly benign face with a grain of salt. Within the agency there remain powerful groups promoting continued support of "old friends" in Latin America and Southeast Asia. The China/Cuba lobby has traditionally been one of the most influential within the CIA, and there is little reason to believe that the situation has seriously changed. Finally, the agency has laid low of late, as the Carter administration has lobbied for a relaxation of constraints placed upon it by Congress in the wake of the seventies' exposés of CIA horror stories.

In addition to, or rather behind, the CIA's new official policy there is also an unofficial one. It manifests itself in such matters as the manipulation of the DEA to perform what previously had been CIA dirty work, and in the toleration, if not encouragement of a large, apparently independent army of Cuban exile terrorists, available for action in Latin America at the request of the presiding dictators.

The evidence suggests that the forces behind the unofficial policy were able to place many of their loyal CIA agents in the DEA, and in such private intelligence agency covers as Intertel and Wackenhut, where they continue their tasks while letting the agency wash its hands.[1] Intelligence is still gathered by the CIA, but some of the dirtiest operations are now performed by "former" agents.

We cannot, of course, discount the possibility that the unofficial policy is in fact executed by former agents who had either been purged from the agency, or left in protest against its more moderate line. However that implies that a renegade CIA faction now runs an independent secret service, aided by lobby interests –i.e., not Intertel, but an even more powerful "third force."[2] If that is so, I can come up with only one lobby group with the relevant motives as well as the power to back them–the World Anti-Communist League (WACL). WACL can mobilize CIA agents closely associated with the China/Cuba/Chile lobby, especially the large contingent of former agents of the Gehlen/Vlassov organization (the intelligence agency run by Hitler's masterspy Reinhard Gehlen, which became the BND, the West German equivalent of the CIA).[3]

E. Howard Hunt was clearly the China/Cuba/Latin America lobby's man. That he is also tied to WACL is suggested by the fact that William F. Buckley, Hunt's close friend for twenty years and the god-father of his children,[4] was one of WACL's top U.S. supporters.[5] Also connected to the same lobby groups are Lucien Conein and the State Department's former intelligence chief, Ray S. Cline, who continues to be a frequent guest at the Taiwan WACL stronghold.[6]

Hunt and Conein were the vital forces behind the White House's great heroin coup. Hunt secured the Cuban exiles their necessary footing; and he got his friends Bernard Barker and Manuel Artime to set up "hit teams" to kidnap and murder Latin American narcotics traffickers. According to Frank Sturgis, those traffickers included members of Auguste Ricord and Christian David's Grupo Francés. Hunt persuaded Egil Krogh to bring CIA agents into the White House narcotics apparatus. He told Krogh that he knew "key CIA officers who could be temporarily detached from the agency and employed by the new liaison group."[7] It was Hunt who recommended Lucien Conein to head the group. Finally, it was intelligence reports from the CIA and Conein's group which made White House narcotics actions focus almost exclusively on the Corsicans.

Conein's close friend Mitch WerBell III told journalist Jim Hougan he "found it difficult to believe that a lifelong spy of Conein's stature could ever really leave the CIA. Accustomed to the use of other government agencies as CIA covers, WerBell quite naturally held open the possibility that Conein's DEA job was no more than an exercise in 'sheep-dipping' the backgrounds and identities of the Dirty Dozen, all of whom were CIA veterans."[8]

The desire to help its old friends in Southeast Asia and Latin America was not the CIA's only motive for promoting the heroin coup. The Gaullists in France, including their loyal adherents in intelligence agency SDECE, and their dirty tricksters in SAC were, in the de Gaulle era, the CIA's arch enemies as well as rivals for control of the world heroin trade. One can well imagine the CIA joining forces with Georges Pompidou and other pro-U.S. forces in France, in crushing the old Gaullist intelligence network.

In 1973, with the Corsicans finally pushed out of the picture, the White House reorganized the narcotics effort to form the DEA. Almost immediately, heroin began flowing to the U.S. from new sources of supply. Journalist Ron Rosenbaum cites the following statement by a U.S. customs official: "BNDD and Customs are finally getting somewhere, they break up the French Connection, they're getting big conspiracy cases. Suddenly they [the White House] step in and there's this big shake-up, and by the time people get back to work the Mexican Connection is set up, protected and doing big business. What's that say to you?"[9]

He might have added that the Southeast Asian connection was also protected and doing big business.

The emergence of the DEA was the next to last phase of the heroin coup. Hunt and Conein's CIA agents moved into DEA intelligence and operations, Conein locating twelve Latino CIA agents in his Special Operations Group alone. The Dirty Dozen was officially created to combat Cuban and Latin American narcotics smugglers, allegedly following the assassination approach conceived in the darkest corners of the White House.

It must have been a gag. Conein's forces were apparently directed, for the most part, against small-time independents who had competed with the big-time traffickers in on the heroin coup. The biggest Cuban network, Santo Trafficante's, went untouched. Miami's 1974-75 murder wave in Little Havana might even have been connected to the activities of Conein's Cubans. The victims had opposed Orlando Bosch's drive for solidarity in terrorism, a drive which—as suggested by writer Hougan[10]—might well have enjoyed the support of Trafficante and Robert Vesco. Of the latter two, certainly the first and quite possibly the second as well were central figures in the heroin coup.

That brings us to the last, the political phase of the heroin coup, which began with the DEA's 1974 takeover of the CIA's Latin American torture and repression apparatus, and ended with the 1976 creation of CORU, Bosch's terrorist mercenary army. "Ended" is, however, the incorrect word, since the brutalities financed by the heroin coup continue. The DEA—or that part of it penetrated by the CIA—protects the major narcotics dealers. The latter, in turn, support—financially and through gun-running—anti-Communist paramilitary groups which work hand in hand with Latin American police and military forces, whose death squads and torturers are supervised by agents of the DEA.

The infiltration of the DEA, and the variety of political assignments for its agents, have caused such violent splits within the bureau that one can speak of two wings which fight one another. One wing carries out guns-for-drugs-and-protection programs; the other tries desperately to combat the drug traffic carried out or protected by the first! Among the expressions of this bitter internal strife, apparently, are the Sicilia-Falcon and WerBell cases, and the dismissal of DEA director Bartels for suspected corruption.

Recently, the use of drug profits to finance right wing terrorism has been placed in a new perspective by revelations of Cuban exile teamwork with European and Latin American Fascists, and the economic support of WACL for the same anti-Communist groups.[11] And that brings us to the final link in the chain of drugs, intelligence, and fascism.

Notes

1. Wackenhut was founded in Miami in 1954, at the height of the Cold War, McCarthyism, and domestic witch hunts, by George Wackenhut, a former FBI gym instructor. The firm reportedly has archives containing files on everyone investigated by the old House Committee on Un-American Activities (HUAC), and publishes a monthly bulletin, *The Wackenhut Corporation Security Review: Communism and You.* In 1974 it was awarded a $15 million contract to guard the trans-Alaska pipeline.

International Intelligence, Inc. (Intertel) was created in 1970 by former Naval Intelligence, National Security Agency and Justice Department investigator Robert Peloquin. It grew out of the latter's association with James Crosby (a partner in the Mary Carter Paint Company which became Resorts International, and a close friend and business associate of Nixon crony Bebe Rebozo) whose entry into the Bahamas gambling casino scene was facilitated by a U.S. Justice Department probe, led by Peloquin, of Bahama gamblers' links to the Mob. Once Crosby had built his own casino on Paradise Island, Peloquin ran the security firm that policed it. Resorts International later helped Peloquin found Intertel, whose more prominent clients have included Howard Hughes and ITT. Thus was Intertel involved in the Thanksgiving 1970 whisking away of Hughes to the Bahamas, and the 1972 affair involving the Dita Beard memo on ITT's buy-off of a Justice Department antitrust action. Besides industrial security, Intertel's specialties include economic intelligence, data processing, systems engineering, and the behavioral sciences. See G. O'Toole: *The Private Sector* (Norton, 1978).

2. Intertel might indeed be very important in this connection, as the Justice Department's DeFeo report reveals the close relationship between Intertel and the DEA on such matters as Operation Silver Dollar and Operation Croupier. Consider DEA agent Santo Allesandro Bario, who seems to have been in on many of the operations discussed in this book. Intertel employed him on a 1971 security project in Las Vegas. He later infiltrated New Orleans Mafia circles as a BNDD undercover agent. In 1972-73 the BNDD/DEA sent him to France, where he infiltrated the key Corsican Guerini family. In May 1974 Lucien Conein recommended Bario as an undercover agent to help

Intertel on Operation Croupier. Croupiers at the Paradise Island Casino were allegedly involved in narcotics smuggling. In July 1974 Bario, Conein and acting DEA chief inspector Phillip Smith met with Intertel director Robert Peloquin. In August Bario was off on his mission to Nassau. Smith and Bario alike have been under investigation for cases of fraud and misconduct involving Intertel. Bario worked for the DEA in Mexico from 1975 until he was caught in 1978 in a mysterious fraud setup in San Antonio. He went to jail, where he was allegedly poisoned, and was unconscious in a hospital until he died a few months later.

3. Spearheading WACL's Latin America drive is the Confederacion Anti-comunista Latinoamericana (CAL), which is connected to the Federacion Mexicana Anticomunista (FEMACO). Financial support for these organizations is allegedly supplied through Shuen Shigh Kao, a Mexico-based agent of Taiwan intelligence – see P. Chairoff: *Dossier Neo-Nazisme* (Éditions Ramsay, 1978). WACL's tolerant attitude towards heroin smuggling was never more evident than in the case of Chao Sopsaisana, who in 1977 was arrested in Paris with sixty kilos of pure heroin in his valise. Diplomatic immunity got him back to Laos, where he continued in his role as vice president of the National Assembly as if nothing had happened. He remains today the president of the Laotian chapter of WACL – see *Asian Outlook*, January 1979.

4. E.H. Hunt: *Undercover* (Berkeley-Putnam, 1974); T. Szulc: *Compulsive Spy* (Viking, 1974).

5. According to Frederic Laurent in *L'Orchestre Noir* (Stock, 1978), documents of the neo-Fascist terrorist group Aginter Press, recovered by the Portuguese army in 1974, included correspondence between Buckley and Aginter agent Jay Salby; see chapter twenty-three on the terrorists.

6. *Asian Outlook*, June and October 1978.

7. E.J. Epstein: *Agency of Fear* (Putnam, 1977).

8. J. Hougan: *Spooks* (William Morrow, 1978).

9. R. Rosenbaum: "The Decline and Fall of Nixon's Drug Czar," *New Times*, 5 September 1975.

10. Hougan, *op. cit.*

11. *ABC*, 27 January 1977; *Latin America*, 27 August 1976; *Cuadernos para el Dialogo*, 19 February 1977; *Triunfo*, 12 February 1977; Chairoff, *op. cit.*; Carlos Barbeiro Filho, the Brazilian head of the South American branch of the WACL, runs an Asunción, Paraguay finance company, Financiera Urundey, which launders dirty money from Saudi Arabia and South Korea through Paraguay's wide open foreign exchange market. Barbeiro, who has been linked to the Argentine and Brazilian Anticommunist Alliances, the terrorist AAA and AAB, reportedly arranges training courses in Taiwan for the Paraguayan police (see *The Leveller*, October 1979).

PART III
THE MIAMI CONSPIRACY

TWENTY-TWO
MY FRIEND PATRICE

In the spring of 1976 I went to France to see people who might tell me something about Christian David, the Ben Barka affair, or the great heroin coup, which still had not fully crystallized for me. Among those I met with, three people filled in holes, and at least one opened up exciting new perspectives.

The first was Patrice Chairoff, the author of *Dossier B . . . comme Barbouzes*, whose disclosures of SAC activities had caused a sensation. A former SAC and later narcotics agent, Chairoff appeared to have come over to the socialist camp, as he was now employed as a journalist for the left wing French newspaper, *Liberation*. Just the man to see. We met for the first time on Monday, April 26.

Highly cooperative, Chairoff told me he knew a good deal about Christian David. Chairoff himself had been in Venezuela when Beau Serge sought to infiltrate Douglas Bravo's guerilla band. He also said that gun-running had been as important a part of David's Latin American operations as drug trafficking. Furthermore, he knew of proof that David had murdered Georges Figon in connection with the Ben Barka affair. David had retained the murder weapon, a 32 caliber Ruby automatic which was found in his arsenal when he was arrested in Brazil. It was now in the custody of the Americans, explained Chairoff, who added: "David is a psychopath, a born killer who goes berserk at the sight of blood. Though he has a certain amount of charm, he should be in an asylum."

Before parting we agreed to meet again that Wednesday. In the meantime he would try to get hold of documents and other additional information. When I mentioned my trying to run down Daniel Guerin, Chairoff amicably suggested that we together see the highly es-

teemed journalist and author of a string of political-philosophical
works.[1] He, too, had been wanting to meet Guerin, and would contact
him for the two of us.

That evening I met Claude, who was a fugitive in France.[2] A former
military officer and OAS terrorist, he had been part of Commando
Delta in Algeria and witnessed the demolition of Barbouze headquarters at Villa Andrea. He had also taken part in a plot to murder
Charles de Gaulle and been sentenced to death after his arrest in 1962.
Several years afterward, he was pardoned and released after de
Gaulle's general amnesty for the OAS. When we spoke, Claude was
commuting between Switzerland and Spain, where, like other OAS
figures, he was an agent of the neo-Fascist Paladin group as well as
the Spanish intelligence agency, Direcion General de Seguridad
(DGS), both run by the Nazi war hero/criminal Colonel Otto Skorzeny
until his death in 1975.

During our conversation – overheard by my able assistant on
matters French, Niels Levinsen, Paris correspondent of the Danish
daily, *Jyllands-Posten* – Claude made no secret of having been one of
Chairoff's sources for *Dossier B*. Claude had been a DGS agent in 1972
when, as described earlier, SAC leader Charles Lascorz fled to Spain
and was captured by Spanish intelligence.[3] Lascorz had with him SAC
archives, which DGS agents photographed before extraditing him to
France.

"At the moment," said Claude, "I am working for people quite
seriously on the rise again in French politics." Though he would not go
any further, he must have been referring to an emergent, powerful
coalition centered around former OAS leaders, who are farther to the
right than their longtime arch enemies, the Gaullists. This very
rivalry could explain recent years' leakage of material embarrassing
to SAC, as well as a chain of incidents which have rocked France.

Claude's description of Christian David clashed with Chairoff's:
"That he murdered 54 people in Algeria is an exaggeration. David was
neither better nor worse than the other barbouzes... He could
appear to be no more dangerous than a common criminal, but that is
how he has fooled people through the years. He is cool, calculating and
intelligent, has no politics and always puts money first. But he was
also true to his gangster friends, who revered him."

Claude knew more about Beau Serge than he was willing to let on,
as we discovered after a few more drinks. He then told us he would
soon be off on a mission having much to do with Christian David.
Claude's benefactor was interested in knowing just who was regularly

sending David funds, and so he was going to America to find out.

On Wednesday morning, Patrice Chairoff phoned me to say that Guerin was out of town, but that he himself would be interested in meeting with me at 1:30 PM in a restaurant on Ile Saint-Louis. I was there at the appointed time, but waited in vain for two hours. As I was on my way out, the manager called me to the phone. It was Chairoff, apologizing. He was at an important meeting with one of his contacts, and included in the topics of discussion were my investigation and the possibility of obtaining confidential material. We would meet the next evening at the Drug Store restaurant.

That night I phoned Daniel Guerin despite Chairoff's claim that he was away. Guerin was indeed at home. He had gone nowhere at all, and was already mad at Chairoff for not appearing at a meeting they had arranged for that same afternoon. In fact, the meeting was to have coincided with the one Chairoff had set up with me. The next morning I went to see Guerin. When I arrived he was visibly upset. Following our conversation the previous evening, he had met his U.S. embassy contact, who informed him that Chairoff had spent that entire afternoon in the office of DEA chief Paul Knight. That was the "contact" with whom Chairoff had discussed my investigation.

Guerin also said that his friend had told him not to believe "the garbage about David's having the Figon murder weapon on him when he was captured, and its presently being in the custody of the Americans." In the following hours Guerin supplied me with much additional information and allowed me to read a letter he had received from David in prison.

That evening I was at the Drug Store as agreed, and this time Chairoff appeared. He was a changed man. The helpfulness had gone and it was his turn to pump me. I did not let on that I knew of his whereabouts the previous day. The meeting was short. He said that I would receive the material he had promised if at 5:30 PM the next day, Friday, I came to a restaurant in the Place de la Republique.

Chairoff was not there the next day, and when I phoned his newspaper and publisher on Monday, I was told he had left on Friday for an extended weekend planned days in advance. In fact, Chairoff did not show up at all that week, nor the following one, and his employers were no less irate than I.

Not until weeks after my return to Denmark was the true Chairoff revealed. It was then that the Italian magazine *L'Europeo* and the French *L'Express* ran exposés of his escapades.[4] The "left wing" writer had been a leading force in European neofascism and neonazism. Only as a leftist was he known as Chairoff. His true name was Dominique Calzi. By age fifteen he belonged to the Nazi movement, Jeune Nation. In 1961 he and the British Nazi leader Colin Jordan chartered an international Nazi movement. In 1962 he began publishing the newspaper *Le Viking Provencal*, a mouthpiece for Jean-Claude Monet's National Socialist Party. He joined SAC briefly in 1968, but otherwise operated with figures from the OAS.

Calzi/Chairoff was also known as Yvan Dieter Calzi and Dieter von Freudenreich. In 1971 he was in Greece, thriving under the colonels as Dr. Siegfried Schoenenberg, a narcotics agent for the Americans and special agent for the head of Greek security forces, Colonel Georghis Ioannidis. There he coordinated joint actions of the CIA, Ioannidis' police, and European neo-Fascists, under cover of the World Service "press" bureau, a branch of the right wing terrorist network that included Aginter Press in Lisbon. Like Aginter, World Service had stations in many countries; the main, according to Chairoff, in Miami.[5]

This was the man who, on an afternoon in April 1976, was in the DEA Paris office discussing my interest in Christian David.[6]

Notes

1. The author of *Les Assassins de Ben Barka* (Guy Authier, 1975), Guerin has dedicated his life to unravelling that affair.
2. Though Claude is indeed his first name, he prefers not disclosing his surname.
3. See chapter twelve.
4. *L'Express*, 24 May 1976.
5. *Ibid.*
6. The publication of Chairoff's *Dossier B . . . comme Barbouzes* suited perfectly the CIA's struggle against the Gaullist intelligence network and associated heroin traffickers.

TWENTY-THREE
THE MIAMI CONSPIRACY

Early in 1980 Alan Pringle, head of the DEA's Miami office, told an Associated Press reporter that Miami banks constitute "the Wall Street" of the drug dealers. To the reader of this book that should come as no surprise. Nor should Patrice Chairoff's claim to me that Miami was the main station of the Fascist front organization, World Service. Yet the significance of Miami in the netherworld of international fascism remains one of America's better kept secrets.

In June 1976 Herve de Vathaire, the financial director for Mirage jet manufacturer Marcel Dassault, spent a week in Miami together with soldier of fortune Jean Kay of Spain's neo-Fascist Paladin group.[1] While there they had several meetings with Cuban exiles. Upon their return to France the two disappeared with over $1.5 million in aircraft corporation funds. It was then reported that the money went to support Christian Falangists fighting in Lebanon, but some French observers believe it financed two great French bank robberies.

On the weekend of 17-18 July 1976, twenty men set out on an expedition through the sewers of Nice to the Société Générale Bank. There they stole upwards of $10 million. When the robbery's mastermind, Albert Spaggiari, was arrested that October, he fingered La Catena, cover name for a coalition of Spanish and Italian Fascists, the Paladin group in particular. Most of the take went to finance their operations.

A second sewer heist was executed in August 1976, this time at the Société Générale Paris branch on Ile Saint-Louis. The amount was $5 million.

Immediately after the Nice heist, Spaggiari travelled to the U.S. and contacted the CIA. According to a confidential source, he had also been in Miami shortly *before* the heist. The French *Le Point* and *L'Aurore* reported that the agency was compelled to pass on its information about Spaggiari to French authorities.

In early 1977, Spanish police arrested Jorge Cesarsky of Argentina's Fascist terror organization, the AAA, and Carlos Perez, a Miami-based Cuban exile, in connection with a string of murders of young Spanish leftists. According to the Spanish daily *El Pais*, Perez and a large number of other Cuban exiles were in Spain as part of a newly created Fascist International.[2]

In 1976 OAS and Aginter Press terrorist Jean-Denis Raingeard was in the United States seeking the support of such right wing leaders as Senator Strom Thurmond of South Carolina for an OAS coup in the Azores in the wake of Portugal's left wing military revolution. The coup, if successful, would bring a rightist government and U.S. control over the militarily strategic Atlantic archipelago. According to an FBI investigation of Raingeard, on 19 November 1969 the Bureau had sent Portuguese police a questionnaire on his connection to an OAS front (Aginter Press). The questions concerned a prior Raingeard trip to Miami, during which he had a run-in with the law. When asked about Raingeard's troubles, the State Department's Portugal desk officer in 1975, William Kelly, said: "I would prefer not to address the question of the French Connection."[3]

What are European Fascists doing in Miami before and after major operations? Why are Miami-based Cuban exiles executing contracts on young Spaniards? Why was the main station of the CIA-supported Fascist front World Service in Miami? Why did bank robber Spaggiari contact the CIA in the United States?

Miami is the center of a huge conspiratorial milieu whose personnel wind through the Bay of Pigs, attempts on Castro's life, the JFK murder and the great heroin coup, and which is now reaching out with a vengeance to Latin America and Europe.

To trace the roots of this milieu we must refer to the immediate aftermath of World War II, when the CIA began its close cooperation with Adolf Hitler's espionage chief, Reinhard Gehlen, and the Soviet general, Andrei Vlassov, of Russia's secret anti-Communist spy network. Vlassov's organization was absorbed into Gehlen's, which evolved into a European subsidiary of the CIA. U.S. and German agents mingled in Berlin and West Germany, paving the way for inroads into U.S. intelligence by former Nazis, SS agents, and Russian czarists.

Headquarters of the CIA/Gehlen/Vlassov combine, staffed in the mid-fifties by 4000 full-time agents, were in Pullach, near Munich.[4] There Gehlen sang to the tune of more than one piper, having remained in touch with the old Nazi hierarchy relocated in Latin America, whose coordinator, Otto Skorzeny, was in Spain. Skorzeny had infiltrated the Spanish intelligence agency DGS, and effectively controlled it single-handedly.

With the onset of the Cold War, Gehlen's agents were recruited by the CIA for assignments in the United States, Latin America and Africa. One agent, reportedly, was Frank Bender, allegedly alias Fritz Swend, a key figure in the Bay of Pigs invasion.[5]

U.S. historian Carl Oglesby sees the origin of much of the CIA's later sinister record in the alliances it forged almost immediately upon its birth, with the Gehlen/Vlassov organization and, through Operation Underworld, with the Lansky crime syndicate: "Everything after this [the Gehlen alliance], on top of Operation Underworld, was probably just a consequence of this merger. How can a naive, trusting, democratic republic give its secrets to crime and its innermost ear to the spirit of Central European fascism and expect not to see its Constitution polluted, its traditions abused, and its consciousness of the surrounding world manipulated ultimately out of all realistic shape."[6]

Well put. Moreover, it is ironical that Europe's contribution to U.S. fascism is now returning home and threatening the continent in a conspiracy supported by U.S. economic and clandestine forces. The forces Oglesby speaks of were united during and after the Bay of Pigs affair, and their bedfellows were big businessmen with their own private interests. The merger was toasted in Miami.

The Bay of Pigs invasion itself was not the most important phase in the development. That was CIA Station JM/Wave and its Operation 40, the agency's secret war on Cuba from the summer of 1961 until the end of 1965 – four years during which a truly conspiratorial powerhouse was forged in Miami. Station JM/Wave was unique in the annals of the CIA, as attested to by then Deputy Director of Intelligence Ray S. Cline: "It was a real anomaly. It was run as if it were in a foreign country, yet most of our agents were in the state of Florida. People just overlooked the fact that it was a domestic operation."[7]

With the start of its secret war, the new station became the agency's largest and the command post for its anti-Castro operations worldwide. Its annual budget of $50-100 million financed the activities of 300 permanent employees, most of them case officers who controlled an additional several thousand Cuban exile operatives. Each major CIA station had at least one case officer assigned to Cuban operations who ultimately reported to Miami. In Europe all Cuban matters were routed through the Frankfurt station, which in turn reported to JM/Wave.

JM/Wave covered anything and everything Cuban, wherever in the world it might be. Cuban representatives were shadowed in Japan, and a Cuban exile-led commando unit was sent to Helsinki to sabotage the 1962 International Socialist Youth Conference.[8] As JM/Wave was closing down in 1967, the agency sent another team of saboteurs to France to contaminate a shipment of lubricant bound for Cuba with a bacterial substance developed under its mind-control project, MK-ULTRA. When poured in oil, it would ruin motors and other machines.[9]

I mention these scattered incidents only to elucidate the situation around the October 1965 murder of the exiled Moroccan opposition leader Mehdi Ben Barka in Paris. Ben Barka must have been JM/Wave's number two target after Fidel Castro between the fall of 1963 and the end of 1965. Castro in 1963 had asked Ben Barka to arrange the first Tricontinental Congress, which was to be held in Cuba in January 1966. The conference, aimed at Third World solidarity against U.S. imperialism and support for Castro and Cuba, would signal a major setback for JM/Wave and the CIA's plans for Latin America, where all the agency's major operations in the 1962-66 JM/Wave era were focussed.

In 1963 the agency masterminded a revolution in Honduras, another in the Dominican Republic, and a third in Guatemala. In 1964 it assisted in General Branco's military coup in Brazil. In 1965 the Special Forces joined U.S. Marines in suppressing civil war in the Dominican Republic, and in 1966 the CIA aided and abetted Colonel Ongania's military coup in Argentina.

Cuba was an especially hot number in 1965. Led by JM/Wave personnel, the CIA had planned a new invasion of the island to follow one of its attempts to assassinate Castro. The planners included Howard Hunt and James McCord.[10] Unlike the Bay of Pigs invasion, this time the agency was offering leadership in addition to training and financing. However, one by-product of the 1965 intervention in the Dominican Republic was the aborting of the plan to invade Cuba.

The CIA, station JM/Wave in particular, must have been anxious to know Ben Barka's plans for the Tricontinental Congress, and to sabotage them if possible. And time was running out after Ben Barka's September 1965 visit with Castro. Thus the key to solving the

Ben Barka murder case appears to lie with three men: JM/Wave chief Theodore Shackley, Morocco station chief Robert Wells, and the head of the CIA station in Frankfurt.[11] CIA contract agent Fernand Legros is also known to have associated with Ben Barka in Geneva – the same Legros who frequented Miami, the Bahamas, and other spots in the Caribbean.[12]

When JM/Wave was dismantled, Shackley and his staff left Miami for Laos, leaving behind a highly trained army of 6000 fanatically anti-Communist Cubans allied to organized crime and powerful elements of the U.S. far Right.

In 1966, following the Tricontinental Congress which proceeded without Ben Barka, a counterfront, the World Anti-Communist League (WACL), was chartered in Seoul, South Korea by hardline reactionaries from the world over. That same year Aginter Press, sponsored by WACL and the intelligence agencies of the United States, France, and Portugal, was created in Lisbon as a cover for OAS terrorists and other European Fascists. Led by the Frenchman Yves Guerin-Serac, its aim was the subversion, through espionage, sabotage and murder, of all that the Tricontinental Congress had stood for.[13]

In that same period Cuban exile activist organizations sprouted all over Miami's Little Havana. They spawned, in turn, terrorist subgroups like Alfa 66 and Omega 7, whose more notorious leaders – Guillermo and Ignazio Novo, Orlando Bosch, and Nasario Sergen – had all been trained by the CIA. Between 1965 and 1971 they staged sporadic acts of sabotage and assassinations, with Guillermo Novo repeatedly arrested only to be released each time. Cubans, terrorists among them, were also being paid by Santo Trafficante and the Syndicate to help spin their intricate U.S. narcotics web. And they also found the time for dirty tricks on behalf of Richard Nixon and his White House staff.

However, incidents like Operation Eagle of 1970 – when the BNDD rounded up Cuban exile drug traffickers and found many to have been trained by the CIA – had made the Cubans an increasing embarrassment to the agency. As the seventies began the CIA's Cubans had become an angry, confused, and divided lot, who felt betrayed by their former employer. Still, they experienced a comeback midway through 1971, when the powers-that-be, CREEP in the fore, again sought their services. And in 1973, with the military in power in Chile, they found a new employer in the ruthless Chilean secret police, DINA. Other dictators south of the border have since followed suit.

In 1974-75 a reign of terror struck Miami's Cuban community as opponents of Orlando Bosch were liquidated.[14] The campaign continued well into 1976, during which Miami was rocked by over 700 bombings.[15] And that year there was a notable upsurge in Cuban exile activity beyond the territorial U.S.

On April 6 two Cuban fishing boats were attacked and destroyed, and one fisherman was killed. On April 22, a bomb exploded at Cuba's Lisbon embassy, killing two and seriously wounding several others.

In June 1976 in the Dominican Republic town of Bonao, the Cuban Action Movement, Cuban National Liberation Front, Brigade 2506, F-14 and the Cuban Nationalist Movement merged as Bosch's Coordination of United Revolutionary Organizations (CORU).[16]

On July 5 a bomb exploded at the office of Cuba's UN delegation. On July 9 another went off at Kingston airport in Jamaica, in baggage about to be loaded onto a Havana-bound Cuban flight. The next day there was an explosion at the Bridgetown, Barbados office of British West Indian Airways, which also represented Cubana de Aviacion.

On July 17 bombs went off in the Cuban airline office and embassy in Bogotá, Colombia. On July 23 a Cuban technician was killed in Merida, Mexico trying to stop the abduction of the Cuban attaché. On August 9 terrorists kidnapped two diplomats assigned to the Cuban embassy in Buenos Aires. On August 18 a bomb exploded at the Cubana de Aviacion office in Panama.

On September 21 Chile's former Secretary of State, Orlando Letelier, and his coworker Ronni Karpen Moffitt were killed in Washington when a bomb decimated their car. On October 6 yet another explosion gutted a Cuban airliner off Barbados, killing seventy-three. On November 7 one exploded at the Cubana de Aviacion office in Madrid. Finally, on November 9 kidnappers seized an Argentine employee of the Buenos Aires Cuban embassy.

Orlando Bosch's army of anti-Castro Cuban terrorists was responsible for all these acts. When the Cuban airliner went down, Bosch himself was arrested in Venezuala.

But the extremists had not waited until 1976 to take part in international terrorist operations. In 1975 one hundred anti-Castro Cubans joined European Fascists in the Army for the Liberation of Portugal (ELP). From neighboring Spain, the ELP – whose core comprised Aginter Press OAS veterans – attempted to overthrow Portugal's progressive military regime.[17]

The 1975 attempt in Rome on the life of Chilean Christian Democratic Party leader Bernardo Leighton was a joint action of DINA, the youth wing of the Italian Fascist party, MSI, and anti-Castro Cubans.[18] The 1976 murder of Letelier and Moffit, a DINA/CORU job, was planned in Miami. Four of the five Cubans involved in it were CIA veterans of the Bay of Pigs invasion.[19] The Leighton attempt and Letelier murder were each coordinated by the American/Chilean DINA agent, Michael Townley.

The common denominator in CORU, as well as Internacional Fascista—a combine of anti-Communist extremist organizations chartered at an October 1976 meeting in Rome attended by CORU representatives[20]—appears to have been the CIA, or at least a faction thereof. CORU's headquarters are in Miami. Originally, it was sustained by tight collaboration with the CIA and the Chilean junta's secret police. According to the Cuban former CIA agent Manuel d'Armas, the CIA coordinated DINA's acts with CORU's, and supplied the latter with funds, advisors and explosives. The head of DINA's Miami-based force was reportedly Eduardo Sepulveda, the Chilean attaché in Miami and a top dog in DINA.[21]

Internacional Fascista is the outgrowth of many years of planning in Madrid by the late Nazi, Otto Skorzeny, who in the fifties had worked for the CIA. On its rolls are former SS agents, OAS terrorists, hatchet men for Portugal's dreaded secret police (PIDE), terrorists from Spain's Fuerza Nueva, Argentine and Italian Fascists, Cuban exiles, French gangsters from SAC, and former CIA agents hardened by terror campaigns in Operation 40, Guatemala, Brazil, and Argentina.

Besides CORU, Internacional Fascista's militants have at various times numbered the Army for the Liberation of Portugal (ELP) and its Aginter Press contingent under Yves Guérin-Sérac; the Italian Ordine Nuovo led by Salvatore Francia and Pierluigi Concutelli; Spain's Guerillas of Christ the King, Associacion Anticomunista Iberica and Alianza Anticomunista Apostolica (AAA), which is not to be confused with the Argentine AAA that is also represented in Internacional Fascista; and the Paladin group.

SS Colonel Skorzeny was the kingpin of the Paladin mercenary group until his death in 1975.[22] Dr. Gerhard Hartmut von Schubert, formerly of Joseph Goebbels' propaganda ministry, was its operating manager.[23] Headquartered in Albufera, Spain,[24] its actual nerve centers were Skorzeny's Export-Import offices and cover firm M.C. located at a Madrid address shared with a front for the Spanish intelligence agency SCOE under Colonel Eduardo Blanco,[25] and also an office of the U.S. Central Intelligence Agency.[26] The cozy relationship of Spanish right wing terrorists with U.S. and Spanish intelligence is further underlined by the SCOE's purchase in the mid-seventies of WerBell's silenced M10 machine pistols, prior to which the ideal terrorist weapon had been unavailable in Europe.[27] Shortly thereafter, the M10 turned up in the hands of Spanish and Italian terrorists.[28]

A mélange of former OAS and SAC figures, and West German rightist activists and mercenaries, Paladin joined terrorist actions in Europe, Africa, Latin America, and even Southeast Asia. Along with Italian Fascists, Paladin is responsible for the 17 December 1973 bombing of Rome's Fiumicino airport which claimed thirty-two lives.[29] On behalf of the Spanish government Paladin kidnapped and murdered leaders of the Basque ETA and in 1974-76 engineered some fifty bombings in Basque country.

Paladin's bankrollers included Skorzeny's weapons empire and Libyan head-of-state Moammer Qadaffi.[30] The Skorzeny-controlled World Armco, with main offices in Paris, was registered in the name of Paladin manager von Schubert.[31] Upon the death of Skorzeny in 1975, von Schubert moved to Argentina, but returned six months later to reorganize. In the spring of 1976 he raised eyebrows with a want ad in the *International Herald Tribune* for a pilot, navigator, captain, three demolitions experts, two camouflage experts, two specialists in Vietnamese, and two in Chinese. Applicants were directed to a Paladin office in Spain.

Internacional Fascista was a crucial first step toward fulfilling the dream not only of Skorzeny, but also of his close friends in Madrid exile, Jose Lopez Rega, Juan Peron's grey eminence, and Prince Justo Valerio Borghese, the Italian Fascist money man who had been rescued from execution at the hands of the World War II Italian resistance by future CIA counterintelligence whiz James J. Angleton.[32] They, and other Nazi and Fascist powers throughout Europe and Latin America, envisioned a new world order built on a Fascist Iron Circle linking Buenos Aires, Santiago, Lima, La Paz, Brasilia and Montevideo.

In 1973 their goal seemed near. Chile's President Allende had been overthrown. Peron had regained the Argentine presidency after seventeen years of exile. Hugo Banzer was still in control in Bolivia, as was Alfredo Stroessner in Paraguay, and other right wing military regimes ruled Brazil and Uruguay. When he returned to Argentina, Peron brought with him Lopez Rega as an advisor. The latter would wield great influence over both the aging president and his wife Isabel, and import hatchet men from Spain to help the Argentine Anticommunist Alliance (AAA) slaughter the Argentine Left.

In 1976, however, Fascist plans suffered a setback. Isabel Peron, who had succeeded her late husband, was ousted from office and Lopez Rega was chased out of Argentina.[33] Argentina's contingent of international terrorists then followed Lopez Rega back to Spain, and were joined there by several of their Argentine colleagues, among them Commissioner Morales and Colonel Navarra.[34] Portugal's revolution, and the liberation of Mozambique and Angola that followed, further complicated the Fascist game plan. However, Third World terrorist actions continued.

In 1976 a seven-man Fascist commando group dispatched from Spain was arrested in Algeria following an act of sabotage. Its leader identified himself as Aurelio Bertin. In truth he was Jay S. Sablonsky, a native Philadelphian also known as Jay Salby.[35] Another member of the unit disclosed that he had contacted it in Madrid through one Gille Maxwell, an American working for a real estate agency run by the former U.S. Air Force colonel August Woltz.[36]

Salby was a ringleader of Aginter Press, and later the ELP.[37] Together with Guérin-Sérac and other Euro-Fascists, he had worked for the CIA in Guatemala from 1968 to 1971 in the unprecedented terror campaign which followed the August 1968 assassination of U.S. ambassador Gordon Mein.[38] The campaign, allegedly set in motion by Mein's successor Nathaniel Davis, was modelled after Vietnam's Phoenix program. It afforded an early glimpse at the teamwork of European Fascists with Miami-based, CIA-trained Cuban exiles. According to Amnesty International, some 30,000 people were either killed or disappeared in Guatemala in the decade beginning in 1962, the worse of it coming in 1970-71.[39]

A later-released FBI document revealed that Salby and former OAS terrorist Raingeard (mentioned at the start of this chapter) had been in Miami in 1969, on leave from participating in mass murder in Guatemala.[40] Correspondence in 1971 from Aginter Press leader Sérac to Sablonsky is addressed to Jay Salby, Seaboard Holding Corp., 1451 NE Bayshore, Miami.[41] Raingeard again shuttled between Miami and Guatemala in late 1973.[42]

As to Ambassador Davis, he moved on to bigger things in Chile.[43] A terrorist contingent which would train commandos for the Chilean Fascist party, Patria y Libertad (whose co-leader was reportedly Davis's next-door neighbor), followed soon on his heels from Guatemala. After a coup d'état replaced Salvador Allende with Augusto Pinochet's military junta, some terrorists moved on to Argentina, while others, Salby among them, rejoined Aginter Press in Portugal.

As Fascist terror then struck Europe, Davis became the U.S. ambassador in Bern, Switzerland. By coincidence, DINA's chief of foreign operations, Pedro Ewing, set up an office in the same city. The southern European Left, most vocally the Italians, then protested repeatedly against the presence of Davis, who was regarded as a coordinator of the terror. Eventually he was relegated to the happy hunting ground of the foreign service, the Naval War College in Newport, Rhode Island.

In 1976-77 Internacional Fascista made its presence felt often in Europe. West Germany's Fascist and neo-Nazi groups doubled. After Spain and Italy, though, it was in France that the Fascists were most industrious, with the old standbys from SAC assuming a new role. When 7000 SAC agents were fired in 1972-73, many joined Fascist groups in Spain – Paladin in particular. Paladin's OAS contingent let bygones be bygones.[44]

What has made sleuth work difficult is Internacional Fascista's attempts to camouflage itself as an arm of the Left. When General Joaquín Zenteno Anaya, Bolivia's ambassador to France, was shot down in Paris in May 1976, a caller to the police claimed the Che Guevara Brigade had murdered him to avenge the 1967 capture of Guevara in Bolivia. An eyewitness, moreover, claimed to have recognized the assailant as the infamous left wing terrorist Carlos. However, one month later the *Nouvel Observateur* reported that the assassination had been planned at Madrid's Consulade Hotel by Bolivian intelligence agent Saavedra and three terrorists from the Paladin group. Furthermore, inspection of Zenteno Anaya's politics revealed his opposition to Bolivian President Banzer, and allegiance to ex-President Torres, whose murder in Argentina followed shortly after Zenteno's. Then it was the turn of former Chilean foreign minister Orlando Letelier to be murdered by Chilean and Cuban terrorists in Washington – soon after which the establishment U.S. press, citing CIA and FBI sources, pointed the finger at the Chilean left.

In connection with these assassinations it's appropriate here to quote, in its entirety, a recent report entitled "Latin America: Murder Inc.": "A still classified staff report on 'questionable foreign intelligence operations' in the United States, prepared for the Senate Foreign Relations subcommittee on international operations, sheds some new light on cooperation in security matters between Argentina, Bolivia, Brazil, Chile, Paraguay and Uruguay. According to the Senate report, which has been leaked to the press in the United States, the joint operation is known as 'Condor.' The Senate report mentioned a 'phase three' of Operation Condor, which involved the formation of special teams to carry out 'sanctions,' including the assassination of the enemies of its constituent governments.

"The best known killing of this type was the bomb attack on Orlando Letelier in September 1976 in Washington. Condor's role in this emerged during the testimony of the FBI agent, Bob Scherer, who investigated the case and gave evidence at the trial of Michael Townley. He testified to the use of Condor as the channel by which the Chilean DINA chief, General Manuel Contreras, tried to get U.S. visas for two of the agents involved.

"An impressive list of murders may now be laid at the door of Operation Condor. These include the killings of General Carlos Prats of Chile and Juan José Torres of Bolivia in Argentina, the Uruguayan politicians Héctor Gutiérrez Ruiz and Zelmar Michelini, also in Argentina, Bolivia's General Joaquín Zenteno Anaya and Uruguay's Colonel Ramón Trabal in Paris, and the attempted assassination of the Chilean senator, Bernardo Leighton.

"The Senate report disclosed that Condor had considered establishing its own operational base in Miami in 1974, but that this was headed off by a CIA protest 'through regular intelligence channels.' In this case, the CIA informed the Chilean DINA of United States displeasure and no Miami station was opened. According to the Senate report, the FBI concluded early in its investigation of the Letelier assassination that the murder might have been carried out as a third phase of Operation Condor.'

"Presumably 'third phase' will now go into the lexicon of euphemisms alongside the CIA's 'to terminate with extreme prejudice.' The fact that the operation was well known to the United States at least five years ago makes nonsense of its shocked surprise at the time of Letelier's death."[45]

The advent of democracy in Spain was fought bitterly by Internacional Fascista. At least seventy lives fell victim to the struggle within the first half of 1977. On January 24 Fascists armed with machine pistols stormed a midtown Madrid attorneys' office and opened fire on twelve lawyers who had defended leftists. Six of the lawyers were killed, the rest were seriously wounded. Over the next three days right wing terrorists murdered four others, two of them students, which led to the arrest of Carlos Perez, the Cuban exile associated with the Argentine AAA.

On 22 February 1977 Madrid police discovered a factory where Italian Ordine Nuovo Fascists had manufactured hand guns. The building had been rented from an order of nuns by Otto Skorzeny's friend, Mariano Sanchez Covisa.[46] Following up their discovery, the police investigated a bankbox in the name of Italian Fascist kingpin Elio Massagrande. In it they found a small fortune and three gold bars traceable to the $10 million bank robbery masterminded by OAS alumnus Albert Spaggiari.[47] This led to the roundup of most of Spain's Italian Fascist elite: Stefano della Chiaie, Marco Pozzan, Elidore Pomar, Clemente Graziani, Salvatore Francia, Flavio Camp, Mario Rossa, Enzo Salzioli, plus Massagrande and his wife Sandra Cricci.[48]

Spanish authorities, however, were pressured by the Italians' local protectors, and the terrorists were soon released. Many of them headed to Argentina and eventually returned to Europe.[49] Massagrande and one Gaetano Orlando went to Paraguay, where they were arrested in December 1977 and released within days on orders from dictator Stroessner. There they remained.[50]

In August 1977 the Spanish AAA stole jewels worth $20 million from the cathedral at Oviedo. The police recovered most of the jewels when several terrorists were stopped at the Portuguese border. That same month Internacional Fascista's Italian, Spanish, Argentine, and Cuban exile terrorist contingents were represented at a Taiwan assembly of the World Anti-Communist League.[51]

In April 1978 the parties behind Internacional Fascista formed an umbrella organization, Euro-Droit (Euro-Right) as a response to Eurocommunism.[52] Charter members included Georgio Almirante's Italian Fascist party (MSI), Spain's Fuerza Nueva led by Blas Pinar, France's Forces Nouvelles (PFN) led by Jean-Louis Tixier-Vignancour, Belgium's Front National and Greece's Rassemblement General.[53] In May Almirante and others represented Euro-Droit at the WACL assembly in Washington.[54] On 27 June 1978 Euro-Droit met in Paris,[55] and on July 18 its leaders met in Madrid with Latin American observers including Ricardo Courutchet of Argentina.[56] Its representative at the April 1979 WACL assembly in Paraguay was Fuerza Nueva's Pinar.[57] Finally, in 1979, several Euro-Droit members were elected to the first European Parliament.

The springboard of this chapter was what I deem The Miami Conspiracy. Inevitably I am drawn to suspect that international Fascist operations are, to some degree, directed from Miami. World Service, the cover organization Patrice Chairoff told me was based in Miami, was of the same ilk as Aginter Press, whose agents Raingeard and Salby were in and out of Miami. Miami Cubans joined Aginter Press terrorists in Guatemala. The Nice bank robber Albert Spaggiari was allegedly in Miami before his heist, and was definitely in touch with the CIA in the U.S. after it. Ten months later money and gold stolen from the bank were in the safe-deposit box of an Italian terrorist leader in Spain. Mirage director de Vathaire and Paladin agent Kay flew to Miami before their theft of Mirage millions, and met there with Cuban exiles.[58] One hundred Florida-based Cubans joined the Aginter Press-ELP army in Spain, where they became involved in acts of terrorism. Michael Townley and other DINA agents were in Miami to plan the murder of Orlando Letelier, and Townley also engineered an attempt on Bernardo Leighton's life in Rome.

The old JM/Wave operation is born again. Only it is no longer confined to Cuba and the Third World, but now encompasses a bitter struggle against a new enemy, Eurocommunism. The home town of CIA fronts like the Sea Supply Corporation, Double-Chek Corporation, Zenith Technical Enterprises, Gibraltar Steamship Corporation, and Vanguard Service Corporation, and the site of ominous Fountainebleau Hotel meetings between Santo Trafficante, Sam Giancana, John Roselli, Robert Maheu, William Harvey, and Meyer Lansky, remains the birthplace of conspiracy. And to close the circle, let us not forget that gangsters and former espionage agents among Internacional Fascista and CORU's minions were knee-deep in the heroin trade; that still floating in the quagmire are extraordinary, international agents E. Howard Hunt and Fernand Legros[59]; and that several Spaggiari gang bank robbers had been the close associates of both Francois Chiappe and Christian "Beau Serge" David, whom this book was, at one time, to have been all about.[60]

Notes

1. *L'Express*, 13 September 1976.

2. *El Pais*, 3 February 1977.

3. F. Strasser and B. McTigue: "The Fall River Conspiracy," *Boston*, November 1978.

4. E.H. Cookridge: *Gehlen, The Spy of the Century* (Random House, 1971).

5. L. Gonzalez-Mata: *Cygne* (Grasset, 1976).

6. C. Oglesby: *The Yankee and Cowboy War* (Sheed Andrews and McMeel, 1976).

7. T. Branch and G. Crile III: "The Kennedy Vendetta," *Harper's*, August 1975.

8. *Ibid.*

9. J.D. Marks: *The Search for the Manchurian Candidate* (Timès Books, 1979).

10. T. Szulc: *Compulsive Spy* (Viking, 1974).

11. According to Patrice Chairoff: *Dossier B...comme Barbouzes* (Alain Moreau, 1975), three agents assigned to the CIA's West German station were in on the plot: Otto-Karl Dupow, Friedrich Stoll and Paul Welles.

12. It was while station JM/Wave was in full swing that the Cuba-based French intelligence (SDECE) agent Thyraud de Vosjoli teamed up with the CIA. Particularly interesting is de Vosjoli's close friendship with Leroy-Finville, who was jailed in the Ben Barka case. Furthermore, in his book *Le Comité* (Éditions de l'Homme, 1975), de Vosjoli refers to a certain Legros in the same affair.

13. It is interesting, in light of the 1965 murder of Ben Barka and the 1966 appearance of Aginter Press, to note that CIA agent Howard Hunt was in Madrid in 1965-66, following cancellation of the planned second invasion of Cuba (Szulc, *op. cit.*). In Madrid, Hunt's family lived in an apartment owned by the brother of his good friend, William Buckley, as reported by Hunt in *Undercover* (Berkeley-Putnam, 1974). Buckley was one of the Americans instrumental in the creation of WACL, and was later in contact with an agent of Aginter Press, according to Frederic Laurent in *L'Orchestre Noir* (Stock, 1978).

14. Portugal's revolution and the ensuing defeat in Angola of the CIA-supported FNLA by the Cuba-supported MPLA no doubt conspired to make Bosch's work easier.

15. S. Landau: *They Educated the Crows* (Transnational Institute/Institute for Policy Studies, 1978).

16. Anon.: "Miami, Haven for Terror," *The Nation*, 19 March 1977.

17. *Counterspy, Vol. 3*, No. 2, 1976.

18. J. Dinges: "Chile's Global Hit Men," *The Nation*, 2 June 1979.

19. Landau, *op. cit.* Recently the FBI reportedly assigned "highest priority" to seizing members of the Union City, New Jersey-based Omega 7, a group of anti-Castro Cubans responsible for twenty bombings in the New York City metropolitan area between 1 February 1975 and 13 January 1980 (*New York Times*, 3 March 1980).

   According to the well-informed investigative reporter Jeff Stein ("Inside Omega 7," *Village Voice*, 10 March 1980), high-ranking New York City law enforcement officials "believe that nothing can be done to stop the terrorist wave without vigorous federal intervention – and so far Washington has remained silent." Stein also reports that Omega 7 has been supported by other anti-Castro groups including the Cuban Nationalist Movement (Northern Zone), five of whose members were indicted in connection with the Letelier murder.

The name of Gustavo Marin – president of another, university-based exile group, Abdala, headquartered on Twenty-Ninth Street in New York City – appears on police files as an Omega 7 suspect. In 1974 Marin and Abdala teamed up politically with Reverend Sun Myung Moon's Unification Church in support of the Moonies' fast to save Richard Nixon.

Stein also reports rumors of an alliance of anti-Communist terrorist groups involving the Croations, in particular, whose bombing activities have recently been on the rise. Its funding, according to FBI sources, is coming from Paraguay and that Nazi haven's recent arrival from Nicaragua, Anastasio Somoza. Yugoslavia recently requested a U.S. crackdown on the Croation National Congress headed by Janko Skrbin, whose extradition as a war criminal the Yugoslavs seek for his collaboration with the Germans in the "independent" Fascist state of Croatia from 1941 to 1945 (*New York Times*, 23 March 1980).

These allegations are particularly interesting in lights of the revelations in *Latin America Political Report* (29 April 1977) that the Croation representative of the World Anti-Communist League (WACL) in Paraguay, Dinko Zakic, had used $3.5 million from the WACL's regional organization, the Confederacion Anticomunista Latinoamericana (CAL), to finance Croatian terrorist activities. These included the murders of the Uruguayan ambassador in Paraguay (an apparent mistake) and the Yugoslav ambassador in Sweden (not a mistake).

20. *Information*, 22 February 1977; prior to the Rome meeting there had been planning sessions in Lyons in 1974 and Barcelona in 1975.

21. *Litteraturnaja Gazeta*, November 1976.

22. *Liberation*, 24 and 25 March 1974.

23. *Le Nouvel Observateur*, 23 September 1974.

24. Chairoff, *op. cit.*

25. *Le Nouval Observateur*, 7 June 1976.

26. L. Gonzalez-Mata: *Cygne* (Grasset, 1976).

27. Laurent, *op. cit.*

28. *Cambio 16*, 20 February 1977; *Time*, 2 February 1977; Laurent, *op. cit.*

29. *Le Nouvel Observateur*, 23 September 1974.

30. *Ibid.*

31. E. Gerdan: *Dossier A...comme Armes* (Alain Moreau, 1974).

32. Laurent, *op. cit.*

33. Since 1976, when General Jorge Videla led a military coup in Argentina, some 15-20,000 Argentines, according to Amnesty International, have disappeared. At a 4 February 1980 news conference in London, Amnesty related reports of former Argentine concentration camp inmates, that prisoners are "tortured with electric cattle prods...drugged and dropped unconscious from a plane into the sea" (*Boston Globe*, 5 February 1980). Just prior to that report, President Jimmy Carter's special envoy, Lt. Gen. Andrew Goodpaster, had told Argentine officials that the Carter administration would consider asking Congress to revoke 1978 human rights legislation prohibiting U.S. weapons sales to Argentina.

34. *Cuadernos para el Dialogo*, 5 February 1977.

35. *El Moudjahid*, 5 March 1976.

36. *Ibid.*

37. In Portugal Salby/Sablonsky was known as Joaquín Castor. Colonel Corvacho, the commandant at Oporto, confiscated Salby's false Guatemalan passport, issued to him in the name of Hugh C. Franklin, by Guatemala's Montreal consulate.

38. *Liberation*, 11 and 12 December 1974 and 19 July 1976.

39. Amnesty International recently announced that 2000 Guatemalans had been killed for political reasons during the "alarming upsurge" in violence in the eighteen-month period ending in December 1979. Many of the murders are carried out by "semi-clandestine death squads" created to combat the left, which, according to an earlier Amnesty report, "act with complete impunity" from the nation's military rulers (*New York Times*, 6 December 1979). Total U.S. military aid to Guatemala for the 1946-75 period was $39.3 million – see N. Chomsky and E.S. Herman: *The Washington Connection and Third World Fascism* (South End Press, 1979).

40. *Boston Phoenix*, 14 March 1978.

41. Laurent, *op. cit.*

42. *Ibid.* Guatemala has always had a magnetic attraction for right wing terrorists. According to René Louis Maurice's *The Heist of the Century*, bankrobber Albert Spaggiari, a former member of the OAS, stopped over in Guatemala before his 1976 visit in the U.S. with the CIA.

43. Nathaniel Davis and William H. Sullivan, who presided over the CIA's secret war in Laos and later over the Tehran embassy during the fall of the Shah, each graduated in the class of 1947 from the distinguished Fletcher School of Law and Diplomacy at Tufts University outside Boston.

44. What remains to be seen is whether the Gaullist party presently led by Jacques Chirac has also teamed up with Fascists by way of SAC. In May 1976 Marseilles' mayor and one of France's leading Socialists, Gaston Deferre, accused the Gaullists of reestablishing "the notorious SAC barbouze corps" to crack down on leftists – see H. Krüger and N. Levinsen: *Fascismens Internationale Net i Dag* (Bogan, 1977). Deferre charged the Gaullists with exploiting their position in power to once again open prison gates to release murderers and other hardened criminals, as extensively as during the 1960-61 recruitment for the battle against the OAS in Algeria. The rebuilding of the barbouze corps convinced Deferre that the Gaullists would use force to remain part of the ruling coalition. He and other leftist politicians demanded a National Assembly debate on whether to dissolve SAC as a threat to French democracy, comparing it to the Nazi SS. Within SAC and the Gaullist party as well, old-timers who would not dream of working with the OAS have struggled with new blood more interested in power than the prolongation of past vendettas. It is in light of this and SAC's role in Internacional Fascista that one should view the many "affairs" that shook France in 1976 – e.g., the Agret and de Vathaire affairs, the murders of journalist René Trouve and former Vice Foreign Minister Jean de Broglie, and the two great bank robberies.

45. *Latin America Political Report*, 17 August 1979.

46. *Cuadernos para el Dialogo*, 5 March 1977; *International Herald Tribune*, 24 February 1977.

47. According to the 18 October 1979 issue of *Rolling Stone*, Massagrande was himself in on the heist.

48. *Cuadernos para el Dialogo*, 5 March 1977.

49. *Information*, 21 July 1977.

50. *The Leveller*, October 1978.

51. *Cuadernos para el Dialogo*, 1 October 1977.

52. Agence France-Presse, 20 April 1978; *Triunfo*, 29 April 1978; *Metro*, 19 July 1978.

53. *Metro, op. cit.*

54. *Washington Post*, 28 May 1978.

55. *Metro, op. cit.*

56. *Politiken*, 19 July 1978.

57. *Fuerza Nueva* weekly magazine, 19 May 1979.

58. *Journal de Dimanche*, 5 September 1976.

59. A great art forgery trial, which the French spent three years preparing against Legros, was dropped in early 1977 when the star witness, the Hungarian painter Elmyr de Hory, died of an overdose of pills in his home on Ibiza shortly after he was informed of his extradition to France to testify. Legros' army of defense lawyers then wasted little time having the case dismissed – see *L'Aurore*, 26 January 1977. At nearly the same time, fate claimed another of Legros' close acquaintances, the gangster Didier Barone, who had been closely in touch with the Felix Lesca mob and Christian David. Barone was shot and wounded by three men as he and his wife Gisele were on their way home one day. Gisele fled. Barone disappeared without a trace. In Alain Jaubert's *Dossier D . . .comme Drogue* (Alain Moreau, 1974), Barone is also described as a specialist in forged paintings.

60. *France Soir*, 27 October 1976.

POSTSCRIPT

The more things change, say the French, the more they remain the same. And who knows better than the French, for whom scandal at government's highest levels is as common as the new moon. The current talk of Paris is the cover-up in the investigation of the Christmas 1976 murder of Prince Jean de Broglie, former French cabinet member and co-founder of his brother-in-law President Giscard d'Estaing's Republican party. When he left the government in 1967 de Broglie plunged into the shadowy side of "export-import", choosing as his associates traffickers in arms, counterfeit dollars and drugs. Following a five-day investigation, then Interior Minister Michel Poniatowski fingered two members of the neo-Fascist OAS underground, who were later released for lack of evidence. Poniatowski's lame attempt to minimize the president's embarrassment is now being compared to the Ben Barka affair cover-up of a decade earlier.[1]

Which is not to imply that the sensation of déja vu is a monopoly of the French. One needn't be an apologist for Russia's involvement in Afghanistan to see history repeat itself in CIA support for the side financing its operations with opium. By the time the agency admitted supplying arms to Afghanistani insurgent groups,[2] it had long been known that the same groups supported themselves via the drug traffic. As reported a year earlier

> Feudal landlords whose buildings are threatened with confiscation by the Taraki government are bringing the produce from their poppy crops into Pakistan, and use the proceeds to buy rifles, explosives, and other weapons. Pakistani arms merchants report that their new customers come in daily and business is booming.[3]

Guns for drugs, the same scenario as in Laos, Burma and Latin America.

In a *New York Times* portrait, Afghanistani rebel leader Sayed Ahmed Gailani was described as an aristocrat tied to former King Zaher Shah and the owner of a Peugeot dealership in Kabul. His ancestral holdings confiscated, he was now underwritten by Saudis.[4] Gailani's followers, reports *Counterspy* magazine, are for the most part Pathan tribesmen, traditional harvesters of opium.[5]

Not long after the major dislocations began, tribal areas of Pakistan and Afghanistan were replacing Southeast Asia's "Golden Triangle" as the major source of heroin in Western Europe, and beginning to ship heroin to the United States.[6] This was reported *prior* to the Russian invasion, by DEA director Peter Bensinger. He added that the Afghanistani police were vigorously combatting the narcotics traffic (Afghanistan's 1979 opium harvest was twenty times Mexico's[7]), thanks to their Russian advisers and the decrease in corruption. Most of Europe's heroin was arriving in West Germany by way of Turkish migrant workers. The Turkish Fascist party and its storm troopers, the "Grey Wolves," were said to be organizing the traffic and using their profits to purchase arms.[8]

As in Afghanistan, Iran's problems, too, have been a shot in the arm for the drug trade. That this is not taken lightly by the Ayatollahs was shown by the recent firing squad execution in Teheran of 20 drug traffickers.[9] Americans, meanwhile, have been learning about a quarter century of CIA teamwork with its Gestapo-like creation, the Shah's secret police SAVAK (which had long been operating against progressive forces *in Afghanistan*). Among the more notable developments was one evoked by the April 1980 trial in Wilmington, Delaware of SAVAK agent Sharokh Bakhtiar, cousin of Iran's last prime minister under the Shah and son of SAVAK's founder, on charges of selling heroin to Federal agents. One week before the trial was to open, former CIA agent Donald Deneselya, who met Bakhtiar while working for SAVAK, threatened to reveal the names of 7500 CIA agents – hostages in Iran included – unless the charges against Bakhtiar were dropped.

Although Deneselya's initial threat proved idle, when Bakhtiar was found guilty and sentenced to fifteen years in prison, Deneselya gave a list of names to the *Wilmington News-Journal,* which chose not to print them. The same newspaper reported, however, that Bakhtiar and his two co-defendants were among a group of Iranian intelligence operatives who resorted to the smuggling of heroin to finance a counterrevolution in Iran. Moreover, according to Deneselya, SAVAK's heroin traffic into the U.S. had long been tolerated by U.S. authorities, who also ignored the fact that as the Shah's downfall approached, Iranians brought in large amounts of heroin via the diplomatic pouch.

A member of the State Department Iranian Task Force confirmed that the Iranian aristocracy cashed the local currency into heroin as they escaped the revolution. Furthermore, DEA sources acknowledged that until shortly before the Shah's departure, all SAVAK drug arrests were automatically dropped.[10]

In August 1979 two Cuban exiles and the Turkish-American owner of a Manhattan restaurant were arrested selling four pounds of Middle Eastern heroin to an undercover agent, prompting the *Times'* Nicholas Gage to speculate that Latino drug dealers were in business with Turkish suppliers.[11] Five months later DEA regional director John Fallon reported that 48 percent of all heroin confiscated in New York could be traced to the Middle East and Asia.[12] In late February Attorney General Benjamin Civiletti targeted Baltimore, Boston, New York, Philadelphia, and Washington for stepped-up enforcement to halt the flood of high-grade heroin from Iran, Afghanistan and Pakistan[13] – where the DEA reported a combined 1979 harvest of 1600 tons, ten times the figure for the Golden Triangle and one hundred times the tally for Mexico.[14]

As noted earlier, drug trade realignments of this magnitude are generally paralleled by realignments in the underworld. The 12 July 1979 gangland slaying in Brooklyn of Carmine Galante might have been connected to the fight for control of the East Coast heroin trade. Galante was the reported boss of the New York Bonnano crime family which, according to a 1978 N.Y. Police Dept. report, "controls the large majority of the heroin shipped through Canada into the United States."[15]

On 21 March 1980, a day after appearing before the New Jersey State Commission on Investigation, Angelo Bruno, reputed capo of the Philadelphia-southern New Jersey crime organization, was shot to death in front of his home. Speculations as to why included Mafia squabbling over half-a-billion dollars' worth of service industry growth since legal gambling came to Atlantic City, and control over the New Jersey numbers racket – which Bruno reportedly refused to share with such interested parties as the late Galante and the New York crime family of the late Carlo Gambino. Philadelphia police, however, felt Bruno's killing might have been related to his reported aversion to dealing in narcotics.[16] Coincidentally, three days before the Bruno murder, two of Gambino's cousins had been arrested in their Cherry Hill, New Jersey restaurant on charges of conspiring to smuggle $10 million worth of heroin into New York.

Rosario and Giuseppe Gambino, who Federal law enforcement officials say ran 200 southern New Jersey pizza joints employing illegal aliens, had allegedly masterminded the smuggling of 90 pounds of heroin from Afghanistan, Iran, and Pakistan by way of Milan, Italy. What makes their case all the more intriguing is the Gambinos' connection to the powerful Milan-based financier Michele Sindona.[17] Sindona was convicted in New York in late March on counts ranging from bank fraud to perjury after looting $45 million from the Franklin National Bank—America's twentieth largest—which he controlled and brought to ruin. In June a New York judge sentenced him to twenty-five years imprisonment, a record for white collar crime. He is similarly accused of looting $225 million from his banks in Milan.

On 2 August 1979, three weeks after the assassination in Milan of the lawyer chosen to liquidate Sindona's bankrupt Banca Privata Italiana, and one month before the scheduled opening of his New York trial, Sindona disappeared—supposedly kidnapped by left wing Italian extremists, as he later reported—only to reappear two and a half months later on 42nd Street and Tenth Avenue with a bullet wound in his thigh and with documents, miraculously gathered during his "abduction" in Europe, which he claimed would exonerate him. That was not all. On 24 January 1980 it was announced that three high-standing clerics from the Vatican—whose immense financial holdings had once been in Sindona's hands—were going to be his character witnesses (an offer the Vatican would later retract).

Sindona's fortunes suffered another setback, however, when Italian and U.S. agents established that he had arranged his own disappearing act—booking, for example, his own European flights—and that his accomplices had included the Gambino brothers. The Gambinos, it seems, had a long record in the import-export and protection of criminals and other illegal aliens, among them the family of Sicilian Mafia chieftain Tomasso Buscetta[18]—who, recall, was dispatched to South America to take over the Ricord network, but wound up joining Christian David's heroin connection.

As to Sindona, his co-defendant in the U.S., Carlo Bordoni, reportedly told the Italian magazine *Panorama* that "Michele Sindona was (and still is) one of the mafia's bankers, the route through which organized crime money passes across the Atlantic."[19] Back in 1967 Interpol had asked the Italian police if they could verify that he and others were "involved in the illicit movement of depressant, stimulant and hallucinogenic drugs between Italy, the United States and possibly other European countries." The response was negative.[20]

Sindona's connections to the presidential administration of Richard Nixon are more firmly established. Sindona's Italian banks were investment partners with the Continental Illinois Bank headed by David Kennedy, Nixon's first treasury secretary and a director of Fasco International, Sindona's Luxembourg-based holding company. Sindona's interests were represented in the United States by Mudge, Rose, Guthrie and Alexander, the law firm of Nixon's attorney general John Mitchell. In Italy, Sindona orchestrated the efforts of the neo-Fascist deputy Luigi Turchi to garner Italian support for Nixon's election campaign.[21] Sindona even offered $1 million, on condition of anonymity, to CREEP treasurer Maurice Stans. The offer was refused.

While Sindona was out-Vescoing Robert Vesco himself, the CIA was exploiting Sindona's far Right political sympathies and connections in Italy. According to the House of Representatives' Pike Report on CIA activities, Sindona was a key channel for the millions distributed by the agency to centrist and right wing Italian political parties, affiliated organizations and candidates. Part of the payoff helped finance an abortive Fascist coup in December 1970. Another portion was allocated to the Fascist "Strategy of Tension," in which Italian intelligence officers and neo-fascists conspired to shift Italian voters rightward through bombings–that were attributed to "leftists"–including the 1969 explosion at Milan's Piazza Fontana which claimed seventeen lives.[22]

(A key figure in the 1969 bombing and the 1970 coup attempt was the Italian Stefano delle Chiaie. As we go to press, we find confirmation of his role in the 1975 attempted assassination of Bernardo Leighton in Rome, in John Dinges and Saul Landau's penetrating book *Assassination on Embassy Row* (Pantheon 1980). Delle Chiaie had been contacted for the hit by Michael Townley of the Chilean DINA and Virgilio Paz of the Miami and Union City, N.J.-based Cuban Nationalist Movement.)

While it's not certain just who is controlling the U.S. end of the heroin bonanza from Southwest Asia (Santo Trafficante's the sentimental favorite), there is no disputing the fact that the United States–its heroin capital New York City in particular–is again experiencing a major heroin wave. The New York State Division of Substance Abuse Services reports that, compared with 1978, drug-related deaths increased in 1979 by 77 percent and hospital emergency room admissions for heroin by 46 percent.[23]

The 1980 outlook is even gloomier. In the first quarter of 1979 the DEA rarely found heroin purities in excess of 20 percent. One year later the laboratories were reporting purities between 20 and 90 percent. An addict from Manhattan's Lower East Side reports: "It's all over the neighborhood. You can get it on the street corners, even in the candy stores. And it's superior to the earlier stuff." The head of New York's Phoenix House, a drug treatment center, says: "There is no question that we are going to have another heroin crisis."[24]

In Boston the story is the same. "It's getting worse all the time," says a detective in the Police Department's Drug Control Unit (DCU), which handled twice as many cases from December 1979 to mid-April 1980 as it had in the same period one year before. When asked how many heroin addicts there were in Boston, a city of under one million inhabitants, DCU head Lt. David Walsh replied: "If your figure was 3500 it would be a conservative estimate."[25]

What has been the federal government's response? While enforcement officials like Attorney General Civiletti promise intensified efforts to control the heroin deluge, the reelection-minded Carter administration has added $15 billion to the military budget while proposing *cuts* of $40 million in the $160 million national drug abuse treatment program. The White House Strategy Council on Drug Abuse, appointed by President Carter in November 1977, has not convened, despite the urgings of its members, in seven and a half months. In the words of two of those members:

> Our requests for information that by law we are entitled to receive have been met in some instances by delays of years, at other times with only superficial responses. The council has working groups and subcommittees about which we are given only the sketchiest information.
>
> Since November 1977, we have never received classified information, although we cannot understand how we can serve any supervisory function without it. For example, we worry about the growing of opium poppies in Afghanistan and Pakistan by rebel tribesmen who apparently are the chief adversaries of the Soviet troops in Afghanistan. Are we erring in befriending these tribes as we did in Laos when Air America (chartered by the Central Intelligence Agency) helped transport crude opium from certain tribal areas?[26]

NOTES

1. *L'Express,* 26 April 1980. Speaking of Ben Barka, his old arch enemy, King Hassan II of Morocco, is currently waging war against nationalists in Western Sahara with the aid of US aircraft, a $200 million Westinghouse Tactical Air Defense system and a PR campaign run by a firm chaired by former N.Y. senator Charles Goodell, which is primarily directed (according to Justice Dept. records) at improving "public and political understanding in the United States of Moroccan interests, including obtaining US approval of the right of Morocco to purchase armaments in the US." In 1975 Hassan's air force bombed and napalmed camps set up for refugees from the guerilla war waged by the Polisario independence movement. (See S. Talbot: "Arms for Peace", *Inquiry,* 26 May 1980) According to a medical team sent to Morocco by the Belgian Association of Democratic Jurists, political prisoners there are regularly left in total isolation, chained to the ground, suspended head down or beaten on the soles of their feet until they lose consciousness (*New York Times,* 22 May 1980).

2. *New York Times,* 16 February 1980.

3. *McLean's,* 30 April 1979.

4. A. Khan: "With the Afghan Rebels", *New York Times Magazine,* 13 January 1980, cited in *Counterspy Vol. 4,* No. 2 (1980).

5. *Counterspy, op. cit.* An added irony of the situation in Afghanistan is to be found in President Carter's promotion, in response, of a military draft that would include women. In the wake of the April 1978 Taraki takeover, school-teachers rushed to the Afghanistani countryside to spread education to women. Many of the schoolteachers were assassinated by villagers with more traditional views on the status of women. (See D. Johnstone in *In These Times,* 27 February 1980)

6. *Washington Post,* 10 October 1979.

7. *Counterspy, op. cit.*

8. *Stern,* 13 October 1979; *Arbeiterkampf,* 29 October 1979. Turkey, by the way, is in the throes of long-standing, violent political convulsions, in which the frequency of murder makes Latin America's bloodbath seem like child's play.

9. *New York Times,* 22 May 1980.

10. J. Trento and R. Sandza in the *Wilmington News-Journal,* 30 March and 3 May 1980.

11. *New York Times,* 11 January 1980.

12. *New York Times,* 18 January 1980.

13. *Boston Globe,* 20 February 1980.

14. *New York Times,* 15 May 1980.

15. *New York Times,* 4 March 1980.

16. C. Winans in the *Boston Globe*, 23 March 1980. One year before the Bruno hit, Anthony "Little Pussy" Russo, the reputed mob boss in northern New Jersey, had been knocked off – by the same hit team, according to a "top-ranking underworld federal informant."

17. N. Pileggi: "Sindona: A Little Help from his Friends", *New York*, 7 April 1980.

18. *Ibid.*

19. C. Mann and D. McAdoo: "Sindona: An Investigative Report", *Attenzione*, December 1979. A different opinion was apparently held by U.S. Ambassador John Volpe in January 1974 when, at a luncheon at the American Club in Rome, he presented Sindona with the "Man of the Year" award.

20. B. Rostron: "A Chapter from 'The Godfather'?", *Village Voice*, 21 January 1980.

21. Mann and McAdoo, *op. cit.*

22. *Ibid.*

23. *New York Times*, 15 May 1980.

24. *Ibid.*

25. *Boston Globe*, 11 May 1980.

26. J.H. Lowinson and D.F. Musto, *New York Times*, 22 May 1980.

INDEX

AAA (Alianza Anticomunista Apostolica-Spain), 209, 224

AAA (Argentine Anticommunist Alliance), 7, 11, 13, 85, 106, 113, 165, 168n, 204, 209, 211, 214

AAB (Brazilian Anticommunist Alliance), 196n

Abdala, 217n

Abourezk, Sen. James, 165

Afghanistan, opium traffic in, 221-224, 226

AFL (American Federation of Labor), 15, 34

Aginter Press, 10-11, 20-22, 196n, 202, 204, 207-208, 211-212, 215, 216n

Agret affair, 218n

AID – see USAID

Air America, 125, 136, 137n, 226

Air Opium, 133-134

Albertini, Dominique, 101

Alcohol, Drug Abuse and Health Administration, 171

Aleman, José, 147

Alessio, John, 155

Alfa 66, 207

Allen, Richard V., 21-22, 26n

Allende, Pres. Salvador – 1973 CIA coup against, 146, 151n, 177, 210, 212

Allied Military Government (Sicily), 15

Alliegro, Anselmo III, 8, 23n

Alliegro, Anselmo IV, 8, 21, 182

Almirante, Giorgio, 214

Alo, Vincent, 150n

Altmann, Klaus – see Berbie, Klaus

Ambrose, Myles, 152n, 160, 162-163

Ambrosiono, Louis, 117n

American Bankers Insurance Co., 130

American Nazi Party, 168n

American Security Council, 182

Amit, Meir, 63

Amnesty International, 168n, 211, 217n-218n

Anastasia, Albert, 85n, 142

Anderson, Jack, 85, 165

Andréani, André, 98

Angleton, James, 14, 210

APACL (Asian Peoples Anti-Communist League), 124-125

Arantez, Haide, 105, 107

Arbenz, Pres. Jacobo – see Guatemala, 1954 CIA coup in

Argoud, Col. Antoine, 43, 56-57

(d')Armas, Manuel, 209

Artime, Manuel, 144, 161, 193

Assassination on Embassy Row, 225

(Les) Assassins de Ben Barka, 72, 202n

Associacion Anticomunista Iberica, 209

Association of Former Intelligence Officers, 12

Atlanta Penitentiary, 29, 31, 32n, 117n

Attia, Jo "The Terrible", 30, 35, 40-43, 44n, 51-52, 54-57, 64, 85, 115

Attia, Nicole, 42-43

Auge, Jean, 54, 58n, 85, 112, 114-115

(L') Aurore, 204

Auto gang, 41

Aviles-Quintero family, 177

Azores, plan for liberation of, 20-21

Bakhtiar, Sharokh, 222

Ball, George, 47

Banca Privata Italiana, 224

Banzer, Pres. Hugo, 210, 212

Barbeiro Filho, Carlos, 196n

Barberot, Col. Roger, 34, 52, 54, 76-77, 91, 94, 102n

Barbie, Klaus ("Killer of Lyons") alias Klaus Altmann, 83-84, 85n

Barbouzes, 3, 40, 52-56, 67-68, 110, 114, 200, 218n

Bario, Santo Allesandro, 195n-196n

Barker, Bernard, 2, 126, 161, 163, 193

Barone, Didier, 54, 56, 76, 116n, 218n

Baroudi, Eduardo, 184

Barrera, Enrique, 117n

Bartels, John R., 163, 195

Batista, Fulgencio, 89, 141-142, 144, 153

Bauer, Josette, 97-98

Bay of Pigs invasion, 16, 126, 131, 134, 137n, 144-145, 151n, 154, 156, 161, 177, 204-206, 209

Bayard, Col. Robert F., 185

Bayo, Eddie, 146

BDPA (Bureau pour le Developpement de la Production Agricole), 91, 94

Beau Serge – see Christian David

Beaujolin, Gilbert, 102n

Beaumont, Col. René alias Bertrand, 42, 46

Becker, Felix, 92

Behr, Edward, 69

Beidas, Yussef, 103n, 184-185

Bellemin-Noel, Lt., 108

Belmondo, Jean Paul, 44n

Ben Barka, Mehdi, 4-5, 59-70, 72, 73n, 199, 206-207, 227n

Ben Barka affair, 30-31, 32n, 43, 46, 59-74, 78, 99, 109, 206-207, 216n, 221

Ben Bella, Ahmed, 103n

Bender, Felix alias Don Federico, Drecher, Droller and Swend, 144-145, 150n, 205

Bennett, Robert F. 19

Bensinger, Peter, 7, 168n, 177, 222

Berdin, Richard, 37-38, 90n, 98-99, 115

Berg, Donald, 154

Berg, Robert, 167n

Bernier, Philippe, 64

Bernstein, Carl, 19

Bertin, Aurelio – see Jay S. Sablonsky

Bertrand, Col. René – see Col. René Beaumont

Bianchi, Cesar, 92-93

Bimini Run, 151n

Binder, David, 12

Bird, William, 130

Bird, Willis, 130

Bistoni, Albert, 111, 115

Black Commandos, 52, 58n, 94

Black Mafia, 126
Black Panthers, 161, 167n
Blackburn mob, 143
Blanco, Col. Eduardo, 209
Blémant, Robert, 55
BND (West German intelligence), 192
BNDD (Bureau of Narcotics and Dangerous
  Drugs), 84, 98-100, 103n, 107, 122-126, 135,
  145, 147, 149, 152n, 161-163, 183, 190, 193,
  195n, 207
Bokassa I, Emperor, 81n
(La) Bolita, 143
Bongo, Pres. Omar, 49, 81n
Bonnano, Joseph, 99, 103n, 110n
Bonnano family, 223
Bonnay, Thierry de, 70, 76, 99
Bonsignour, Louis, 76
Bordaberry, Pres. Juan Maria, 80, 81n
Border Patrol (U.S.), 179
Bordoni, Carlo, 225
Borghese, Prince Justo Valerio, 10, 210
Borsalino (film), 44n
Bosch, Orlando, 11, 13-14, 144-145, 183, 187n,
  194, 207-208
BOSS (Bureau of Special Services), 160
Boucan, Marcel, 99-101, 117n, 184, 190-191
Bouchard, Conrad, 184
Boucheseiche, Georges, 41-42, 54-56, 64-68,
  71-72, 115
Bourdoulous, Robert, 105
Bourguiba, Pres. Habib, 46
Bozzi, Jean, 39, 48
Bradlee, Ben, 151n
Branco, Gen., 206
Bravo, Douglas, 77, 199
B.R. Fox Co., 163, 181
Bricole gang—see Lesca gang
Brigade 2506, 208
Broglio, Prince Jean de—murder of, 218n, 221
Brotherhood of Love, 175n, 187n
Brown, Irving, 15, 25n, 34
Bruno, Angelo—murder of, 223-224, 228n
Buckley, William F., 193, 196n, 216n
Bureau of Alcohol, Tobacco and Firearms, 178
Burma, opium traffic in, 2, 15, 132
Burnstine, Kenneth G., 8, 181, 185
Bursten, Leonard, 155, 157n
Buscetta, Benedetto, 106
Buscetta, Tomasso, 105-106, 109, 123, 225

Cabinet Committee on International Narcotics
  Control, 126, 161
Caille, Jean, 58n
Cain, Richard, 145
CAL (Confederacion Anticomunista
  Latinoamericana), 196n, 217n
Callejas, Mariana, 10
Calzi, Dominique—see Patrice Chairoff
Camp, Flavio, 214
Campora, Pres. Hector, 113
Canazzi, Francois, 105
Cape Florida Development Co., 154
Capone, Ralph, 85n

Carbone-Spirito gang, 38, 44n
Carlson, Alex E., 151n
Carter, Pres. Jimmy—administration of, 21,
  81n, 157n, 174-175, 217n, 226, 227n
Casalini, Guglielmo, 113, 200
Castro, Fidel, 142, 145, 206
  —actions against 11, 143-144, 147, 185n,
  204-206
CAT (Civil Air Transport) 130, 132, 134, 137n,
  151n
(La) Catena, 203
Cecchini, Achilles, 95-96
Cellini, Dino, 21, 187n
Cellini, Ed, 155
Cerny, Howard, 26n
Cesari, Jo, 25n, 38, 88, 101-102, 103n, 115
Cesarsky, Jorge, 10-11, 204
Chairoff, Patrice alias Yves Dieter Calzi, Dieter
  von Freudenreich and Dr. Siegfried
  Schoenenberg, 54, 199-203, 214
Chang Chi-fu, 174
Chang Yu Ching, 149
Che Guevara Brigade, 212
Chennault, Anna Chan, 131, 156
Chennault, Gen. Claire, 16, 129, 131, 137n,
  144
Chesler, Lou, 155
Chiang Ching-kuo, 132, 138n
Chiang Kai-shek, 130, 132
Chiappe, Francois "Big Lips", 76-77, 84, 105,
  109, 112-114, 165, 215
China Lobby, 14, 18, 122, 129, 131-132, 138n,
  144, 146, 192-193
Chinese Mafia, 87-88, 148
Chirac, Jacques, 218n
Chiu Chao Chinese, 88, 173-174
Cho, Sammy, 149
Chotiner, Murray, 17, 153, 157n
Christian Democratic Party (Italy), 14
Chtouki—see Mohammed Miloued
Chu Chi-fu, 174
Chung, Dr. Margaret, 137n
Church Committee report, 43, 142
CIA (Central Intelligence Agency), 1-21, 24n,
  30, 32-35, 38, 43, 57, 60-65, 67-73, 73n-74n,
  78, 80n, 87, 92-93, 95, 99, 103n, 107, 109,
  114, 116n, 122, 124-126, 127n, 130-136,
  137n-138n, 143-149, 150n-151n, 159-165,
  173, 175n, 177-179, 182-186, 189-194, 202,
  202n, 204-207, 210-211, 213, 215, 216n,
  218n, 221-222, 225-226
Ciacomazzo, Giuseppe, 98
CID (U.S. Army Criminal Investigation Divi-
  sion), 135
Cirillo, Louis, 143
Cisculli massacre, 105
Civiletti, Benjamin, 223, 226
Claude, 200, 202n
Clement, Gen. Claude, 74n
Cline, Ray S., 138n, 151n, 193, 205
Cobray International, Inc., 186n
Cochran, Col. Barney, 186n
Cohen, Mickey, 153

General Development Corp., 131, 155
Genovese, Vito, 15, 25n
Gentile, Nick, 15
Gestapo, 38, 41, 75, 83
Giancana, Sam, 143, 145-146, 152n, 178, 215
Gibraltar Steamship Corp., 215
Gigante, Paul Lilio, 106
Giscard d'Estaing, Pres. Valery, 40, 49, 81n, 221
Golden Triangle, 2, 88, 122, 132-133, 148, 172-174, 191, 222-223
Goebbels, Joseph, 209
Gonzalez, Felipe, 126
Gonzalez-Mata, Luis, 72, 93, 167n
Goodell, Charles, 227n
Goodpaster, Lt. Gen. Andrew, 217n
Grasso, Sonny, 117n
Gray, Gordon, 22
Graziani, Clemente, 214
Green Gang, 14
Grey Wolves, 222
Gross, Nelson, 161
Grossin, Gen. Paul, 46
Groves, Wallace, 155
Grupo Francés, 29, 85, 163, 193
Guatemala, 1954 CIA coup in, 16, 130, 144
Guerin, Daniel, 72, 74n, 199-201, 202n
Guerini, Antoine, 25n, 38-39, 55
Guerini, Barthélémy "Mémé", 38, 40, 55, 75
Guerini, Francois, 38, 40
Guerini, Lucien, 38
Guerini, Pascal, 38
Guerini, Pierre, 38
Guerini gang, 15, 35, 38, 40, 42, 55, 58n, 75, 195n
Guérin-Sérac, Yves, 8-10, 207, 211
Guibaud, Gen. Eugene, 46
Gutiérrez Ruiz, Hector – assassination of, 213

Haig, Gen. Alexander, 191
Haldeman, H.R., 18
Hall, Bobby, 185
Hall, Loren, 146
Hammarskjöld, Dag, 65
Harper & Row, 127n
Harvey, William 145, 215
Hassan II, King, 59-63, 69, 71, 74n, 227n
Health, Education and Welfare Department (U.S.), 171
Helliwell, Paul, 15-16, 18, 24n-25n, 130
Helms, Richard, 19
Hemming, Gerry Patrick, 8, 181-182, 185n-186n
Hernandez-Cartaya, Guillermo, 148
Hernandez Rumbaut, Carlos, 13, 26n, 164
(The) Heroin Trial, 4
Herrera family, 177
Hevia Cosculluela, Manuel, 80n
Hill, Amb. Robert C., 113, 165
Hillenkoetter, Rear Adm. Roscoe, 34
Hip Sings gang, 15
Hirsch, André, 85, 97-98, 185

Hirsch, Evelyne, 98, 185
Hitchcock, William Mellon, 175n
Hitler, Adolf, 204
Hoffa, Jimmy, 130, 143, 154, 156, 157n
(The) Hoffa Wars, 191
Hoffman, Carl O., 137n
Hoffman, William, 165
Hoge, Warren, 81n
Hoover, J. Edgar, 123, 161, 178
Hougan, Jim, 13, 183-184, 193-194
Hory, Elmyr de, 76, 218n
House Committee on International Narcotics Control, 171
House Select Committee on Assassinations, 21, 146
House Select Committee on Narcotics Abuse and Control, 171
HUAC (House Un-American Activities Committee), 195n
Hughes, Howard, 153, 155, 186n, 195n
Humphrey, Hubert, 162
Hunt, E. Howard, 2, 16, 18, 20, 124, 126, 129-131, 139n, 144, 150n-151n, 154, 160-164, 189, 193-194, 206, 215, 216n
Huston Plan, 123, 126, 159, 162

IACB (International Anti-Communist Brigade), 145
Ianni, Francis, A.J., 90n
ILGWU, (International Ladies Garment Workers Union), 34
Indiviglio, Benedetto "Beni the Cringe", 143
Indiviglio brothers, 143
Ingersoll, John, 124, 161, 163
Ingram, Gordon, 182
Ingram M-10 machine pistol, 8, 21, 182-183, 210
INC (International Narcotics Control program), 165, 179
Interarmco, 6
Intercontinental Corp., 137n
Intermountain Aviation, Inc., 151n
International Commission of Jurists, 61
Internacional Fascista – see Fascist International
International Herald Tribune, 210
International Penetration Force (Interpen), 181, 185n, 186n
International Police Academy, 164
International Police Services, 165
International Socialist Youth Conference, 205
Interpol, 9, 107, 225
Intertel, 192, 195n-196n
INTRA Bank, 184
Intrattor, Max, 99
Ioannidis, Col. Georghis, 202
IOS (Investor's Overseas Service), 155-156, 184-185, 187n
IRS (Internal Revenue Service), 123
Italian Mafia, 1-3, 14-15, 37, 88, 105, 138n
ITT (International Telephone and Telegraph), 195n

Marcellin, Raymond, 97, 122
Marcello, Carlos, 16, 103n, 110, 147, 152n
Marenches, Alexandre de, 46, 91, 93
Marin, Gustavo, 217n
Marion Penitentiary, 32n, 111
Markovic, Stefan, 58n, 91
Martin, Jacky, 98
Martin, Patricia Richardson, 184
Martinez, Eugenio Rolando, 126, 144, 146, 151n, 161
Martino, John, 146
Mary Carter Paint Co., 155, 195n
Masia, Jacques, 103n
Massagrande, Elio, 214, 218n
Mattei, Enrico – assassination of, 47, 106
Mauduit, Simone, 75
Maxwell, Gille, 211
Mayfield Road Gang, 155
McClellan Hearings, 130, 143
McCord, James, 126, 206
McCoy, Alfred W., 127n, 138n, 173-174
McGovern, Sen. George, 162
McGregor, Clark, 168n
McHale, William, 47
McNabb, Donald, 93, 102n
Mechere, Belkacem, 73
Mein, Amb. Gordon – assassination of 211
Meo tribesmen, 134, 136, 146, 148, 165
Mercier, Col. Marcel, 46, 65
Mertz, Michel Victor, 54, 95-96
Messick, Hank, 18, 148, 182
Mexican Bar Association, 180
Meyer, Cord Jr., 127n
MI5 (British intelligence), 3
Miami National Bank, 90, 131, 157n
Michelet, Edmond, 41
Michelini, Zelmar – assassination of, 213
Military Armaments Corp., 8, 182
Miloued, Mohammed alias Chtouki, 63, 66
Minnick, Walter, 159-160, 163
Mishler, Judge Jacob, 30
Mitchell, John, 122, 147, 168n, 225
Mitrione, Dan A., 6, 78, 80n, 165
MK/ULTRA (CIA operation), 15, 206
MNC (Cuban Nationalist Movement), 10-11, 208, 216n, 225
Moffitt, Ronni Karpen – see Orlando Letelier
Moldea, Dan, 191
(Le) Monde, 1-3, 6, 9, 12, 15, 21
Mondolini, Paul, 54, 89, 111
MONGOOSE (CIA operation), 17
Monet, Jean Claude, 202
Montaldo, Jean, 58n
Montoneros, 113
Morales, Commissioner, 211
Morgenthau, Robert, 155
Mori, Robert, 97
Mosca, Etienne, 111, 115
Mossad (Israeli intelligence), 63
Moulin, Raymond, 98
Mouvement pour la Communauté, 53
MSI (Italian Fascist party), 209, 214
Mudge, Rose, Guthrie and Alexander, 225

Mullen and Co., 19
Muravnik, Aron, 92
Murder Inc., 142
Murphy, Rep. Morgan, 123
Murphy Steele report – see World Heroin Problem
Muskie, Sen. Edmund, 162

Narcotics Control Action Plan for Mexico, 162
Nardi, John, 185
National Bulk Carriers, 155
National Commission on Marijuana and Drug Abuse, 162
National Security Council, 20, 160
National Socialist Party (France), 202
Naval War College, 212
Navarra, Col., 211
Nesmoz, Louis, 54, 56, 69, 112, 115
New Hebrides secessionist movement, 26n
New Republic, 2
New Right, 138n
Newsday, 4-5, 16
Newsweek, 11, 69
New York Times, 2, 6, 9, 12, 22, 182
Ng Sik-ho ("Limpy Ho"), 149
Nhu, Ngo Dinh, 129
Nicolet, Raymond, 97
Nicoli, Michel, 3, 54, 76, 84, 105-106, 109, 112
Nitze, Paul, 22
Nixon, Donald, 156
Nixon, Edward, 156
Nixon, Richard M., 2-4, 17-20, 87, 91-92, 102, 103n, 116, 121-124, 126-127, 131, 136, 148-149, 152n, 153-157, 159-160, 163-164, 166, 167n, 171, 183, 191, 195n, 207, 217n, 225
Noto, Mario T., 152n
(Le) Nouvel Observateur, 212
Novo Sampol, Guillermo, 10-11, 207
Novo Sampol, Ignacio, 10, 24n, 207

OAS, (Organisation de l'Armée Sécrète), 3, 9, 11, 21-22, 48, 50n, 52-57, 62, 96, 113-114, 200, 202, 204, 207-211, 218n, 221
Occorsio, Judge Vittorio, 8-9, 183
ODALE (Office for Drug Abuse Law Enforcement), 125, 162-163, 166
Office of Price Administration, 153
Oglesby, Carl, 205
Oliveira, Ademar Augusto de alias Fininho and Irineu Bruno da Silva, 166
Oliver, Michael, 26n
Omega 7, 207, 216n-217n
Ongania, Gen., 206
ONI (US Naval intelligence), 14
ONNI (Office of National Narcotics Intelligence), 126, 161, 163, 167n
Operacao Bandeirantes, 165-66
Operation 40, 16, 161, 177, 181, 205, 209
Operation Cointelpro, 161, 167n
Operation Condor, 213

237

Taylor, Gen. Maxwell D., 22
Teamsters Union, 130, 143, 154, 157n
Thai border police, 13, 24n, 133, 173
Theresa, 78-79
Thieu, Nguyen Van, 135
Thurmond, Sen. Strom, 20, 204
Time, 44n, 47, 72
Tisslenkoff, Alexandre, 53-54
Tixier-Vignancour, Jean-Louis, 214
Torres, Juan José – assassination of, 212-213
Torrijos, Gen. Omar, 161
Touré, Pres. Sekou, 46
Townley, Michael, 10, 12, 209, 213, 215, 225
Trabal, Col. Ramón – assassination of, 213
Trafficante, Santo Jr., 1, 3, 7, 14, 16, 85n,
    89-90, 100, 103n, 110n, 122-124, 127, 131,
    134, 141-149, 150n, 156, 160-163, 172-173,
    183, 189-191, 194, 207, 215, 225
Trafficante, Santo Sr., 141
Transmaritima Bolivia, 86n
Treasury Department (U.S.), 160
Triads – *see* Chinese Mafia
Tricontinental Congress, 5, 32n, 61-64,
    206-207
Trinquier, Col. Roger, 133
Trouve, René – murder of, 218n
Trujillo, Rafael, 144, 150n
Tsai Chien Cheng, 174
Tshombé, Moise, 65, 70, 99
Tupamaros, 5, 6, 78-79, 81n, 165
Turbay, Pres. Julio Cesar, 168n
Turchi, Luigi, 225
Turkey, opium traffic in, 2-3, 38, 87, 115,
    124, 149, 152n, 166, 222
Turkish Fascist party, 222
Turner, Stansfield, 146

UDR (Gaullist Party), 34, 39, 50n, 52, 55,
    58n, 72, 92, 96, 218n
Ulmer, Ralph, 157n
UNFP (Union Nationale des Forces
    Populaires), 60
Ungerleider, Dr. J. Thomas, 162
Unification Church, 217n
Union Casualty Agency, 130
United Fruit Co., 130-131
USAID (U.S. Agency for International
    Development), 124, 164-165, 173
U.S. Labor Party, 168n, 182
U.S. Life Insurance Co., 130

Vaky, Amb. Viron, 26n
Valenzuela family, 177
Valeriano, Napoleon, 144
Vanguard Service Corp. 215
Vathaire, Herve de, 203, 215, 218n
Venturi, Dominique, 39, 54, 88-89
Venturi, Jean, 39, 50n, 89
Vesco, Robert, 8, 14, 16, 20-22, 26n, 127,
    155-156, 157n, 164, 175n, 182-185, 187n,
    190-191, 194, 225
Videla, Gen. Jorge, 114, 217n
(Le) Viking Provencal, 202

Vlassov, Gen. Andrei, 204
Vlassov organization, 192, 204-205
Voitot, Roger, 64-65, 68
Volpe, Amb. John, 228n
Vosjoli, Philippe T. de, 5, 46-47, 65, 73n,
    216n

Wackenhut, 192, 195n
Wackenhut, George, 195
WACL (World Anti-Communist League), 13,
    16-17, 124, 152n, 182, 192-193, 195, 196n,
    207, 214, 216n-217n
Waldron, Bert, 186n
Wallace, George, 162
Walsh, Lt. David, 226
Warner, John, 124
Washington Post, 2, 19
Washington Star, 11
Watergate affair, 1-2, 18-20, 126, 129,
    144-145, 160, 163, 185
Weiller, Paul Louis, 184
Welles, Paul, 216n
Wells, Robert, 61, 207
WerBell, Mitch III, 8, 14, 16, 21, 26n, 137n,
    164-165, 168n, 181-187, 193, 195, 210
Westinghouse Tactical Air Defense System,
    227n
Whattley, Richard, 145
White, George, 15-16, 25n
White House Strategy Council on Drug
    Abuse, 226
Willauer, Whiting, 16
Williams, Edward Bennett, 22
Williams, Phillip M., 4-5
Wilmington News-Journal, 222
WI/ROGUE, 43
Withers, Paul, 136
Wofford, Tatum "Chubby", 153, 156n
Woltz, August, 211
Woods, Rose Mary, 160
Woodward, Bob, 19
World Armco, 210
World Finance Corp., 148
World Heroin Problem, 123-124
World Service press bureau, 202-204, 214
Wroth, John, 97

Yaras, David, 143
Young, David, 160
Youngman, William, 130

Zakic, Dinko, 217n
Zemmour, William, 111
Zenith Technical Enterprises, 137n, 215
Zenteno Anaya, Gen. Joaquín, 212
Zero (Cuban exile group), 10
Zippo, Carlo, 106, 110n
Zurita, Joseph, 66, 69